© **Copyright 2022 - All rights reserved.**

The content contained within this book may not be reproduced, duplicated or transmitted without direct written permission from the author or the publisher.

Under no circumstances will any blame or legal responsibility be held against the publisher, or author, for any damages, reparation, or monetary loss due to the information contained within this book, either directly or indirectly.

Legal Notice:

This book is copyright protected. It is only for personal use. You cannot amend, distribute, sell, use, quote or paraphrase any part, or the content within this book, without the consent of the author or publisher.

Disclaimer Notice:

Please note the information contained within this document is for educational and entertainment purposes only. All effort has been executed to present accurate, up to date, reliable, complete information. No warranties of any kind are declared or implied. Readers acknowledge that the author is not engaged in the rendering of legal, financial, medical or professional advice. The content within this book has been derived from various sources. Please consult a licensed professional before attempting any techniques outlined in this book.

By reading this document, the reader agrees that under no circumstances is the author responsible for any losses, direct or indirect, that are incurred as a result of the use of the information contained within this document, including, but not limited to, errors, omissions, or inaccuracies.

Table of Contents

Introduction 14
Meal Prepping Basics 16
   Why Meal Prep? 17
   Different Ways To Meal Prep 21
   Tips To Manage Time More Efficiently 22
Meal Prep Essential Equipment 24
Safely Cooking, Storing And Reheating Foods 28
Mistakes to Avoid During Meal Prep 31
How To Have A Successful Meal Prep? 34

Chapter 01: Plant-Based Meal Prep Meal Plans 36
   Meal Plan 1 37
   Meal Plan 2: High Protein Meal Plan 41
   Meal Plan 3: Weekly Meal Plan For The Family 45
   Menu Plan 4: Easy, Fast And Quick Weekly Meal Plan 49
   Menu Plan 5: Light Dishes Weekly Meal Plan 53
   Menu Plan 6: Asian Dishes Weekly Meal Plan 57
   Menu Plan 7: Lunches & Dinners Plus Kid Friendly Meal Plan 61

Chapter 02: Breakfast Recipes 65
   Vegan Quiche 66
   Vegan Breakfast Burrito 67
   Chickpea Omelets 68
   Vegan Pumpkin Muffins 69
   Cranberry Orange Muffins 70
   The Best Vegan Banana Bread 71
   Veggie Tofu Scramble 72
   Strawberry Almond Baked Oatmeal 73
   Vegan Tater Tot Breakfast Casserole 74
   Blueberry Almond Oatmeal (Vegan, High-Protein) 75
   Savoury Vegan Muffins 76
   Chickpea & Sweet Potato Breakfast Hash 77
   Quiche Muffins With Sun-Dried Tomatoes And Spinach 78
   Peanut Butter And Banana Mini Muffins 79
   Breakfast Enchiladas 80
   Coconut Chia Oats 81
   Berry Smoothie Bowls 82

Tropical Smoothie Bowls ... 83
Pumpkin Pie Quinoa ... 84
Carrot Quinoa Bars ... 85
Thumbprint Cookies ... 86
Vegan Waffles ... 87
Bircher Muesli ... 88
Breakfast Cookie Bites ... 89
Breakfast Cookies ... 90
Grain Free Granola ... 91
Green Smoothie Bowl ... 92
Avocado Toast ... 93
Breakfast Burrito ... 94
Overnight Zoats ... 95
Blueberry Muffins ... 96
Fruity Flapjacks ... 97
Chocolate Baked Oatmeal ... 98
Zucchini Bread ... 99
Apple Cinnamon Waffles ... 100

Chapter 03: Lunch Recipes ... 101

Mushroom Broccoli Stir Fry ... 102
Green Bean Curry ... 103
Mediterranean Vegan Bowls ... 104
Tempeh Vegetable Quinoa Bowls ... 105
Lunch Wrap ... 106
Mushroom Cauliflower Rice ... 107
Vegan Bowl With Cashew Pesto ... 108
Bbq Tofu Wraps ... 109
Tofu With Zucchini Noodles ... 110
Korean Barbeque Tofu ... 111
Jerk Spiced Tofu ... 112
Curried Chickpea Bowls ... 113
Greek Couscous Salad ... 114
Thai Quinoa Salad ... 115
Tempeh Stir Fry ... 116
Vermicelli Soup ... 117
Broccoli, Carrot And Potato Soup ... 118
Vegan Borsch Soup ... 119
Cream Of Broccoli Soup ... 120
Greens Soup ... 121

Soup Of Broccoli And Spinach	122
Chickpeas Creme Soup	123
Italian Chickpea Soup	124
Lentil Soup	125
Lentil Soup With Mixed Veggies	126
Penne Pasta With Pesto Sauce	127
Pasta Salad With Tomato And Broccoli	128
Pasta With Lentil Sauce	129
Sauteed Zoodles	130
Penne Pasta With Tomato Sauce	131
Three Colors Pasta	132
Vegan Poke Bowl	133
Rice With Vegetables	134
Rice With Chopped Carrots	135
Black Rice Meal	136

Chapter 04: Dinner Recipes — 137

Stuffed Aubergine Rolls	138
Tofu And Rice Platter	139
Vegetable Meatballs With Zucchini Noodles	140
Noodles With Tofu	141
Eggplant Casserole	142
Vegetarian Eggplants Stew	143
Pasta With Vegetables And Chickpeas	144
Salad With Roasted Eggplant And Kale	145
Farfalle Pasta With Chickpea	146
Spicy Tomato Soup	147
Rustic Gnocchi Pasta	148
Mushroom Soup	149
Lentil Soup With Mushrooms	150
Mushroom Soup With Green Vegetables	151
Miso Soup With Mushrooms	152
Cutlets Cauliflower	153
Mushroom Tofu Soup	154
Chickpea Rice	155
Stinky Tofu	156
Steamed White Beans In Tomato Sauce	157
Grilled Eggplant Rolls	158
Mushrooms Broccoli Stir Fry	159
Traditional Pizza	160

Stuffed Cabbage Rolls 161
Rice Stuffed Butternut Squash 162
Potato Kale Burger 163
Broccoli, Mushrooms Quinoa Bowl 164
Vegetarian Meal Salad.. 165
Edamame Quinoa Salad 166
Rotini Pasta Salad With Arugula 167
Rigatoni with Tomatoes, and Zucchini... 168
Lemon Sauteed Cabbage 169
White Rice Cakes 170
Kimchi... 171
Herbed Couscous 172

Chapter 5: High Protein Meals 173
Boiled Red Beans 174
Stewed White Beans With Pumpkin 175
Tofu Stuffed Pastry 176
Tofu Falafel Wraps 177
Cereal Almonds Bars 178
Muesli Bars... 179
Saucy Navy Beans 180
Black Chana Fry.. 181
Red Lentil Potato Soup 182
Mixed Lentil Stew 183
Korean Eggplant Stew 184
Tuscan White Beans 185
Brussels Sprout Broccoli Stew... 186
Tofu Curry 187
Crispy Tofu Platter 188
Glazed Tofu 189
Rice with Brown Lentils 190
Vegetable Tempeh Stew 191
Vegetable Gyoza 192
Tofu Mushroom Dumplings 193
Water Chestnut Mushroom Fry 194
Rice Bean Platter.. 195
Chickpea and Carrot Stew.. 196
Spaghetti with Falafel Balls.. 197
Brussel Sprout Tofu Fry 198
Pappardelle Pasta 199

Chapter 6: Sheet Pan, Instant Pot, Freezer Meals 200

- Steamed Cabbage Rolls 201
- Eggplant Ratatouille 202
- Eggplant Stir Fry 203
- Eggplant Lasagna 204
- Scalloped Potatoes 205
- Mushroom Pasta Bake 206
- Eggplant Stuffed Bread 207
- Puff Pastry Pesto Bites 208
- Pumpkin Chickpea Stew 209
- Eggplant Pie 210
- Shiitake Mushroom Soup 211
- Potato Tomato Bake 212
- Stir-Fried Eggplant 213
- Green Bean Stir-Fry 214
- Sauteed Potatoes And Mushrooms 215
- Sandwich with Roasted Vegetables 216
- Sheet Pan Vegetables 217
- Cauliflower Cakes 218
- Mushroom Bisque 219
- Beans Pasta Soup 220
- Garlicky Roasted Potatoes 221
- Roasted Polenta Pizza 222
- Sheet Pan Buns 223
- Potato Tomato Stew 224
- Roasted Veggies with Baby Corn 225
- Mushroom Tomato Risotto 226
- Saffron Risotto 227
- Instant Pot Chickpea Stew 228
- White Bean Salad 229
- Green Bean Mushroom Medley 230
- Potato Pasta Soup 231
- Potato Vermicelli Soup 232
- Instant Pot Butternut Soup 233
- Barley Vegetable Stew 234

Chapter 7: Kid Friendly Recipes 235

- Cauliflower Mash 236
- Mash Potatoes 237
- Crispy and Creamy Pasta 238

Creamy Pasta	239
Zucchini Cranberry Muffins	240
Tofu Patties	241
Strawberry Pops	242
Mashed Carrot	243
Mango Cream Bowl	244
Strawberry Popsicles	245
Kid's Carrot Rice Soup	246
Potato Croquettes	247
Cinnamon Apple Meal	248
Baby Oatmeal	249
Orange Mini Cookies	250
Star Cookies	251
Butternut Squash Puree	252
Pink-and-Yellow Cookies	253
Animal Pasta Soup	254
Bow Tie Pasta Soup	255

Chapter 8: Snack Recipes — 256

Zucchini Sticks	257
Fried Blossoms	258
Caramel Popcorn	259
Bake Buffalo Cauliflower Wings	260
Tofu Sticks	261
Sweet Potato Fries	262
Potato Stuffed Rolls	263
Vegetable Spring Roll's	264
Eggplant Fries	265
Apple Chips	266
Cassava Croquettes	267
Chocolate Bombs	268
Chocolate Peanut Balls	269
Orange Thumbprint Cookies	270
Beetroot Chips	271
Roasted Chickpeas	272
Crusted Kale Chips	273
Air Fried Tofu Nuggets	274
White Beans Meatballs	275
Chickpea Stuffed Zucchini Boats	276
Vegan Buckwheat Muffins	277

Tahini Date Cookies	278
Chocolate Chip Zucchini Muffins	279
Carrot Oat Balls	280
Chili Garlic Baked Parsnip Fries	281
Raw Hemp Seed Brownies	282
Carrot Fries	283
Avocado Fries	284
Onion Rings	285
Crispy Pepper Poppers	286

Chapter 9: Sauces, Condiments and Dressing Recipes 287

Chilli Garlic Sauce	288
Vegan Buffalo Sauce Recipe	289
Gochujang Sauce	290
Sweet Chilli Sauce	291
Avocado Hummus	292
Pumpkin Hummus	293
Beet Root Hummus	294
Chickpea Hummus	295
Mango Chutney	296
Cashew Sauce	297
Peri Peri Sauce	298
Green Sauce	299
Chimichurri Sauce	300
Walnut Spinach Pesto	301
Basil Pesto	302
Thousand Island Sauce	303
Vegan Tzatziki Sauce	304
Cranberry Sauce	305
Satay Peanut Sauce	306
Dairy-Free Béchamel Sauce	307

Conclusion	308
References	309
Alphabetic List of Recipes	310
Ingredients Index	314

Special Bonus!

Want This Bonus Challenge + Book for FREE?

Get **FREE**, unlimited access to it and all of my new books by joining the Fan Base!

Scan W/ Your Camera To Join!

Before we get started, I'd like to offer you this gift. It's my way of saying thank you for spending time with me in this book. Your gift is a special report titled **"The 30-Day Plant-Based Challenge."** As a bonus, you will also receive **"The Plant-Based Nutrient Cheat Sheet & Micronutrient Guide."** This is a 30-day challenge, and an easy-to-use guide that pulls together tons of analysis and fun activities you can enjoy doing every day. This guide will help you understand what exactly could be missing in your plant-based diet to achieve your health and fitness dreams. This guide will make sure you are eating clean and making sure you are getting all the nutrients you need daily to help you along with whatever fitness dreams you have. Whether you want to lose weight, burn fat, build lean muscle, or even bump up your confidence, this challenge and guide are just for you.

Paulgreencookbook.com

This 2 in 1 gift includes:

- ✓ Complete 30 days of daily plant-based fun and activities you will love
- ✓ 80+ detailed micronutrient information of the most common plant-based foods at your fingertips
- ✓ Basic Beginner steps to cover all the basic information you need to hop into the plant-based lifestyle
- ✓ The micronutrient guide will provide you with essential information about the body's vitamin and mineral requirements
- ✓ The cheat sheet guide will make your transition to a whole foods plant-based diet very simple

I'm willing to bet you'll find at least a few ideas, tools and meals covered in this gift that will surprise and help you. This guide will set you up for success and is a proven system when starting your plant-based journey. With this guide, you will be armed with the info & focus you need. You will be giving your body nutritious fuel and enjoy eating plant-based foods. With downloading this guide, you're taking a solid step to the path of your health and fitness dreams.

How can you obtain a copy of **The 30-Day Plant-Based Challenge** and the **Plant-Based Nutrient Cheat Sheet & Micronutrient Guide?** It's simple. Visit paulgreencookbook.com and sign up for my email list (or simply click the link above). You'll receive immediate access to the guides in PDF format. You can read it online, download it or print it out. Everything you need to get started and stay on your plant-based journey is included when you sign up for my email list.

Being on my email list also means you'll be the first to know when I release a new book. I plan to release my books at a steep discount (or even for free). By signing up for my email list, you'll get an early notification.

If you don't want to join my list, that's fine. This just means I need to earn your trust. With this in mind, I think you will love the information I've included in the ultimate guide. More specifically, I think you will love what it can do for your life.

Without further ado, let's jump into this book.

Join The Plant-Based Health, Fitness, And Nutrition Facebook Group

Looking for a community of like minded individuals who love all things plant base, working out, fitness, nutrition and health? If so, then check out my Facebook community: The Plant-Based, Health, Fitness and Nutrition Community.

This is an amazing group of plant-based health enthusiast who focus on getting results with their lives. Here you can discover simple strategies along your health journey, build powerful habits and relationships, find accountability partners, and ask questions about your struggles. I also host free book giveaways and share other helpful free resources that will be the key to reaching your health and fitness goals as fast as possible. If you want to "level up" in your health and fitness journey then this is the place to be.

**Just scan the QR code below
to join The Plant-Based, Health, Fitness and Nutrition Community**

Attention

Do Not Turn The Page Until You Have Read Everything Below

Scan the QR code below to receive the ebook version of this cookbook that includes all the pictures of each receipe!

Scan W/ Camera Now!

Due to printing costs, we are not able to provide you with a print book with colors and pictures. Instead, I have provided you the ebook version for you to download completely for free with the full cookbook for your ultimate plant-based experience. I want my book to be easily accessible for everyone in the world and since we are a small publishing company, this is the best we can offer to still keep the price for you as low as possible. Hopefully, in the near future, we would like to change this by offering the best quality of books in the world for the lowest prices. Thank you for your understanding and we greatly appreciate your support.

Introduction

Perhaps now more than ever, time has become precious. Every second, every minute we waste, is time we could spend making money or memories. Not all of us can afford to spend too much of it in the kitchen.

Without the time or energy to cook nutritious meals every day, many of us choose fast, unhealthy options. These poor dietary choices rely heavily on processed or fast foods which provide little nutrition and contribute to chronic disease. While that's nothing to feel guilty about, it isn't the way it has to be. With a little knowledge and preparation, we can all learn to create fast, healthy and nutrient rich meals to support our bodies and minds for the demanding world that is our everyday lives.

When it's understood that time is valuable and nutrition is paramount, the next natural question pertains to the kind of diet that provides quick and healthy options. As far as I can see, there's only one option that optimally balances health benefits, cost and prep time. That option, that solution, is a plant-based diet.

People have asked me why I chose a plant-based diet. My answer always pertains to my first-hand experiences. I've suffered from high blood pressure and elevated blood sugar levels for years. These conditions came hand-in-hand with the risk of chronic diseases such as diabetes, obesity, hypertension, and cardiovascular disorders. I was stuck in that vicious cycle of fast unhealthy food combined with a sedentary lifestyle.

The problem I had to solve was how to eat healthier in a practical way that would promote a more active lifestyle. I approached this problem in steps so that I could construct a solid plan. It started with the basics. What kind of food should I eat?

Of all the foods that are available to us on a daily basis, plants provide the most bang for your buck. They are rich sources of the macronutrients, vitamins, minerals, and fibers that we need to heal our minds and bodies. Those major benefits aren't the only reason to create a diet around plant-based meals. There is a versatility to plants that most other food groups don't have. You can eat them raw. You can steam, fry, grill, stew and even make plants into soups. And as far as availability and affordability go, they can be found in almost any grocery store for reasonable prices.

Devising a healthy diet plan is difficult. The pace of modern life, combined with the abundance of unhealthy dining options makes it hard to eat out without compromising said plan. Though on the rise in urban centers, vegan cuisine is generally hard to come by. Most people aren't on plant-based diets making dinners at friends and families' houses hard. Add to that the money you will save by relying on home-cooked meals, and it becomes clear that utilizing the recipes in this book is a wise decision.

This plant-based cookbook is a collection of my own meal prep experiences with the plant-based diet. When I first started meal prepping my plant-based meals, it felt a little tedious. Micromanaging every little detail of a weekly menu took a lot of time. I spent hours in the kitchen on weekends, pre-cooking, prepping, and storing food for the week to come. Though it was a lot of work, the fruits of my labor came during the following week.

Meal prepping makes life more convenient. This book not only contains easy-to-make recipes but also tips pertaining to the meal prepping process. Armed with this knowledge there's nothing holding readers back from enjoying the revelation that is a plant-based diet and a more active lifestyle.

Meal Prepping Basics

Why Meal Prep?

Meal prepping may appear to be a weekend chore at first, but once you discover all of the benefits that this healthy culinary practice can provide, you won't be able to resist giving it a try. Making and preparing your meals ahead of time makes it much easier to keep track of your dietary preferences. It also singles out their more unhealthy eating habits. But the benefits don't stop there. Here are some ways in which meal planning can aid in building a healthier lifestyle.

Affordability

With modern life being as hectic as it is, a lot of people think they don't have time to cook. That leaves little alternative options other than eating out or ordering take out. After a while, that can get pretty expensive. Plus, food in most restaurants is cooked with too much salt and a lot of butter. But when you cook your own food, you save money by making enough for more than one meal and you have full control over the ingredients. Therefore, the quality and cost are completely up to you.

Convenient Grocery Shopping

We've all been in the supermarket, without a plan or the faintest idea of what we're going to get. Unless you go there with a list compiled from ingredients needed from recipes, you're doomed to stroll around and improvise. That leads to buying more than you need, unhealthy impulse buys and forgetting to get small but essential foods, necessary to cook complete meals. Walking through those automated doors without a game plan is akin to inviting disaster.

Portion Control

One of the biggest problems people have while trying to eat healthier is portion control. There's this false notion, a lie that many people tell themselves, that if it's healthy you can eat however much you want of it. That's a dangerous game to play. Anything in life, whether it be food, drink or pleasure, can be a problem if done to excess. So how do you control the size of your portions?

Meal prepping is one of the best ways to practice and develop portion control in your diet. The fact that you are making meals ahead of time means that there's always going to be a more finite amount of any given food. Plus, the containers you use to store the meals already limit each serving size. Not to mention it makes keeping track of calories and nutrients easier. There's a big difference, in theory and in practice, between going to the stove top and scooping a couple more portions of what you cooked than taking out another container and heating it up. Having to do the latter makes you think about the choice you're making.

End to Food Wastage

Do you ever feel bad about wasting and discarding food that you couldn't eat? Food wastage is not just a personal issue for us, but it is becoming a societal issue. So, while it is generally recommended not to waste food, no one has really developed a practical solution. Meal prep, according to most experts, is an effective way to reduce food waste. Because all of the food we prepare for meal prep is packed and stored for a certain day in predetermined portion sizes, so there is very little or no food wastage.

Saves Time

There's no getting around the fact that meal planning and prepping takes time. Most effectively done on the weekends, it can take up some of your free time. But it's best to think about that time as an investment. You're not only investing in easy, quick, nutritious meals during the week, but you're investing in your health and therefore, your future. After a long day of work, when you don't feel like doing much of anything, you'll be thankful that you took the time out of your weekend to provide yourself with a meal that just needs to be heated up. And before you know it, the prepping on the weekend won't feel like a chore, you'll start looking forward to it.

Improves Health

Nothing in life is free or without consequence. This applies to food as well. When we're younger the negative effects of fast food, processed meals and store-bought products aren't as readily apparent. Faster metabolisms and more active lifestyles can cover up a lot of the damage we do to our bodies. But when you get older, those two factors slow down. And it's almost impossible not to see and feel the effects of our dietary choices.

What meal prepping provides is a more direct personal study of what you eat and its effects on your health. Controlling your portion sizes and knowing every ingredient in what you're putting into your body can help you compensate for the natural rigors of aging. It starts with your digestional health. Then you will start to see the pounds burn off. Before you know it, you'll start physically feeling better, be more energetic, and clear minded. At that point, you'll be wondering why you waited so long to make this change.

Keeps you Motivated

It is never easy to follow a healthy lifestyle or to stick to a health-oriented diet plan. People give up quickly when they lose all their motivation and willpower. Meal prepping can help you achieve that much-needed consistency. You will be able to stick to this routine without losing the desire to eat if you cook and store all of the nutritious meals in your refrigerator according to a fixed menu and schedule. And once meal prepping is put into reality, it boosts a person's motivation even more.

Stress-Free

Every day, deciding what to eat and cook is a huge source of stress, especially when you have other things to do. Meal planning can help you avoid unnecessary anxiety and stress. You may breathe a sigh of relief and enjoy delicious food every day, knowing that a home cooked supper is already saved in the refrigerator.

Food With Variety

There's a misconception about the variety available in a healthy diet. Most people think it begins and ends with something green, maybe different varieties of salads. But nothing could be further from the truth. No restaurant or delivery service in existence has a wider menu than nature. And that's what a plant-based diet follows, the menu of the very planet itself. Plants, fruits, nuts, legumes, and vegetables come in endless varieties with just as much, if not in some cases more ways to prepare them than anything that comes in a box or is served through a drive through window. The only limit is your imagination and willingness to try something new.

Weight Control

The modern diet has been overrun with carbohydrates, trans fats, saturated fats, sugar, and salt. As a result, people are more obese than they've ever been in our history as a species. With obesity comes poor health and harmful chronic conditions. But, by making your own meals, you control every aspect of the food you eat. There won't be any of those unpronounceable mystery ingredients you might see on the side or back of a box. Everything you put into your meals and therefore your body, comes from nature. Once you get in the habit of eating better, you'll find that controlling your weight and BMI will be much easier.

Different Ways To Meal Prep

Meal prepping may appear to be a weekend chore at first, but once you discover all of the benefits that this healthy culinary practice can provide, you won't be able to resist giving it a try. Making and preparing your meals ahead of time makes it much easier to keep track of your dietary preferences. It also singles out their more unhealthy eating habits. But the benefits don't stop there. Here are some ways in which meal planning can aid in building a healthier lifestyle.

Make-Ahead Meals

Every day, deciding what to eat and cook is a huge source of stress, especially when you have other things to do. Meal planning can help you avoid unnecessary anxiety and stress. You may breathe a sigh of relief and enjoy delicious food every day, knowing that a home cooked supper is already saved in the refrigerator.

Batch Cooking

In this method, you can cook large batches of food, then divide them into individual portions to store for different days of the week. This can save time and in some cases money as some produce is cheaper bought in bulk. Out of all the meal prep methods, this is one of the most balanced as it can be used for lunches and dinners.

Meals That Are Portioned Out Individually

Fresh meals are cooked and portioned into individual grab-and-go servings, chilled and consumed over several days. This is ideal for quick lunches.

Keep Ready-to-Cook Ingredients

To save time in the kitchen, prepare the materials needed for specific dishes ahead of time. For instance, you can store the pre-made sauces, gravies, curries, and pickled veggies or fruits to add to the meals. Cutting up and portioning ingredients ahead of time is also ideal for people who prefer freshly cooked meals instead of re-heated ones.

Tips To Manage Time More Efficiently

The whole idea of meal prepping revolves around the concept of time management. By using few simple techniques and employing some basic meal prepping methods, you can also save your time during meal preparation and storage:

Maintain a Regular Routine

Much like dieting and working out, meal prepping is most effective when done regularly. This is essential. Picking a day(s) ideal to go shopping and prepping your meals will develop into a habit. That habit will flow into a routine. Before too long, it will feel odd or off not following that routine promoting consistency.

Choose the Right Recipe Combination

There's going to be some experimentation at first. It's the only way to choose the best recipe combination for you and your goals. This is also useful in planning your meal prepping. Choosing recipes that require a variety of cooking processes will allow you to cook quicker and more efficiently. For example, if you cook your main course in the oven, you can cook sides on the stove top at the same time. This way you'll get hot freshly cooked food without having to wait for other aspects of your meal to finish.

Plan Your Cooking Times

A well-thought-out kitchen workflow will save you a lot of time. To efficiently organize your prep and cook times, start with the recipe that has the longest cook time. Typically, this is a soup or an oven meal. After that has begun cooking, concentrate on the rest of the meal. Cold meals should be made last because they can simply be prepared while the other meals are cooking. Automated appliances like a rice cooker or a slow cooker can help you optimize your process even more. Use the cooking time of one recipe to prepare other ingredients and recipes for another. You'll be surprised how much time can be saved using these simple techniques.

Make a Shopping List

Shopping for groceries may be a huge waste of time. Keep a precise grocery list sorted by supermarket categories to cut down on your time at the grocery store. This will save your time by not having to go back to a previous section and will allow you to finish your purchasing faster. Limiting your grocery shopping to once a week and using a supermarket delivery service are two strategies you can utilize to cut down on your shopping time.

Meal Prep Essential Equipment

Without the proper tools, meal prep can be close to impossible. To prepare numerous meals in a short period of time, more likely than not, you'll need to invest in the proper kitchen equipment. Before stepping foot in the grocery store and trying your first recipes, you should make sure you have some of these essential tools in your home.

Food Processor, Spiralizer, Chopper, and Dicer

One of the most time-consuming tasks while meal prepping involves cutting, chopping, and dicing fruits and vegetables. As a rule of thumb, you should always assume it will take longer than you think. Not to mention it takes a lot of energy to take the knife to these ingredients. So, it's essential to have a good food processor, dicer, spiralizer or automated chopper in your kitchen. There are tons of options that can accommodate the way you like to cook, the amount of storage space you have, and of course, your budget. If that's not enough to convince you, know that many recipes call for the use of these machines making ownership vital in order to achieve the culinary results you're aiming for.

Sealable Mason or Canning Jars

Storage is often just as important as the equipment you use to cook your meals. When it comes to food that comes in liquid form like soups, stews, broths, pickled/poached vegetables and certain fruits, using sealable mason or canning jars is ideal. Easily available at most supermarkets, make sure to choose jars that are appropriate for your needs. Often they come in sets meaning that for one price you can get a whole variety of sizes. Make sure that these jars are cleaned and sterilized before use.

Silicone Baking Cups, Molds and Muffin Cups

One thing that kitchen equipment doesn't lack is variety. There's more than one way to make a certain piece and various materials to make them out of. When it comes to baking cups, molds, and muffin cups, silicone is often the best option to choose. BPA-free, they don't contain plastic and are reusable. Flexible, silicone molds and cps can withstand high temperatures while not sticking to food. They are an excellent choice, well-worth seeking out.

Stackable Steamer Racks

There are few things better when it comes to meal prep then the ability to cook numerous foods at once. Using stackable steamer racks/baskets, you can steam vegetables over boiling water, cooking soup or stew.

Meal Prep Essential Equipment

Eco-Friendly Food Wraps

The emphasis on sourcing from nature doesn't have to begin and end with your food. There are other eco-friendly options, especially when it comes to storage. In particular, bee's food wrap is ideal for covering and storing food in the fridge. Free of any plastic or chemical components that could contaminate food, it's easy to find online and is even washable. That means you can re-use it instead of wasting more money on plastic wrap that will just end up taking up space in a landfill.

Glass-lock Storage Containers

Another great more eco-friendly food storage option are glass-lock containers. Unlike plastic, they're chemical and BPA free. You can reheat meals in them without risking the same contamination you do with the plastic versions. They come in a variety of shapes and sizes. Leak-proof, their tops prevent spills and stack easily in the refrigerator. They often come in sets providing a container for your every need.

Electric Cookers, Instant Pot

Sometimes we simply don't have time to cook in or on the stove. Years ago, there weren't really any other options. But now we have electric cookers and instant pots. Not only do they provide quicker avenues to freshly cooked meals, they provide different ways to do it. Whether you need anything from an air fryer to a rice cooker, there's a piece of equipment for practically every need. And if you want to take a more hands-off approach crock pots and slow cookers can be set up and then forgotten about for as long as a whole day.

Reusable Storage Food Bags

While they are the old standard, plastic bags are not suitable for storing food. With them comes the risk of micro-plastic and chemical contamination which over time gets absorbed into our meals and therefore our bodies. Luckily reusable silicone bags are available to purchase. Besides being safer, they can sustain more damage, are machine washable, non-stick, and are more cost effective.

Notes or Weekly Meal Planner

One of the best ways to approach meal planning is to treat it like school. Before stepping into the kitchen to cook, you should do your homework. Research the foods you like, foods that you want to eat, learn about their nutritional value, appropriate portion size, and what to pair them with. Then schedule out your weekly meals. It's important to know what has the longest shelf life and what you need to eat first before it goes bad. Keep a list of ingredients, so that most of your grocery list is done before even thinking about going. You may want to try using labels as well, putting down the dates that any meal was cooked so you can keep track and waste as little as possible.

Safely Cooking, Storing And Reheating Foods

Meal prepping is pointless without proper storage techniques. The point, after all, is to make food to have for an entire week. If not stored properly, your meals will go bad and you'll be throwing food and money into the garbage. Here are some simple steps to help you get the most out of your meal prep efforts.

Safely Cooking, Storing And Reheating Foods

01. Consider the Expiration Date

Pay attention to expiration dates on food before buying it. That minimizes the chances of early spoilage. It's also important to realize that most grocery stores push their oldest products to the front of the shelf or top of the pile. Make sure that any expiration date gives you at least a 2-3 week window if possible. Certain products like dairy present a bigger risk if consumed after they've gone bad. So, pay special attention to those labels.

02. Don't Haste

Haste can make waste. This applies to a common mistake people make. Don't rush to pack food into a container after it's cooked. When stored immediately after cooking even in a sealed container, the food keeps cooking. This can spoil the food. A good policy is to wait for 10-15 minutes before putting a cover on anything. But make sure not to wait too long because that can have just as harmful of an effect as packing away too quickly.

03. Select the Right Container

Choosing the right container is another important step. Firstly, the size of the container should match the serving size of the food you want to enjoy later. Then the type of container or storage is also important to look into. Use glass jars or boxes to store liquid items like juices, soups, broths, and juices. Use bee wraps to store dry solid items or plastic bags to keep vegetables, fruits, tofu etc. By using different storage containers, you can easily manage the space inside your refrigerator. Plus, it makes it easier to reheat your meals, saving time and effort which is the crux of meal prepping.

04. Label What you Store

You might have a fantastic memory. But it's still wise to label the containers of food you cooked. That makes it considerably easier to keep track of and identify each meal. This even pertains to frozen food. Often, it's harder to identify a meal when it's been in the freezer for a while.

Safely Cooking, Storing And Reheating Foods

05. Store After Vacuum Sealing

Vacuum sealing is an effective method to not only store but add days if not weeks to a meal's shelf life. With all the air removed, there's less fuel for bacteria and mold to feast upon, preserving the food for a substantially longer time. You don't necessarily even need a machine to do this. You can do it with a sealable bag by immersing it in water while keeping the open end dry. All the air will be removed from said bag allowing you to immediately close it and preserve it a lot longer than you would in a Ziplock.

06. Set temperature of the refrigerator

Most of us don't think about it, but the temperature inside our fridge is important. It can make a huge difference when it comes to keeping stored food fresh. If the temperature goes above 40 degrees Celsius, it becomes ideal for growing bacteria. That is why the temperature of the refrigerator should be maintained below this tipping point. In summers, especially when the outside temperature is high, or your refrigerator is overstuffed with food, its temperature can rise, and that's one of the biggest reasons for food spoilage most meal preppers usually complain about. Constantly keep the temperature in your mind and keep it under 40 degrees C.

07. Manage Storage Space Properly

Keeping the storage space neat and clean is another important part of meal prepping. Whether it is the refrigerator or the freezer, both spaces must be kept well organized for your convenience. It is better to use the different compartments of the refrigerator to store different types of meals. For instance, you can divide the spaces according to days or according to the mealtime, like one section for breakfast only, the other for lunch, one section for snacks, and the other for dinner. This will help you instinctively choose the right meal for the right time.

Mistakes to Avoid During Meal Prep

It is usually the early stages of meal prepping when the dieters lose the will and motivation of carrying it on, largely because of some common mistakes. These minor errors are barely recognizable. But when you repeat these missteps, it makes this vital skill close to impossible. Here are some things to avoid in order to help your meal prepping go as smooth as possible.

Mistakes to Avoid During Meal Prep

 ## Over-complication

Go easy on yourself. Do not dive into the deep end of the pool without learning how to swim first. Start with less complicated recipes that require minimal ingredients. Slowly work your way up to those involving more complex cooking or prepping techniques. Try not to beat yourself up if you make mistakes. Because you will make mistakes. This time and effort is an investment, just like the equipment/tools you bought and the research you've done. Unlike a lot of investments though, patience while learning how to cook almost always pays off in the long run.

 ## Wrong Containers Size

For most beginners, container size doesn't seem like a big deal. This is especially true if you are busy managing other important parts of your meal plan. But it makes a big difference when you don't select the right sized container to store your meal. When you use the wrong size, it can throw off the storage of the other food you've prepared and deviate from the routine and habits you're trying to establish. It won't take long for you to be able to visualize the right size you need. Don't take the easy way out and just choose whatever is clean.

 ## Not adding Snacks

Most people focus on making 3 three main meals for the day and forget about storing some snacks. When you add snacks to the menu, it reduces the serving size for the main meals. Such a meal plan can guarantee a constant boost of energy along with a variety of flavors on the menu. It will also satisfy all your cravings and will stop you from getting something to eat from outside the diet. This also aids in a healthy metabolism. The importance of healthy snacks cannot be overlooked, including frozen berries, frozen fruits, carrots, cookies, granola bars etc.

 ## Not Freezing

You will often find yourself in a situation where you cooked a little more than you can store in the fridge or possibly eat before it spoils. That's when you utilize your freezer. This the most effective way to store food long term. You can store meals for as long as 6 months when frozen. This is an essential habit to get into, that especially pays off when life gets in the way of your meal prepping routine.

Mistakes to Avoid During Meal Prep

No Set Targets

Without having a fixed health goal, you cannot follow a healthy plant-based meal plan. To stay oriented and well on course while meal prepping, a person must have a goal or aims to shoot for. Set up a small health target for each week; in this way, you can change your unhealthy eating habits into healthy ones over time. And you lessen the possibility of being overwhelmed.

Disorganized Storage

Disorganization can hamper your meal prep efforts. Not labeling food, storing containers in random places in the fridge or freezer, and not having a system leads to chaos. Therefore, it is imperative to not only label your meals but stack and place them in their correct order.

How To Have A Successful Meal Prep?

Preparing a week's worth of meals, especially for first timers, might be intimidating. It doesn't have to be difficult, though. A simple step-by-step strategy to streamlining your meal planning procedure can be found below. These are a few basic techniques and key takeaways to successfully pull meal prepping while being on a plant-based diet plan.

- Select a meal prepping method that suits your lifestyle. Keep your daily routine, your nutritional needs, weight goals and meal timings in mind before selecting the meal prep method. Be realistic rather than being idealistic!

- Select a specific day in a week to do all the meal prepping. You can also choose any two days as well, like Saturday and Sunday, to plan your meal, and grocery shop on one day, and cook the meal the next day.

- Keep your daily schedule in your mind. If there is a dinner you need to attend or a picnic that you should go to, then prepare your meal according to those coming events as well.

- The more the variety, the better! Instead of focusing on a single type of meal, try to keep the variety of flavors by adding different fruits, veggies, pasta, sauces and seasonings to the meals.

- Keep a concise and to the point grocery list with you before entering the grocery store. Categorize the items into sections to hit the specific portions of the store. Go with a game plan.

- Prepare other ingredients while others are cooking. This will save you time.

- Always store properly and label the containers with complete serving details to avoid confusion and wasting your time.

Now that you know how to effectively meal-prep your food, it is about time that you try making some delicious plant-based recipes and store them in your refrigerator and freezer for the days to come.

CHAPTER 01

PLANT-BASED MEAL PREP MEAL PLANS

Meal Plan 1

🌱 MONDAY

Time	Meals	Servings	Storage Tips	Duration
Breakfast	Vegan Breakfast Burrito	2	Wrap the burrito in a paper wrap then place in a container.	• 3-4 days- refrigeration • 1 month-freezer
Lunch	Jerk Spiced Tofu	4	Pack with bread or rice in a partitioned container.	• 3 days- refrigeration • 6 month-freezer
Snack	Fried Blossoms	4	Place the uncooked blossoms in a sealable container then freeze for 2 hours.	• 6 months- freezer
Dinner	Vegetarian Eggplants Stew	4	Pack with bread or rice in a partitioned container.	• 3 days- refrigeration • 6 months- freezer

🌱 TUESDAY

Time	Meals	Servings	Storage Tips	Duration
Breakfast	Left over Vegan Breakfast Burrito	2	Wrap the burrito in a paper wrap then place in a container.	• 5-6 days- refrigeration • 1 month-freezer
Lunch	Korean Barbecue Tofu	4	Pack with bread or rice in a partitioned container.	• 3 days- refrigeration • 1 month-freezer
Snack	Bake Buffalo Cauliflower Wings	4	Store the cauliflower florets in a sealable container	• 6 days- refrigeration • 6 month-freezer
Dinner	Pasta With Vegetables And Chickpeas	4	Pack the pasta with roasted asparagus.	• 3 days- refrigeration • 1 month-freezer

Chapter 01: Plant-Based Meal Prep Meal Plans

🌱 WEDNESDAY

Time	Meals	Servings	Storage Tips	Duration
Breakfast	Chickpea Omelets	4	Pack this omelet with toasted bread and granola bars	• 3 days- refrigeration • 1 month-freezer
Lunch	Bbq Tofu Wraps	4	Wrap with a paper wrap before storage.	• 3 days- refrigeration • 1 month-freezer
Snack	Tofu Sticks	4	Wrap in a paper wrap then store.	• 3 days- refrigeration • 6 month-freezer
Dinner	Eggplant Casserole	4	Enjoy the casserole with flatbread and fresh greens salad.	• 3 days- refrigeration • 1 month-freezer

🌱 THURSDAY

Time	Meals	Servings	Storage Tips	Duration
Breakfast	Chickpea Omelets	4	Pack this omelet with toasted bread and granola bars	• 5 days- refrigeration • 1 month-freezer
Lunch	Vegan Bowl With Cashew Pesto	4	Pack this meal with tofu skewers.	• 3 days- refrigeration • 1 month-freezer
Snack	Eggplant Fries	4	Pack in a sealable container with paper towel.	• 3 days- refrigeration • 6 months- freezer
Dinner	Noodles With Tofu	4	Pack in a partitioned container.	• 3 days- refrigeration • 1 month-freezer

FRIDAY

Time	Meals	Servings	Storage Tips	Duration
Breakfast	Veggie Tofu Scramble	4	Pack with bread or rice in a partitioned container.	• 3 days- refrigeration • 1 month-freezer
Lunch	Lunch Wrap	4	Pack in a partitioned container.	• 3 days- refrigeration • 1 month-freezer
Snack	Apple Chips	4	Pack in a sealable container with paper towel.	• 3-5 days at room temperature (dark and cold place)
Dinner	Vegetable Meatballs With Zucchini Noodles	4	Pack in a partitioned container.	• 3 days- refrigeration • 1 month-freezer

SATURDAY

Time	Meals	Servings	Storage Tips	Duration
Breakfast	Vegan Tater Tot Breakfast Casserole	4	Cover the casserole with a foil sheets for storage.	• 5 days- refrigeration • 1 month-freezer
Lunch	Mushroom Cauliflower Rice	4	Pack in a partitioned container.	• 4 days- refrigeration • 1 month-freezer
Snack	Chili Garlic Baked Parsnip Fries	4	Pack in a sealable container with paper towel.	• 3 days- refrigeration • 1 month-freezer
Dinner	Tofu And Rice Platter	4	Pack all the parts of platter in a different compartment of a container.	• 3 days- refrigeration • 1 month-freezer

Chapter 01: Plant-Based Meal Prep Meal Plans

SUNDAY

Time	Meals	Servings	Storage Tips	Duration
Breakfast	Blueberry Almond Oatmeal	4	Pack this oatmeal with granola bars.	• Upto 7 days-refrigeration • 1 month-freezer
Lunch	Mediterranean Vegan Bowls	4	Pack in a partitioned container.	• 5 days-refrigeration • 1 month-freezer
Snack	Avocado Fries	4	Pack in a sealable container with paper towel.	• 3 days-refrigeration • 6 months-freezer
Dinner	Stuffed Aubergine Rolls	4	Pack in a partitioned container.	• 3 days-refrigeration • 1 month-freezer

Meal Plan 2: High Protein Meal Plan

🌱 MONDAY

Time	Meals	Servings	Storage Tips	Duration
Breakfast	Vegan Quiche	8	Place the quiches in a sealable container.	• 5 days-refrigeration • 1 month-freezer
Lunch	Saucy Navy Beans	8	Pack with bread or rice in a partitioned container.	• 3 days-refrigeration • 1 month-freezer
Snack	Tofu Stuffed Pastry	4	Pack uncooked pastries and freeze.	• 6 months-freezer
Dinner	Tofu Falafel Wraps	4	Pack in a partitioned container.	• 3 days-refrigeration • 1 month-freezer

🌱 TUESDAY

Time	Meals	Servings	Storage Tips	Duration
Breakfast	Vegan Breakfast Burrito	4	Wrap the burrito in a paper wrap then place in a container.	• 3 days-refrigeration • 1 month-freezer
Lunch	Black Chana Fry	4	Pack in a partitioned container.	• 5 days-refrigeration • 1 month-freezer
Snack	Cereal Almonds Bars	8	Store in a cookie jar.	• 3 days-refrigeration • 1 month-freezer
Dinner	Red Lentil Potato Soup	6	Pack in a sealable bowl or ziplock bag	• 3 days-refrigeration • 1 month-freezer

🌱 WEDNESDAY

Time	Meals	Servings	Storage Tips	Duration
Breakfast	Chickpea Omelets	4	Pack this omelet with toasted bread and granola bars	• 5 days-refrigeration • 1 month-freezer
Lunch	Mixed Lentil Stew	6	Pack with bread or rice in a partitioned container.	• 3 days-refrigeration • 1 month-freezer
Snack	Muesli Bars	6	Store in a cookie jar.	• 3 days-refrigeration • 1 month-freezer
Dinner	Korean Eggplant Stew	4	Pack in a partitioned container.	• 5 days-refrigeration • 1 month-freezer

🌱 THURSDAY

Time	Meals	Servings	Storage Tips	Duration
Breakfast	Veggie Tofu Scramble	4	Pack with bread in a partitioned container.	• 3 days-refrigeration • 1 month-freezer
Lunch	Tuscan White Beans	4	Pack with rice in a partitioned container.	• 3 days-refrigeration • 1 month-freezer
Snack	Tofu Sticks	4	Wrap in a paper wrap then store.	• 5 days-refrigeration • 1 month-freezer
Dinner	Brussels Sprout Broccoli Stew	6	Pack with bread or rice in a partitioned container.	• 3 days-refrigeration • 1 month-freezer

🌱 FRIDAY

Time	Meals	Servings	Storage Tips	Duration
Breakfast	Chickpea & Sweet Potato Breakfast Hash	8	Pack with bread in a partitioned container.	• 3 days- refrigeration • 1 month-freezer
Lunch	Rice Bean Platter	6	Pack all the parts of platter in a different compartment of a container.	• 5 days- refrigeration • 1 month-freezer
Snack	Chocolate Peanut Balls	12	Store in a dry cookie jar	• 3-5 days at room temperature (dark and cold place)
Dinner	Vegetable Tempeh Stew	4	Pack with bread or rice in a partitioned container.	• 5 days- refrigeration • 1 month-freezer

🌱 SATURDAY

Time	Meals	Servings	Storage Tips	Duration
Breakfast	Breakfast Enchiladas	4	Pack enchiladas and sauce separately in a partitioned box.	• 3 days- refrigeration • 1 month-freezer
Lunch	Tofu Curry	4	Pack with bread or rice in a partitioned container.	• 3 days- refrigeration • 1 month-freezer
Snack	Roasted Chickpeas	8	Pack in a mason jar.	• 5 days- refrigeration • 1 month-freezer
Dinner	Crispy Tofu Platter	4	Pack all the parts of platter in a different compartment of a container.	• 3 days- refrigeration • 1 month-freezer

Chapter 01: Plant-Based Meal Prep Meal Plans

SUNDAY

Time	Meals	Servings	Storage Tips	Duration
Breakfast	Carrot Quinoa Bars	8	Store in a cookie jar.	• 3 days-refrigeration • 1 month-freezer
Lunch	Glazed Tofu	4	Pack with bread or rice in a partitioned container.	• 5 days-refrigeration • 1 month-freezer
Snack	Air Fried Tofu Nuggets	8	Storage uncooked nuggets in a container in a freezer.	• 6 months-freezer
Dinner	Rice with Brown Lentils	4	Pack all the parts of meal in a different compartment of a container.	• 3 days-refrigeration • 1 month-freezer

Meal Plan 3: Weekly Meal Plan For The Family

🌱 MONDAY

Time	Meals	Servings	Storage Tips	Duration
Breakfast	Breakfast Enchiladas	8	Pack enchiladas and sauce separately in a partitioned box.	• 5 days- refrigeration • 1 month-freezer
Lunch	Tofu With Zucchini Noodles	6	Pack in partitioned container.	• 3 days- refrigeration • 1 month-freezer
Snack	Zucchini Sticks	6	Pack uncooked sticks and freeze.	• 6 months- freezer
Dinner	Lentil Soup With Mushrooms	6	Pack in a sealable bowl or ziplock bag	• 5 days- refrigeration • 1 month-freezer

🌱 TUESDAY

Time	Meals	Servings	Storage Tips	Duration
Breakfast	Peanut Butter And Banana Mini Muffins	6	Pack in an airlock container.	• 3 days- refrigeration • 1 month-freezer
Lunch	Curried Chickpea Bowls	6	Add the fresh herbs or bean sprouts on top then pack.	• 3 days- refrigeration • 1 month-freezer
Snack	Caramel Popcorn	8	Store in a cookie jar.	• 5 days- refrigeration • 1 month-freezer
Dinner	Mushroom Soup With Green Vegetables	6	Pack in a sealable bowl or ziplock bag	• 3 days- refrigeration • 1 month-freezer

🌱 WEDNESDAY

Time	Meals	Servings	Storage Tips	Duration
Breakfast	Quiche Muffins With Sun-Dried Tomatoes And Spinach	6	Store in an airlock container.	• 3 days-refrigeration • 1 month-freezer
Lunch	Italian Chickpea Soup	6	Pack in a sealable bowl or ziplock bag	• 5 days-refrigeration • 1 month-freezer
Snack	Sweet Potato Fries	8	Pack in a sealable container with paper towel.	• 3 days-refrigeration • 1 month-freezer
Dinner	Greens Soup	6	Pack in a sealable bowl or ziplock bag	• 3 days-refrigeration • 1 month-freezer

🌱 THURSDAY

Time	Meals	Servings	Storage Tips	Duration
Breakfast	Savoury Vegan Muffins	8	Store in an airlock container.	• 5 days-refrigeration • 1 month-freezer
Lunch	Thai Quinoa Salad	8	Pack this salad with colorful tofu skewers.	• 3 days-refrigeration • 1 month-freezer
Snack	Potato Stuffed Rolls		Pack in a sealable container with paper towel.	• 3 days-refrigeration • 1 month-freezer
Dinner	Vegan Borsch Soup	6	Pack in a sealable bowl or ziplock bag	• 3 days-refrigeration • 1 month-freezer

FRIDAY

Time	Meals	Servings	Storage Tips	Duration
Breakfast	Strawberry Almond Baked Oatmeal	6	Cover with foil sheet before storing.	• 5 days- refrigeration • 1 month-freezer
Lunch	Greek Couscous Salad	8	Pack with sauteed mushroom or tofu.	• 3 days- refrigeration • 1 month-freezer
Snack	Vegetable Spring Rolls	12	Place the unfried rolls in a sealable container then freeze.	• 6 months- freezer
Dinner	Miso Soup With Mushrooms	6	Pack in a sealable bowl or ziplock bag	• 5 days- refrigeration • 1 month-freezer

SATURDAY

Time	Meals	Servings	Storage Tips	Duration
Breakfast	Vegan Banana Bread	8		• 3 days- refrigeration • 1 month-freezer
Lunch	Tempeh Vegetable Quinoa Bowls	8	Cover the bowl with a foil sheets for storage.	• 3 days- refrigeration • 1 month-freezer
Snack	Cassava Croquettes	8	Place the unfried croquettes in a sealable container then freeze.	• 6 months- freezer
Dinner	Tofu With Zucchini Noodles	6	Pack noodles and tofu separately in a container	• 3 days- refrigeration • 1 month-freezer

Chapter 01: Plant-Based Meal Prep Meal Plans

SUNDAY

Time	Meals	Servings	Storage Tips	Duration
Breakfast	Cranberry Orange Muffins	8	Store in an airlock container.	• 3 days-refrigeration • 1 month-freezer
Lunch	Mushroom Broccoli Stir Fry	6	Pack with bread or rice in a partitioned container.	• 5 days-refrigeration • 1 month-freezer
Snack	Chocolate Bombs	12	Store in an airlock jar.	• 3 days-refrigeration • 1 month-freezer
Dinner	Green Bean Curry	6	Pack with bread or rice in a partitioned container.	• 3 days-refrigeration • 1 month-freezer

Chapter 01: Plant-Based Meal Prep Meal Plans

Menu Plan 4: Easy, Fast And Quick Weekly Meal Plan

🌱 MONDAY

Time	Meals	Servings	Storage Tips	Duration
Breakfast	Vegan Breakfast Burrito	4	Wrap the burrito in a paper wrap then place in a container.	• 5 days- refrigeration • 1 month-freezer
Lunch	Lunch Wrap	4	Wrap the burrito in a paper wrap then place in a container.	• 3 days- refrigeration • 1 month-freezer
Snack	Chocolate Bombs	12	Store the combs in a sealable mason jar.	• 3 days- refrigeration • 1 month-freezer
Dinner	Mushrooms Broccoli Stir Fry	4	Pack with bread or rice in a partitioned container.	• 5 days- refrigeration • 1 month-freezer

🌱 TUESDAY

Time	Meals	Servings	Storage Tips	Duration
Breakfast	Chickpea Omelets	4	Pack with bread in a partitioned container.	• 3 days- refrigeration • 1 month-freezer
Lunch	Mushroom Cauliflower Rice	4	Store the cauliflower rice in a meal box along with sauteed carrots and broccoli for serving.	• 3 days- refrigeration • 1 month-freezer
Snack	Chocolate Peanut Balls	12	Store in a dry cookie jar	• 3-5 days at room temperature (dark and cold place)
Dinner	Grilled Eggplant Rolls	4	Store the rolls in a meal box along with sauteed carrots and broccoli for serving.	• 3 days- refrigeration • 1 month-freezer

WEDNESDAY

Time	Meals	Servings	Storage Tips	Duration
Breakfast	Veggie Tofu Scramble	4	Pack with bread or rice in a partitioned container.	• 5 days-refrigeration • 1 month-freezer
Lunch	Vegan Bowl With Cashew Pesto	4	Pack this meal with tofu skewers.	• 3 days-refrigeration • 1 month-freezer
Snack	Tahini Date Cookies	8	Store in a dry cookie jar	• 3-5 days at room temperature (dark and cold place)
Dinner	Stinky Tofu	4	Pack with bread or rice in a partitioned container.	• 3 days-refrigeration • 1 month-freezer

THURSDAY

Time	Meals	Servings	Storage Tips	Duration
Breakfast	Vegan Tater Tot Breakfast Casserole	4	Cover the casserole with a foil sheets for storage.	• 3 days-refrigeration • 1 month-freezer
Lunch	Bbq Tofu Wraps	4	Wrap the burrito in a paper wrap then place in a container.	• 3 days-refrigeration • 1 month-freezer
Snack	Carrot Oat Balls	6	Store in a dry cookie jar	• 3-5 days at room temperature (dark and cold place)
Dinner	Cutlets Cauliflower	4	Pack the cutlets with whole wheat buns, vegetable salad and tomato sauce.	• 5 days-refrigeration • 1 month-freezer

FRIDAY

Time	Meals	Servings	Storage Tips	Duration
Breakfast	Blueberry Almond Oatmeal	4	Pack this oatmeal with granola bars.	• 3 days-refrigeration • 1 month-freezer
Lunch	Jerk Spiced Tofu	4	Pack with bread or rice in a partitioned container.	• 5 days-refrigeration • 1 month-freezer
Snack	Carrot Fries	6	Pack in a sealable container with paper towel.	• 3 days-refrigeration • 1 month-freezer
Dinner	Miso Soup With Mushrooms	6	Pack in a sealable bowl or ziplock bag	• 3 days-refrigeration • 1 month-freezer

SATURDAY

Time	Meals	Servings	Storage Tips	Duration
Breakfast	Berry Smoothie Bowls	4	Pack this smoothie bowl with baked muffins.	• 3 days-refrigeration • 1 month-freezer
Lunch	Curried Chickpea Bowls	6	Add the fresh herbs or bean sprouts on top then pack.	• 5 days-refrigeration • 1 month-freezer
Snack	Crispy Pepper Poppers	4	Pack the uncooked poppers in a sealable container	• 6 months-freezer
Dinner	Noodles With Tofu	4	Pack in a partitioned container.	• 3 days-refrigeration • 1 month-freezer

Chapter 01: Plant-Based Meal Prep Meal Plans

SUNDAY

Time	Meals	Servings	Storage Tips	Duration
Breakfast	Tropical Smoothie Bowls	4	Pack the smoothie with tropical fruits on top.	• 3 days-refrigeration • 1 month-freezer
Lunch	Greek Couscous Salad	8	Pack with sauteed mushroom or tofu.	• 5 days-refrigeration • 1 month-freezer
Snack	Onion Rings	4	Place the unfried rings in a sealable container then freeze.	• 6 months-freezer
Dinner	Pasta With Vegetables And Chickpeas	4	Pack the pasta with roasted asparagus.	• 5 days-refrigeration • 1 month-freezer

Meal Plan 5: Light Dishes Weekly Meal Plan

MONDAY

Time	Meals	Servings	Storage Tips	Duration
Breakfast	Vegan Breakfast Burrito	4	Wrap the burrito in a paper wrap then place in a container.	• 3 days-refrigeration • 1 month-freezer
Lunch	Steamed Cabbage Rolls	4	Cover the rolls with a foil sheets for storage.	• 3 days-refrigeration • 1 month-freezer
Snack	Zucchini Sticks	6	Place the unfried sticks in a sealable container then freeze.	• 6 months-freezer
Dinner	Eggplant Ratatouille	6	Cover the ratatouille with a foil sheets for storage.	• 3 days-refrigeration • 1 month-freezer

TUESDAY

Time	Meals	Servings	Storage Tips	Duration
Breakfast	Chickpea Omelets	4	Pack this omelet with toasted bread and granola bars	• 3 days-refrigeration • 1 month-freezer
Lunch	Eggplant Stir Fry	4	Pack with bread or rice in a partitioned container.	• 5 days-refrigeration • 1 month-freezer
Snack	Fried Blossoms	4	Place the uncooked blossoms in a sealable container then freeze for 2 hours	• 6 months-freezer
Dinner	Green Bean Stir-Fry	4	Pack with bread or rice in a partitioned container.	• 3 days-refrigeration • 1 month-freezer

WEDNESDAY

Time	Meals	Servings	Storage Tips	Duration
Breakfast	Vegan Pumpkin Muffins	8	Store in an airlock container.	• 3 days- refrigeration • 1 month-freezer
Lunch	Eggplant Lasagna	4	Cover the lasagna with a foil sheets for storage.	• 5 days- refrigeration • 1 month-freezer
Snack	Caramel Popcorn	8	Store in a cookie jar.	• 3 days- refrigeration • 1 month-freezer
Dinner	Stir-Fried Eggplant	4	Pack with boiled rice in a partitioned container.	• 3 days- refrigeration • 1 month-freezer

THURSDAY

Time	Meals	Servings	Storage Tips	Duration
Breakfast	Cranberry Orange Muffins	8	Store in an airlock container.	• 3 days- refrigeration • 1 month-freezer
Lunch	Scalloped Potatoes	6	Cover the potatoes with a foil sheets for storage.	• 5 days- refrigeration • 1 month-freezer
Snack	Bake Buffalo Cauliflower Wings	4	Store the cauliflower florets in a sealable container	• 3 days- refrigeration • 1 month-freezer
Dinner	Potato Tomato Bake	6	Cover the bake with a plastic sheets for storage.	• 3 days- refrigeration • 1 month-freezer

🌱 FRIDAY

Time	Meals	Servings	Storage Tips	Duration
Breakfast	Vegan Banana Bread	8	Wrap the bread in a paper bag then store.	• 3 days-refrigeration • 1 month-freezer
Lunch	Mushroom Pasta Bake	6	Cover the baked with a foil sheets for storage.	• 5 days-refrigeration • 1 month-freezer
Snack	Tofu Sticks	4	Wrap in a paper wrap then store.	• 3 days-refrigeration • 1 month-freezer
Dinner	Shiitake Mushroom Soup	4	Pack in a sealable bowl or ziplock bag	• 3 days-refrigeration • 1 month-freezer

🌱 SATURDAY

Time	Meals	Servings	Storage Tips	Duration
Breakfast	Veggie Tofu Scramble	4	Pack with bread or rice in a partitioned container.	• 3 days-refrigeration • 1 month-freezer
Lunch	Eggplant Stuffed Bread	6	Wrap in a parchment paper to store.	• 5 days-refrigeration • 1 month-freezer
Snack	Sweet Potato Fries	8	Pack in a sealable container with paper towel.	• 3 days-refrigeration • 1 month-freezer
Dinner	Eggplant Pie	4	Cover the pie with a foil sheets for storage.	• 3 days-refrigeration • 1 month-freezer

Chapter 01: Plant-Based Meal Prep Meal Plans

SUNDAY

Time	Meals	Servings	Storage Tips	Duration
Breakfast	Strawberry Almond Baked Oatmeal	6	Cover with foil sheet before storing.	• 5 days- refrigeration • 1 month-freezer
Lunch	Puff Pastry Pesto Bites	12	Pack uncooked pastries and freeze.	• 6 months- freezer
Snack	Eggplant Fries	4	Pack in a sealable container with paper towel.	• 3 days- refrigeration • 1 month-freezer
Dinner	Pumpkin Chickpea Stew	4	Pack with bread or rice in a partitioned container.	• 5 days- refrigeration • 1 month-freezer

Meal Plan 6: Asian Dishes Weekly Meal Plan

🌱 MONDAY

Time	Meals	Servings	Storage Tips	Duration
Breakfast	Vegan Breakfast Burrito	4	Wrap in a paper wrap then store.	• 3 days-refrigeration • 1 month-freezer
Lunch	Tempeh Stir Fry	4	Pack with bread in a partitioned container.	• 3-4 days-refrigeration • 1 month-freezer
Snack	Tofu Sticks	4	Wrap in a paper wrap then store.	• 3 days-refrigeration • 1 month-freezer
Dinner	Tofu And Rice Platter	4	Pack rice and tofu separately in a partitioned container.	• 3-4 days-refrigeration • 1 month-freezer

🌱 TUESDAY

Time	Meals	Servings	Storage Tips	Duration
Breakfast	Veggie Tofu Scramble	4	Pack with bread in a partitioned container.	• 3 days-refrigeration • 1 month-freezer
Lunch	Thai Quinoa Salad	8	this salad with colorful tofu skewers.	• 3-4 days-refrigeration • 1 month-freezer
Snack	Air Fried Tofu Nuggets	8	Place the unfried nuggets in a sealable container then freeze.	• 6 months-freezer
Dinner	Noodles With Tofu	4	Pack in a partitioned container.	• 3 days-refrigeration • 1 month-freezer

WEDNESDAY

Time	Meals	Servings	Storage Tips	Duration
Breakfast	Vegan Breakfast Burrito	4	Wrap in a paper wrap then store.	• 3-4 days- refrigeration • 1 month-freezer
Lunch	Jerk Spiced Tofu	4	Pack with bread or rice in a partitioned container.	• 3 days- refrigeration • 1 month-freezer
Snack	Air Fried Tofu Nuggets	8	Place the unfried nuggets in a sealable container then freeze.	• 6 months- freezer
Dinner	Mushroom Tofu Soup	4	Pack with side salad in a partitioned container.	• 3-4 days- refrigeration • 1 month-freezer

THURSDAY

Time	Meals	Servings	Storage Tips	Duration
Breakfast	Veggie Tofu Scramble	4	Pack with bread in a partitioned container.	• 3 days- refrigeration • 1 month-freezer
Lunch	Korean Barbecue Tofu	4	Pack with bread or rice in a partitioned container.	• 3-4 days- refrigeration • 1 month-freezer
Snack	Tofu Sticks	4	Wrap in a paper wrap then store.	• 3 days- refrigeration • 1 month-freezer
Dinner	Stinky Tofu	4	Pack with rice in a partitioned container.	• 3-4 days- refrigeration • 1 month-freezer

🌱 FRIDAY

Time	Meals	Servings	Storage Tips	Duration
Breakfast	Vegan Breakfast Burrito	4	Wrap in a paper wrap then store.	• 3 days-refrigeration • 1 month-freezer
Lunch	Tofu With Zucchini Noodles	4	Pack tofu and noodles separately.	• 3-4 days-refrigeration • 1 month-freezer
Snack	Air Fried Tofu Nuggets	8	Place the unfried nuggets in a sealable container then freeze.	• 6 months-freezer
Dinner	Brussel Sprout Tofu Fry	4	Pack with bread or rice in a partitioned container.	• 3 days-refrigeration • 1 month-freezer

🌱 SATURDAY

Time	Meals	Servings	Storage Tips	Duration
Breakfast	Veggie Tofu Scramble	4	Pack with bread in a partitioned container.	• 3-4 days-refrigeration • 1 month-freezer
Lunch	Tempeh Vegetable Quinoa Bowls	8	Pack with bread or rice in a partitioned container.	• 3 days-refrigeration • 1 month-freezer
Snack	Tofu Sticks	4	Wrap in a paper wrap then store.	• 3-4 days-refrigeration • 1 month-freezer
Dinner	Vegetable Tempeh Stew	4	Pack with bread or rice in a partitioned container.	• 3 days-refrigeration • 1 month-freezer

Chapter 01: Plant-Based Meal Prep Meal Plans

🌱 SUNDAY

Time	Meals	Servings	Storage Tips	Duration
Breakfast	Vegan Breakfast Burrito	4	Wrap in a paper wrap then store.	• 3-4 days- refrigeration • 1 month-freezer
Lunch	Bbq Tofu Wraps	4	Wrap in a food wraps.	• 3 days- refrigeration • 1 month-freezer
Snack	Bake Buffalo Cauliflower Wings	4	Store the cauliflower florets in a sealable container	• 3-4 days- refrigeration • 1 month-freezer
Dinner	Glazed Tofu	4	Pack with bread or rice in a partitioned container.	• 3 days- refrigeration • 1 month-freezer

Meal Plan 7:
Lunches & Dinners Plus Kid Friendly Meal Plan

🌱 MONDAY

Time	Meals	Servings	Storage Tips	Duration
Breakfast	Cauliflower Mash	4	Pack in small sealable bowls.	• 3-4 days-refrigeration • 1 month-freezer
Lunch	Crispy and Creamy Pasta	6	Cover with a foil sheet to store.	• 3 days-refrigeration • 1 month-freezer
Snack	Zucchini Cranberry Muffins	12	Store in an airlock container.	• 3-4 days-refrigeration • 1 month-freezer
Dinner	Mash Potatoes	12	Pack in small sealable bowls.	• 3 days-refrigeration • 1 month-freezer

🌱 TUESDAY

Time	Meals	Servings	Storage Tips	Duration
Breakfast	Cinnamon Apple Meal	6	Pack in small sealable bowls.	• 3-4 days-refrigeration • 1 month-freezer
Lunch	Creamy Pasta	6	Cover with foil sheet to store.	• 3 days-refrigeration • 1 month-freezer
Snack	Strawberry Pops	4	Keep in the molds for storage.	• 3-4 days-refrigeration • 1 month-freezer
Dinner	Tofu Patties	6	Pack with bread or rice in a partitioned container.	• 3 days-refrigeration • 1 month-freezer

Chapter 01: Plant-Based Meal Prep Meal Plans

🌱 WEDNESDAY

Time	Meals	Servings	Storage Tips	Duration
Breakfast	Mango Cream Bowl	4	Pack in a partitioned container.	• 3-4 days- refrigeration • 1 month-freezer
Lunch	Kid's Carrot Rice Soup	4	Pack in a sealable bowl or ziplock bag	• 3 days- refrigeration • 1 month-freezer
Snack	Mashed Carrot	6	Pack in small sealable bowls.	• 3-4 days- refrigeration • 1 month-freezer
Dinner	Animal Pasta Soup	4	Pack in a sealable bowl or ziplock bag	• 3 days- refrigeration • 1 month-freezer

🌱 THURSDAY

Time	Meals	Servings	Storage Tips	Duration
Breakfast	Cauliflower Mash	4	Pack in small sealable bowls.	• 3-4 days- refrigeration • 1 month-freezer
Lunch	Creamy Pasta	6	Cover with a plastic sheet to store.	• 3 days- refrigeration • 1 month-freezer
Snack	Strawberry Popsicles	6	Keep them in their molds.	• 3-4 days- refrigeration • 1 month-freezer
Dinner	Tofu Patties	6	Pack with bread or rice in a partitioned container.	• 3 days- refrigeration • 1 month-freezer

🌱 FRIDAY

Time	Meals	Servings	Storage Tips	Duration
Breakfast	Cinnamon Apple Meal	6	Pack in small sealable bowls.	• 3-4 days-refrigeration • 1 month-freezer
Lunch	Mashed Carrot	6	Pack in small sealable mason jar.	• 3 days-refrigeration • 1 month-freezer
Snack	Potato Croquettes		Place the unfried croquettes in a sealable container then freeze.	• 6 months-freezer
Dinner	Crispy and Creamy Pasta	6	Store with carrot sticks in a partitioned box.	• 3-4 days-refrigeration • 1 month-freezer

🌱 SATURDAY

Time	Meals	Servings	Storage Tips	Duration
Breakfast	Baby Oatmeal	4	Pack in small sealable mason jar.	• 3-4 days-refrigeration • 1 month-freezer
Lunch	Bow Tie Pasta Soup	8	Pack in a sealable bowl or ziplock bag	• 3 days-refrigeration • 1 month-freezer
Snack	Orange Mini Cookies	12	Store in a dry cookie jar	• 3-5 days at room temperature (dark and cold place)
Dinner	Tofu Patties	6	Pack with bread or rice in a partitioned container.	• 3-4 days-refrigeration • 1 month-freezer

Chapter 01: Plant-Based Meal Prep Meal Plans

SUNDAY

Time	Meals	Servings	Storage Tips	Duration
Breakfast	Pink-and-Yellow Cookies	12	Store in a dry cookie jar	- 3-5 days at room temperature (dark and cold place)
Lunch	Butternut Squash Puree	6	Store this pureed squash with carrot sticks	- 3 days-refrigeration - 1 month-freezer
Snack	Star Cookies	24	Store in a dry cookie jar	- 3-5 days at room temperature (dark and cold place)
Dinner	Animal Pasta Soup	4	Store this soup with roasted asparagus.	- 3-4 days-refrigeration - 1 month-freezer

CHAPTER 02

BREAKFAST RECIPES

Chapter 02: Breakfast Recipes

Vegan Quiche

SERVINGS 8 **PREPARATION TIME** 20 minutes **COOKING TIME** 1 hour 10 minutes

Nutritional Values Per Serving

Calories	353
Total Fat	21.2g
Saturated Fat	2.4g
Cholesterol	0mg
Sodium	374mg
Total Carbohydrate	27.5g
Dietary Fiber	5.1g
Total Sugars	2g
Protein	17.8g

Meal Prep Suggestion:

Reheat the quiche for delayed serving in the microwave for 2 minutes on medium-low heat.

Ingredients:

- 1 ½ cups all-purpose flour
- ¾ teaspoon baking soda
- ¾ teaspoon salt
- ½ cup canola oil
- 3 tablespoons boiling water

Quiche Filling

- 1 tablespoon olive oil
- 1 medium onion, chopped
- 2 cups diced mushrooms
- 1 (5 ounces) bag baby spinach
- 2 (16 oz.) packages of extra firm tofu
- ¼ cup melted vegan margarine
- ½ cup nutritional yeast
- 2 teaspoons salt
- ½ teaspoon black pepper
- ½ cup soy milk
- ⅔ cup vegan cheese, shredded
- 1 tablespoon melted vegan margarine

Instructions:

1. Mix all-purpose flour, salt, and baking soda in a mixing bowl.
2. Stir in 3 tablespoons boiling water and ½ cup oil, then mix well to make a dough.
3. Spread this dough over a piece of parchment paper.
4. Cover this dough with another parchment paper, then roll it into a 1/8 the inch thick sheet.
5. Spread this pie crust in a greased pie dish.
6. At 400 degrees F, preheat your oven.
7. Sauté onion with 1 tablespoon oil in a skillet until soft.
8. Stir in mushrooms, and salt then cook for 5 minutes.
9. Add baby spinach leaves and cook for about 2 minutes.
10. Crumble the tofu and add to a food processor.
11. Stir in black pepper, salt, vegan margarine and yeast, then blend until smooth.
12. Add soy milk spoon by spoon and continue blending.
13. Transfer this tofu mixture to the veggies along with vegan cheese.
14. Mix well and spread this filling in the pie crust.
15. Bake this quiche for 1 hour in the preheated oven.
16. Brush the baked quiche with melted vegan margarine.
17. Allow it to cool, then slice and serve.

Chapter 02: Breakfast Recipes

Vegan Breakfast Burrito

SERVINGS **PREPARATION TIME** **COOKING TIME**
4 10 minutes 15 minutes

Nutritional Values Per Serving	
Calories	339
Total Fat	17g
Saturated Fat	3g
Cholesterol	0mg
Sodium	997mg
Total Carbohydrate	31.2g
Dietary Fiber	6.2g
Total Sugars	4.7g
Protein	21.5g

Meal Prep Suggestion:

Wrap the burritos in Bee's wrap and refrigerate them for storage.

Ingredients:

- 8 (12-inch) tortillas

Tofu

- 2 (14 oz) containers of extra firm tofu
- 2 tablespoons nutritional yeast
- 1½ teaspoons salt
- ½ teaspoon turmeric
- ½ teaspoon garlic powder
- 2 tablespoons olive oil

Others

- 1 cup salsa
- ½ cup cilantro
- 1 cup avocado sliced
- 4 cups baby spinach
- ½ cup hatch green chiles

Vegan Sausage Crumble

- ½ cup water
- 1 tablespoon olive oil
- 1 teaspoon soy sauce
- 1 tablespoon maple syrup
- 1 teaspoon poultry seasoning
- ¼ teaspoon salt
- ¼ teaspoon onion powder
- 1 dash cayenne pepper
- 1¼ cup butler soy curls, crumbled

Instructions:

1. Drain the tofu block and crumble it.
2. Add crumbled tofu and oil to a skillet and sauté for 2 minutes.
3. Stir in salt, turmeric, garlic powder, and yeast.
4. Sauté this mixture for 7 minutes then transfer to a plate.
5. Add soy curls and rest of the sausage crumble ingredients to the same skillet.
6. Sauté for 6 minutes then transfer to a plate.
7. Divide the tofu filling and soy crumble mixture over the tortillas.
8. Divide salsa, avocado, cilantro, baby spinach and green chiles on top of the filling.
9. Roll the tortillas like a burrito and serve warm.

Chapter 02: Breakfast Recipes

Chickpea Omelets

SERVINGS **4**   PREPARATION TIME **15 minutes**   COOKING TIME **15 minutes**

Nutritional Values Per Serving	
Calories	184
Total Fat	9.1g
Saturated Fat	1.2g
Cholesterol	0mg
Sodium	305mg
Total Carbohydrate	20.7g
Dietary Fiber	6.9g
Total Sugars	4.6g
Protein	7.6g

Meal Prep Suggestion:

Serve this omelet with toasted bread and granola bars.

Ingredients:

- ½ cup chickpea flour
- ¾-1 cup water
- 2 tablespoons nutritional yeast
- ½ teaspoon salt
- ½ cup chopped chilllies, carrots and bell pepper
- 2 tablespoons olive oil

Instructions:

1. Mix chickpea flour, water, yeast, salt, and vegetables.
2. Set a suitable pan greased with oil over medium heat.
3. Spread the chickpea batter in the skillet and cook for 4-5 minutes per side.
4. Slice and serve warm.

Chapter 02: Breakfast Recipes

Vegan Pumpkin Muffins

SERVINGS: 8
PREPARATION TIME: 10 minutes
COOKING TIME: 22 minutes

Nutritional Values Per Serving	
Calories	243
Total Fat	7.7g
Saturated Fat	6.4g
Cholesterol	0mg
Sodium	186mg
Total Carbohydrate	42g
Dietary Fiber	1.6g
Total Sugars	21.1g
Protein	2.9g

Meal Prep Suggestion:

Place these muffins in a sealable container, then refrigerate them for storage.

Ingredients:

- 1 cup pumpkin puree
- 1 cup sugar
- ⅓ cup coconut oil melted
- ¼ cup plant-based milk
- 1 teaspoon vanilla

Dry Ingredients

- 2 cups whole wheat flour
- 1½ teaspoon baking powder
- ½ teaspoon baking soda
- 1½ teaspoon cinnamon
- ½ teaspoon nutmeg
- ½ teaspoon salt

Instructions:

1. At 375 degrees F, preheat your oven.
2. Mix vanilla, soy milk, coconut oil, sugar and pumpkin in a bowl.
3. Whisk flour with salt, nutmeg, cinnamon, baking soda, and baking powder in another bowl.
4. Stir in soy milk mixture and mix well until smooth.
5. Mix evenly, then divide this mixture in a greased muffin tray.
6. Bake the muffins for 22 minutes in the preheated oven.
7. Serve.

Chapter 02: Breakfast Recipes

Cranberry Orange Muffins

SERVINGS 8 **PREPARATION TIME** 13 minutes **COOKING TIME** 18 minutes

Nutritional Values Per Serving

Calories	275
Total Fat	14.4g
Saturated Fat	6g
Cholesterol	0mg
Sodium	250mg
Total Carbohydrate	33.6g
Dietary Fiber	1.5g
Total Sugars	8.1g
Protein	3.9g

Meal Prep Suggestion:

Serve these muffins with a smoothie bowl.

Ingredients:

- 2 cups whole wheat flour
- ⅔ cup coconut sugar
- 2 ½ teaspoons baking powder
- ½ teaspoon baking soda
- ½ teaspoon salt
- ¼ teaspoon nutmeg
- 1 cup dried cranberries

Wet ingredients

- ¾ cup plant-based milk
- 1 cup apple sauce
- ⅓ cup olive oil
- 1 ½ teaspoons orange extract

Orange glaze

- ⅓ cup powdered sugar
- 2 teaspoons orange juice
- ½ teaspoon orange extract

Instructions:

1. At 400 degrees F, preheat your oven.
2. Grease and line the muffin cups of a muffin tray.
3. First, mix 2 cups flour with dried cranberries, nutmeg, salt, baking soda, baking powder and sugar in a bowl.
4. Stir in milk, orange extra, apple sauce and oil, then mix evenly.
5. Divide this batter into the muffin cups and bake for 18 minutes at 375 degrees F.
6. Meanwhile, mix orange extract, orange juice and sugar in a bowl.
7. Brush this glaze over the muffins.
8. Allow them to cool and serve.

Chapter 02: Breakfast Recipes

The Best Vegan Banana Bread

SERVINGS 8
PREPARATION TIME 20 minutes
COOKING TIME 50 minutes

Nutritional Values Per Serving	
Calories	324
Total Fat	11.1g
Saturated Fat	2.3g
Cholesterol	1mg
Sodium	236mg
Total Carbohydrate	53.3g
Dietary Fiber	5.5g
Total Sugars	21.4g
Protein	5.9g

Meal Prep Suggestion:

Wrap the bread in a plastic bag, then refrigerate it for longer storage.

Ingredients:

- 3 medium ripe bananas
- ⅔ cup brown sugar
- ¼ cup plant-based milk
- ½ cup applesauce
- 1 teaspoon vanilla extract
- ⅓ cup olive oil
- 2 cups whole wheat flour
- 1½ teaspoons baking powder
- ½ teaspoon baking soda
- ½ teaspoon salt
- ¼ cup dark chocolate chips

Instructions:

1. At 350 degrees F, preheat your oven.
2. Grease an 8½ x 4½ inches loaf pan with cooking spray.
3. Mix ½ teaspoon salt, ½ teaspoon baking soda, 1½ baking powder and 2 cups flour in a bowl.
4. Mash bananas with ⅔ cup brown sugar in a bowl.
5. Stir in 1 teaspoon vanilla, ⅓ cup oil, ¼ cup milk and ½ apple sauce, then mix well.
6. Pour this mixture into the flour mixture, then mix well until smooth.
7. Fold in chocolate chips and mix evenly.
8. Spread this batter in the greased loaf pan.
9. Bake this loaf for 50 minutes in the preheated oven.
10. Slice and serve.

Chapter 02: Breakfast Recipes

Veggie Tofu Scramble

SERVINGS | PREPARATION TIME | COOKING TIME
4 | 10 minutes | 17 minutes

Nutritional Values Per Serving	
Calories	302
Total Fat	21g
Saturated Fat	3.5g
Cholesterol	3mg
Sodium	129mg
Total Carbohydrate	20.1g
Dietary Fiber	6.7g
Total Sugars	11.3g
Protein	15.1g

Meal Prep Suggestion:

Divide the scramble in a partitioned container along with sauteed vegetables and baked muffins.

Ingredients:

- 3 tablespoons olive oil
- 1 small onion, diced
- 2 garlic cloves, minced
- 1 small zucchini, diced
- 1 medium broccoli head, chopped
- 1 lb. extra-firm tofu, drained
- 10 medium cherry tomatoes cut in half
- 3 cups baby spinach
- ½ cup vegan cheese
- 3 tablespoons pesto
- Salt and black pepper to taste
- Sprinkle with pine nuts

Instructions:

1. Sauté onion with garlic, salt and oil in a suitable frying pan for 5 minutes.
2. Stir in broccoli and zucchini, then cook for 2 minutes.
3. Add pesto, and crumbled tofu, then cook for 8 minutes.
4. Stir in cheese, spinach and tomatoes, then cook for 2 minutes.
5. Add chia seeds and pine nuts on top.
6. Serve.

Chapter 02: Breakfast Recipes

Strawberry Almond Baked Oatmeal

SERVINGS PREPARATION TIME COOKING TIME
8   20 minutes   50 minutes

Nutritional Values Per Serving	
Calories	266
Total Fat	8g
Saturated Fat	0.8g
Cholesterol	0mg
Sodium	183mg
Total Carbohydrate	41.6g
Dietary Fiber	7.6g
Total Sugars	8g
Protein	8.2g

Meal Prep Suggestion:

Serve this oatmeal with a smoothie bowl.

Ingredients:

- 2 cups oats
- ⅓ cup slivered almonds
- 2 teaspoon ground cinnamon
- 1 teaspoon baking powder
- ¼ teaspoon sea salt
- 1 ¾ cup almond milk
- ⅓ cup agave
- 2 flax eggs
- 3 tablespoons melted coconut oil
- 2 teaspoon vanilla extract
- 1 pint fresh strawberries chopped
- 1 tablespoon coconut sugar

Instructions:

1. At 375 degrees F, preheat your oven.
2. Mix oats, sea salt, baking powder, cinnamon and almonds in a bowl.
3. Stir in vanilla extract, coconut oil, flax eggs, agave, and nut milk, then mix well.
4. Grease an 8x8 inches baking pan and spread half of the strawberries at its bottom.
5. Spread the oats mixture over the berries, then pour the flax egg mixture on top.
6. Add remaining strawberries and coconut sugar on top.
7. Bake this oatmeal for 45 minutes in the preheated oven.
8. Slice and serve.

Chapter 02: Breakfast Recipes

Vegan Tater Tot Breakfast Casserole

SERVINGS	PREPARATION TIME	COOKING TIME
4	10 minutes	57 minutes

Nutritional Values Per Serving

Calories	302
Total Fat	20.2g
Saturated Fat	3.3g
Cholesterol	0mg
Sodium	315mg
Total Carbohydrate	31.3g
Dietary Fiber	4.9g
Total Sugars	6.7g
Protein	3.5g

Meal Prep Suggestion:

Reheat the casserole covered in the microwave for 1-2 minutes before serving.

Ingredients:

- 2 tablespoons olive oil
- ½ yellow onion, diced
- 1 green bell pepper, diced
- 1 red bell pepper, diced
- 1 teaspoon onion powder
- 1 teaspoon cumin
- 1 teaspoon smoked paprika
- Salt and black pepper to taste
- 2 garlic cloves, diced
- 8 ounces vegan tempeh sausage patties
- 4 ounces vegan cream cheese
- non-stick spray
- 12 ounces flaxseed egg
- 1 bag frozen tater tots

Instructions:

1. At 375 degrees F, preheat your oven.
2. Sauté onion, with oil, black pepper, salt, paprika, cumin, onion powder, and bell peppers in a suitable pan for 7 minutes.
3. Stir in chopped garlic and cook for 30 seconds.
4. Make some space at the center and add the vegan sausage after crumbling.
5. Cook for 3 minutes, then mix with the veggies.
6. Stir in vegan cream cheese and mix well.
7. Spread this mixture in a 10 inch greased iron skillet.
8. Pour the flaxseed eggs over the veggie mixture and bake for 45 minutes in the preheated oven.
9. Slice and serve.

Chapter 02: Breakfast Recipes

Blueberry Almond Oatmeal (Vegan, High-Protein)

SERVINGS 4   **PREPARATION TIME** 10 minutes   **COOKING TIME** 10 minutes

Nutritional Values Per Serving

Calories	249
Total Fat	6g
Saturated Fat	0.6g
Cholesterol	0mg
Sodium	34mg
Total Carbohydrate	45.8g
Dietary Fiber	6.4g
Total Sugars	23.5g
Protein	6.2g

Meal Prep Suggestion:

Enjoy this oatmeal with granola bars.

Ingredients:

- 1 cup oats
- 1 cup oat milk
- 1 cup water
- ½ cup frozen blueberries

Toppings

- 2 tablespoons blueberries
- 2 tablespoons almonds chopped
- 4 tablespoons lemon juice
- 2 tablespoons maple syrup

Instructions:

1. Mix oats with frozen blueberries, water and milk in a saucepan.
2. Cook for almost 10 minutes on medium heat with occasional stirring.
3. Stir in chopped almonds, fresh blueberries, maple syrup and lemon juice.
4. Serve.

Chapter 02: Breakfast Recipes

Savoury Vegan Muffins

SERVINGS	PREPARATION TIME	COOKING TIME
8	10 minutes	35 minutes

Nutritional Values Per Serving	
Calories	217
Total Fat	10.8g
Saturated Fat	6.8g
Cholesterol	0mg
Sodium	299mg
Total Carbohydrate	26.4g
Dietary Fiber	3g
Total Sugars	1.4g
Protein	4.8g

Meal Prep Suggestion:

Pack these muffins in plastic wrap, then keep them in the refrigerator.

Ingredients:

- 2 tablespoons ground flaxseed
- 3 ounces wholemeal flour
- 6 ounces plain flour
- 2½ teaspoon baking powder
- 1 teaspoon salt
- ¼ teaspoon ground pepper
- A pinch of garlic powder
- 2½ tablespoon dried chives
- 1 teaspoon dried thyme
- 1 teaspoon paprika powder
- 2½ tablespoon olive oil
- 1 cup almond milk
- 2 ounces vegan cheese
- 4 ounces zucchini, shredded

Instructions:

1. Mix flaxseed with 6 tablespoons boiling water in a bowl and leave for 10 minutes.
2. Mix flour with paprika, thyme, chives, garlic, black pepper, salt, and baking powder in a suitable bowl.
3. Add almond milk and oil to the flaxseed mixture, then mix well.
4. Stir in the flour mixture and mix until smooth and lump-free.
5. Fold in grated zucchini and vegan cheese.
6. Divide this batter into a greased muffin tray.
7. At 356 degrees F, preheat your oven.
8. Bake the vegan muffins for 35 minutes in the preheated oven.
9. Serve.

Chapter 02: Breakfast Recipes

Chickpea & Sweet Potato Breakfast Hash

SERVINGS **8** | PREPARATION TIME **10 minutes** | COOKING TIME **40 minutes**

Nutritional Values Per Serving

Calories	276
Total Fat	9.2g
Saturated Fat	1.3g
Cholesterol	0mg
Sodium	43mg
Total Carbohydrate	42.7g
Dietary Fiber	9g
Total Sugars	4.4g
Protein	7.7g

Meal Prep Suggestion:

Enjoy this hash with orange segments and sauteed veggies.

Ingredients:

- 1½ lb. sweet potatoes, diced
- ½ large onion, chopped
- 2 red bell peppers, cored and diced
- 1 can (15oz.) chickpeas, drained
- 2 tablespoons olive oil
- 1 teaspoon garlic powder
- 1 pinch of salt
- Black pepper, to taste

Sriracha Tahini Sauce

- 4 tablespoons tahini
- 4 tablespoons water
- juice of ½ small lemon
- 1 pinch of salt
- Sriracha, to taste
- Roasted Peanuts, to garnish
- Chopped parsley, to garnish

Instructions:

1. At 425 degrees F, preheat your oven.
2. Layer a medium sheet pan with parchment paper and grease it with oil.
3. Mix sweet potatoes with black pepper, salt, garlic powder, olive oil, chickpeas, bell peppers and onions in the pan.
4. Spread them evenly, then bake for 20 minutes in the oven.
5. Toss all the veggies once cooked halfway through.
6. Increase the heat to 500 degrees F and continue baking for 20 minutes.
7. Toss all the veggies once cooked halfway through.
8. For dressing, mix tahini with sriracha, salt, water and lemon juice in a bowl.
9. Pour this dressing over the veggies and mix well.
10. Garnish with roasted peanuts and parsley.
11. Serve.

Chapter 02: Breakfast Recipes

Quiche Muffins With Sun-Dried Tomatoes And Spinach

SERVINGS: 6
PREPARATION TIME: 10 minutes
COOKING TIME: 45 minutes

Nutritional Values Per Serving

Calories	163
Total Fat	9.3g
Saturated Fat	4g
Cholesterol	0mg
Sodium	339mg
Total Carbohydrate	10.1g
Dietary Fiber	3.5g
Total Sugars	2.7g
Protein	13.9g

Meal Prep Suggestion:

Enjoy the quiche muffins with a glass of kale smoothie.

Ingredients:

- 16 ounces block firm tofu, lightly pressed
- 1 tablespoon coconut oil
- ¼ cup chopped mushrooms
- 2 cups spinach
- 4 garlic cloves, minced
- 3 tablespoons chopped onions
- Salt and black pepper, to taste
- 7 sundried tomato halves, diced
- 1 cup almond milk
- 3 tablespoons nutritional yeast
- ½ teaspoon sea salt
- ¼ teaspoon black pepper
- 1 pinch of turmeric
- 1 teaspoon dried chives, chopped
- ½ teaspoon baking powder
- 1 pinch black salt

Instructions:

1. At 375 degrees F, preheat your oven.
2. Grease a 12 cup-muffin tray with cooking spray.
3. Sauté mushrooms with spinach, onions, garlic, sundried tomatoes and oil in a skillet for 8 minutes.
4. Stir in black pepper and salt for seasoning.
5. Blend tofu with baking powder, turmeric, black pepper, sea salt, yeast and almond milk in a blender until smooth.
6. Stir in the veggie mixture and give it a stir.
7. Divide the batter into the prepared muffin tray.
8. Bake the muffins for 35 minutes in the oven.
9. Serve.

Chapter 02: Breakfast Recipes

Peanut Butter And Banana Mini Muffins

SERVINGS 6 **PREPARATION TIME** 10 minutes **COOKING TIME** 17 minutes

Nutritional Values Per Serving

Calories	193
Total Fat	4.6g
Saturated Fat	0.9g
Cholesterol	0mg
Sodium	151mg
Total Carbohydrate	35.3g
Dietary Fiber	2.5g
Total Sugars	12.3g
Protein	4.7g

Meal Prep Suggestion:

Enjoy these muffins with a glass of avocado smoothie.

Ingredients:

- ¼ cup unsweetened almond milk
- 1 tablespoon ground flax
- 1 cup all-purpose flour
- 1 teaspoon cinnamon
- 1 teaspoon baking powder
- ½ teaspoon baking soda
- ⅛ teaspoon salt
- ½ cup mini chocolate chips
- 3 tablespoons peanut butter, softened
- 3 tablespoons maple syrup
- 1 teaspoon natural vanilla extract
- 2 large bananas, mashed

Instructions:

1. At 350 degrees F, preheat your oven.
2. Grease an 18 cup-mini muffin pan with cooking spray.
3. Mix ground flax with milk in a bowl.
4. Mix flour with salt, baking soda, baking powder and cinnamon in a bowl.
5. Add mashed bananas, vanilla, maple syrup and peanut butter to the flax mixture.
6. Mix well, then fold in flour mixture.
7. Stir until smooth and lump-free.
8. Fold in chocolate chips, then divide the mixture into the muffin cups.
9. Bake them for almost 17 minutes in the preheated oven.
10. Serve.

Breakfast Enchiladas

SERVINGS	PREPARATION TIME	COOKING TIME
8	12 hours 5 minutes	40 minutes

Nutritional Values Per Serving

Calories	324
Total Fat	5.9g
Saturated Fat	1.1g
Cholesterol	0mg
Sodium	210mg
Total Carbohydrate	52.2g
Dietary Fiber	11.3g
Total Sugars	2.6g
Protein	18.5g

Meal Prep Suggestion:

Store the enchilada sauce and enchiladas in separate containers and pour the sauce over the enchiladas then bake right before serving.

Ingredients:

Filling

- 1 lb firm tofu
- 3 tablespoons salsa
- 1 (15 ounces) can black beans, drained
- 2 garlic cloves, minced
- 1 cup onion, diced
- 1 tablespoon olive oil
- ½ teaspoon black salt
- ½ teaspoon cumin
- ¼ cup fresh chopped cilantro

Other ingredients

- 12 corn tortillas
- 12-ounce jar enchilada sauce
- ½ cup shredded vegan cheese

Instructions:

1. Sauté onions with 1 tablespoon oil in a suitable skillet for 5 minutes.
2. Stir in tofu chunks and cook for 5 minutes.
3. Add spices, salsa, and black beans, then cook until all the liquid is evaporated.
4. Stir in cilantro, then remove this skillet from the heat.
5. At 350 degrees F, preheat your oven.
6. Grease an 11x13 inches casserole dish with oil.
7. Heat the tortillas on a greased skillet for 1 minute per side on medium-high heat.
8. Spread the tortillas on a working surface and add ¼ cup filling at the center of each tortilla.
9. Roll the tortillas, then place them in the prepared casserole dish with their seam side down.
10. Pour the enchilada sauce on top, drizzle cheese on top and bake for 20 minutes.
11. Serve warm.

Chapter 02: Breakfast Recipes

Coconut Chia Oats

SERVINGS **PREPARATION TIME** **COOKING TIME**
4 6 hours 5 minutes 0 minutes

Nutritional Values Per Serving	
Calories	230
Total Fat	8.8g
Saturated Fat	2.1g
Cholesterol	0mg
Sodium	4mg
Total Carbohydrate	32.7g
Dietary Fiber	8.2g
Total Sugars	9.6g
Protein	6.5g

Meal Prep Suggestion:

Store the oats in a mason, seal the lid and refrigerate.

Ingredients:

- 2 cups old fashioned rolled oats
- ⅓ cup unsweetened shredded coconut
- 2 tablespoons chia seeds
- 1 ½ teaspoons matcha tea powder
- 2 ½ cups coconut milk
- 3 tablespoons maple syrup

Garnish

- Unsweetened raw coconut or almond flakes
- Berries

Instructions:

1. Mix oats with matcha, chia seeds, maple syrup and coconut milk in a suitable mason jar.
2. Cover and refrigerate this jar for 6 hours at least.
3. Garnish with berries, nuts, coconut flakes or fresh fruits.
4. Serve.

Chapter 02: Breakfast Recipes

Berry Smoothie Bowls

SERVINGS 4   **PREPARATION TIME** 35 minutes   **COOKING TIME** 0 minutes

Nutritional Values Per Serving	
Calories	202
Total Fat	11.5g
Saturated Fat	0.7g
Cholesterol	0mg
Sodium	96mg
Total Carbohydrate	23g
Dietary Fiber	9.6g
Total Sugars	10.1g
Protein	5.6g

Meal Prep Suggestion:

Enjoy this smoothie bowl with bake muffins.

Ingredients:

- 4 frozen bananas
- 4 tablespoons almond butter
- 2 cups almond milk
- 4 cups fresh raspberries

Garnishes

- 4 bananas, sliced
- 1 cup blueberries
- 1 cup raspberries
- 4 tablespoons chia seeds

Instructions:

1. Blend banana with almond butter, milk and raspberries in a high-speed blender until smooth.
2. Refrigerate this smoothie for at least 30 minutes.
3. Divide the smoothie into four serving bowls.
4. Garnish with fresh berries, banana, and chia seeds.
5. Serve.

Chapter 02: Breakfast Recipes

Tropical Smoothie Bowls

SERVINGS 4
PREPARATION TIME 10 minutes
COOKING TIME 0 minutes

Nutritional Values Per Serving	
Calories	206
Total Fat	6.1g
Saturated Fat	0.6g
Cholesterol	0mg
Sodium	55mg
Total Carbohydrate	38.8g
Dietary Fiber	5g
Total Sugars	27.2g
Protein	3.7g

Meal Prep Suggestion:
Enjoy the smoothie with tropical fruits on top.

Ingredients:
- 4 frozen bananas
- 4 tablespoons almond butter
- 2 cups almond milk
- 1 mango, diced
- 1 papaya, diced

Garnishes
- Mango cubes
- Coconut shavings
- Chia seeds
- Chopped nuts

Instructions:
1. Blend banana with almond butter, milk, mango and papaya in a high-speed blender until smooth.
2. Divide the smoothie into four serving bowls.
3. Garnish with fresh mango cubes, seeds, nuts and coconut as desired.
4. Serve.

Pumpkin Pie Quinoa

SERVINGS 2 | **PREPARATION TIME** 10 minutes | **COOKING TIME** 2 minutes

Nutritional Values Per Serving	
Calories	206
Total Fat	6.1g
Saturated Fat	0.6g
Cholesterol	0mg
Sodium	55mg
Total Carbohydrate	38.8g
Dietary Fiber	5g
Total Sugars	27.2g
Protein	3.7g

Meal Prep Suggestion:

Store this quinoa meal in a sealable container, then refrigerate.

Ingredients:

- ⅓ cup quinoa flakes
- ⅓ cup pumpkin puree
- 2 tablespoons maple sugar
- 1 ¼ cup plant-based milk
- ½ teaspoon cinnamon
- ¼ teaspoon nutmeg
- ¼ teaspoon ginger
- ¼ teaspoon vanilla bean powder
- Pecans, to garnish

Instructions:

1. Mix milk, maple sugar, pumpkin and quinoa flakes in a suitable sauce.
2. Cook this quinoa mixture to a boil, then reduce the heat to a simmer.
3. Stir in spices and cook for 2 minutes.
4. Garnish with maple sugar and pecans.
5. Serve.

Chapter 02: Breakfast Recipes

Carrot Quinoa Bars

SERVINGS
8

PREPARATION TIME
10 minutes

COOKING TIME
26 minutes

Nutritional Values Per Serving	
Calories	201
Total Fat	6g
Saturated Fat	0.6g
Cholesterol	0mg
Sodium	115mg
Total Carbohydrate	28.5g
Dietary Fiber	7.5g
Total Sugars	5.9g
Protein	8.4g

Meal Prep Suggestion:

Wrap the bars in bees wrap and refrigerate in a cookie in a jar for storage.

Ingredients:

- 1½ tablespoons flaxseed meal
- 3 tablespoons water
- 1 cup cooked chickpeas
- ½ cup mashed banana
- ½ cup unsweetened applesauce
- ¾ cup quinoa flour
- ½ cup coconut sugar
- 1 teaspoon ground cinnamon
- ½ teaspoon ground nutmeg
- 1 tablespoon cocoa powder
- ½ teaspoon ground vanilla bean
- ½ teaspoon baking soda
- Pinch of salt
- ¼ cup hemp hearts, finely chopped
- ½ cup grated carrots
- ¼ cup chopped walnuts

Instructions:

1. At 350 degrees F, preheat your oven.
2. Grease an 8x8 inch baking dish with cooking spray, then layer it with parchment paper.
3. Soak flaxseed meal in 3 tablespoons water in a small bowl for 5 minutes.
4. Blend chickpeas with applesauce, cocoa powder and banana in a food processor until smooth.
5. Whisk the rest of the dry ingredients in a bowl, then fold in the chickpea mixture.
6. Mix well until smooth, then fold in walnuts, carrots and hemp hearts.
7. Spread this prepared batter in the greased pan and bake for 26 minutes.
8. Allow the cooked quinoa mixture and cut it into bars.
9. Serve.

Chapter 02: Breakfast Recipes

Thumbprint Cookies

SERVINGS	PREPARATION TIME	COOKING TIME
8	15 minutes	15 minutes

Nutritional Values Per Serving

Calories	291
Total Fat	18.2g
Saturated Fat	6.6g
Cholesterol	0mg
Sodium	157mg
Total Carbohydrate	26.3g
Dietary Fiber	3.8g
Total Sugars	6.9g
Protein	8g

Meal Prep Suggestion:

Keep these cookies in a cookie jar, then seal, refrigerate for longer storage.

Ingredients:

- 1 ¼ cups rolled oats
- ¼ cup oat flour
- ½ cup almond flour
- ½ teaspoon baking soda
- ½ teaspoon fine kosher salt
- ½ cup roasted peanut butter
- ½ cup apple sauce
- 3 tablespoons maple syrup
- 3 tablespoons coconut oil
- 1 teaspoon vanilla extract
- 2 tablespoons flax meal
- 2 tablespoons strawberry jam
- Melted white chocolate to garnish

Instructions:

1. At 350 degrees F, preheat your oven.
2. Layer a cookie sheet with parchment paper.
3. Mix oats, baking soda, salt, almond and oat flour in a bowl.
4. Whisk flax meal with vanilla, coconut oil, maple syrup, applesauce, and peanut butter in another bowl.
5. Stir in oats mixture and mix evenly.
6. Divide the dough into tablespoon-sized balls on the cookie sheet and press each into a cookie.
7. Press each cookie with your thumb at the center.
8. Add fruit jam to each indentation and bake for 15 minutes in the oven.
9. Allow the cookies to cool and serve.

Chapter 02: Breakfast Recipes

Vegan Waffles

SERVINGS
8

PREPARATION TIME
15 minutes

COOKING TIME
10 minutes

Nutritional Values Per Serving	
Calories	290
Total Fat	19.1g
Saturated Fat	12.1g
Cholesterol	0mg
Sodium	30mg
Total Carbohydrate	27.6g
Dietary Fiber	2g
Total Sugars	1.8g
Protein	4.4g

Meal Prep Suggestion:

Serve these waffles with apple sauce on top.

Ingredients:

- 2 cups flour
- 2 tablespoons coconut sugar
- 1 tablespoon baking powder
- 1 ¾ cups almond milk
- ¼ cup olive oil
- 1 pinch of salt

Instructions:

1. At 200 degrees F, preheat your waffle iron.
2. Mix flour with milk, oil and the rest of the ingredients until lump-free.
3. Add a dollop of this batter into the waffle iron and cook as per the machine's instructions.
4. Cook more waffles in the same way.
5. Serve.

Chapter 02: Breakfast Recipes

Bircher Muesli

SERVINGS: 4
PREPARATION TIME: 12 hours 15 minutes
COOKING TIME: 0 minutes

Nutritional Values Per Serving	
Calories	164
Total Fat	4.8g
Saturated Fat	0.5g
Cholesterol	0mg
Sodium	20mg
Total Carbohydrate	27.9g
Dietary Fiber	3.3g
Total Sugars	14.9g
Protein	4.1g

Meal Prep Suggestion:

Add a splash of milk to muesli before serving.

Ingredients:

- 1 cups whole rolled oats
- 1 apple grated
- 1 cup oat milk
- 1 cup soy yoghurt
- ¼ cup raisins
- 1 tablespoon walnuts chopped
- 2 tablespoons flaked almonds
- 1 tablespoon brown sugar
- 1 tablespoon maple syrup
- 1 tablespoon orange juice

Instructions:

1. Mix oats, apple, oat milk, soy yogurt and the rest of the ingredients in a bowl.
2. Cover the oatmeal with saran wrap and refrigerate overnight.
3. Serve.

Breakfast Cookie Bites

SERVINGS	PREPARATION TIME	COOKING TIME
8	1 hour 5 minutes	0 minutes

Nutritional Values Per Serving	
Calories	229
Total Fat	14.4g
Saturated Fat	1.3g
Cholesterol	0mg
Sodium	12mg
Total Carbohydrate	18.6g
Dietary Fiber	7.5g
Total Sugars	7.5g
Protein	7g

Meal Prep Suggestion:

Try the cookie bites with a creamy smoothie.

Ingredients:

- ⅓ cup ground oats
- 1 cup almond flour
- ⅓ cup peanut flour
- 2 tablespoons chia seeds
- ¼ cup natural nut butter
- 1 tablespoon cinnamon
- ¼ cup maple syrup
- ½ teaspoon vanilla
- 1 tablespoon molasses
- 2 tablespoons finely crushed nuts
- Cinnamon sugar to sprinkle on top

Instructions:

1. Grind ½ cup rolled oats in a food processor.
2. Mix the oat flour with chia seeds, almond butter, cinnamon, almond flour and peanut flour.
3. Mix vanilla, molasses and maple syrup in a small bowl.
4. Add this mixture to the oat flour mixture and mix well.
5. Make 1½ inch oat balls out of this dough and roll each in crushed nuts.
6. Place these balls in a baking sheet lined with parchment paper.
7. Cover and refrigerate these balls for 1 hour.
8. Garnish with cinnamon sugar and serve.

Chapter 02: Breakfast Recipes

Breakfast Cookies

SERVINGS	PREPARATION TIME	COOKING TIME
8	15 minutes	25 minutes

Nutritional Values Per Serving	
Calories	241
Total Fat	12.2g
Saturated Fat	3.3g
Cholesterol	0mg
Sodium	24mg
Total Carbohydrate	28.8g
Dietary Fiber	4.9g
Total Sugars	8.5g
Protein	6.3g

Meal Prep Suggestion:

Enjoy the cookies with warmed almond milk.

Ingredients:

- 2 cups rolled oats
- ½ cup almond flour
- 1 small banana, mashed
- 3 tablespoons maple syrup
- ⅓ cup mixed nuts, chopped
- ¼ cup dark chocolate chips
- 1 tablespoon coconut oil
- 1 tablespoon ground flax seeds
- 1 tablespoon chia seeds
- A pinch of vanilla

Instructions:

1. At 325 degrees F, preheat your oven.
2. Layer a large-sized baking sheet with parchment paper.
3. Blend oats in a blender for 1 minute, then mix with the rest of the ingredients in a bowl.
4. Make 1½ inches balls out of this mixture and place them in the prepared baking sheet.
5. Press the balls into cookies and bake for 20-25 minutes until golden brown.
6. Serve.

Chapter 02: Breakfast Recipes

Grain Free Granola

SERVINGS 10 **PREPARATION TIME** 15 minutes **COOKING TIME** 35 minutes

Nutritional Values Per Serving	
Calories	247
Total Fat	20.8g
Saturated Fat	11.7g
Cholesterol	0mg
Sodium	101mg
Total Carbohydrate	11.8g
Dietary Fiber	3g
Total Sugars	5.9g
Protein	5.3g

Meal Prep Suggestion:

Wrap the granola bars in a bee's wrap and refrigerate them for longer storage.

Ingredients:

- 1 cup sunflower seeds
- 1 cup pumpkin seeds
- 1 cup unsweetened shredded coconut
- ¼ cup chia seeds
- 1 teaspoon cinnamon
- ½ teaspoon sea salt
- ¼ cup maple syrup
- ¼ cup coconut oil, melted
- ¼ cup dried cranberries

Instructions:

1. At 300 degrees F, preheat your oven.
2. Layer a large-sized baking sheet with parchment paper.
3. Mix salt, cinnamon, chia, coconut, pumpkin seeds and sunflower seeds in a large bowl.
4. Add coconut oil and maple syrup, then mix well.
5. Spread this granola mixture in the prepared baking sheet and bake for 35 minutes.
6. Once baked, break the granola into pieces.
7. Serve.

Green Smoothie Bowl

SERVINGS	PREPARATION TIME	COOKING TIME
4	35 minutes	0 minutes

Nutritional Values Per Serving	
Calories	160
Total Fat	3.4g
Saturated Fat	0.3g
Cholesterol	0mg
Sodium	53mg
Total Carbohydrate	31.4g
Dietary Fiber	6.6g
Total Sugars	20.4g
Protein	4g

Meal Prep Suggestion:

Add flaxseeds, chopped nuts and chia seeds on top of the green smoothie bowl.

Ingredients:

- 2 cups fresh spinach
- 1 small banana, peeled
- 1 small green apple, peeled
- 1 orange, juiced
- 1 tablespoon chia seeds
- 1½ cups oat milk

Garnishes

- Banana slices
- Blueberries
- Chia seeds

Instructions:

1. Blend spinach with banana, apple, orange juice, milk and chia seeds in a high-speed blender for 1 minute.
2. Refrigerate this smoothie for 30 minutes at least.
3. Serve in a bowl with desired garnishes.

Chapter 02: Breakfast Recipes

Avocado Toast

SERVINGS 4
PREPARATION TIME 10 minutes
COOKING TIME 5 minutes

Nutritional Values Per Serving

Calories	496
Total Fat	18.5g
Saturated Fat	3.1g
Cholesterol	0mg
Sodium	236mg
Total Carbohydrate	67.3g
Dietary Fiber	18.1g
Total Sugars	8.9g
Protein	18.7g

Meal Prep Suggestion:

Add herbs or sauteed vegetables on top of toasts.

Ingredients:

- 4 multi-grain bread slices, toasted
- 1 avocado, peeled
- ½ lime, juiced
- 1 ½ cups cooked chickpeas
- 1 teaspoon smoked paprika
- 1 tablespoon olive oil
- Sea salt, to taste
- Black pepper, to taste

Instructions:

1. Sauté chickpeas with oil, and paprika in a skillet for 5 minutes.
2. Mash avocado with lime juice, a pinch of black pepper and salt in a bowl.
3. Spread the avocado mash over the toast.
4. Add chickpeas on top and garnish.
5. Serve.

Chapter 02: Breakfast Recipes

Breakfast Burrito

SERVINGS 4 | PREPARATION TIME 15 minutes | COOKING TIME 10 minutes

Nutritional Values Per Serving

Calories	574
Total Fat	21.9g
Saturated Fat	2.9g
Cholesterol	0mg
Sodium	488mg
Total Carbohydrate	61.9g
Dietary Fiber	26.2g
Total Sugars	13.2g
Protein	42g

Meal Prep Suggestion:

Serve these burritos with a chimichurri sauce.

Ingredients:

- 4 wholewheat wraps
- 1 green bell pepper, chopped
- 7-8 cherry tomatoes, chopped
- 1 avocado, chopped
- Fresh spinach, chopped
- Salsa

Scrambled Chickpeas

- 1 can (14 oz.) chickpeas, drained
- ¼ teaspoon garlic powder
- ½ teaspoon ground cumin
- ¼ teaspoon chilli powder
- ¼ teaspoon smoked paprika
- 1 pinch ground turmeric

Seitan Bacon

- 3 ½ ounces seitan, sliced
- ½ teaspoon chilli powder
- ¼ teaspoon smoked paprika
- ¼ teaspoon ground cumin
- Salt and black pepper, to taste

Instructions:

1. At 350 degrees F, preheat your oven.
2. Spread the bell pepper and cherry tomatoes on a greased baking sheet and roast for 25 minutes.
3. Mash chickpeas with the spices in a food processor.
4. Cut the seitan into thin strips using a vegetable peeler.
5. Set a pan with 1 tablespoon oil over medium heat.
6. Add chickpeas and seitan to this skillet and cook for 5-10 minutes until warm.
7. Spread the tortilla wraps on the working surface.
8. Divide seitan, chickpeas, roasted peppers, tomatoes, salsa, spinach and avocado over the tortillas.
9. Roll all the tortillas into burritos.
10. Serve.

Chapter 02: Breakfast Recipes

Overnight Zoats

SERVINGS
4

PREPARATION TIME
12 hours 5 minutes

COOKING TIME
0 minutes

Nutritional Values Per Serving	
Calories	249
Total Fat	4.3g
Saturated Fat	0.7g
Cholesterol	0mg
Sodium	79mg
Total Carbohydrate	49.8g
Dietary Fiber	7.7g
Total Sugars	16.8g
Protein	6.9g

Meal Prep Suggestion:

Storage the oatmeal in a container without the fruit garnishes. Garnish right before serving.

Ingredients:

- 1½ cup rolled oats
- 1 teaspoon flax seeds
- 1 medium zucchini, grated
- 2 tablespoons cocoa powder
- ½ teaspoon ground cinnamon
- 2 cups almond milk
- 2 bananas, sliced
- 1 kiwi, sliced
- 1 cup fresh blueberries

Instructions:

1. Mix oats with cinnamon, cocoa powder, zucchini and flaxseeds in a bowl.
2. Stir in almond milk, then mix until smooth.
3. Add this mixture to a glass jar, cover and refrigerate overnight.
4. Garnish with kiwi, berries and banana slices, then serve.

Chapter 02: Breakfast Recipes

Blueberry Muffins

SERVINGS	PREPARATION TIME	COOKING TIME
6	15 minutes	25 minutes

Nutritional Values Per Serving

Calories	207
Total Fat	3g
Saturated Fat	0.5g
Cholesterol	0mg
Sodium	22mg
Total Carbohydrate	41.6g
Dietary Fiber	5.9g
Total Sugars	17.6g
Protein	5.6g

Meal Prep Suggestion:

Serve these muffins with warmed almond milk.

Ingredients:

- 2 cups rolled oats, ground
- 12 dates, pitted and chopped
- ¾ cup soy milk
- ½ teaspoon lemon juice
- ¾ cup water
- 1 ½ tablespoon flaxseeds, ground
- ¾ cup applesauce
- 1 cup blueberries
- 1 tablespoon baking powder
- ½ teaspoon cinnamon
- ½ teaspoon vanilla extract
- Pinch of salt

Instructions:

1. Mix flaxseeds with water, soy milk, vanilla, dates and lemon juice in a bowl for 5 minutes.
2. At 400 degrees F, preheat your oven.
3. Grease a muffin tray with cooking spray.
4. Blend dates mixture in a food processor for 30 seconds.
5. Mix oat ground with the rest of the ingredients in a mixing bowl.
6. Stir in a flaxseed mixture and mix evenly.
7. Fold in blueberries and mix evenly.
8. Divide this mixture into a 12 cup greased muffin tray.
9. Bake for 20 minutes in the preheated oven.
10. Serve.

Chapter 02: Breakfast Recipes

Fruity Flapjacks

SERVINGS   PREPARATION TIME   COOKING TIME
8   10 minutes   30 minutes

Nutritional Values Per Serving

Calories	201
Total Fat	2.9g
Saturated Fat	1.4g
Cholesterol	0mg
Sodium	150mg
Total Carbohydrate	41.6g
Dietary Fiber	4g
Total Sugars	19.5g
Protein	4g

Meal Prep Suggestion:
Keep the flapjacks in a large sealable mason jar.

Ingredients:

- 1½ cup rolled oats
- 1 cup oat flour
- ½ cup desiccated coconut
- 1 teaspoon baking powder
- ½ teaspoon salt
- ⅓ cup full-fat coconut milk
- ½ cup dates pitted
- 2 teaspoon vanilla extract
- 1 cup berry chia jam

Instructions:

1. At 345 degrees F, preheat your oven.
2. Layer an 8x8 inches baking pan with cooking oil and layer it with parchment paper.
3. Mix rolled oats with salt, baking powder, desiccated coconut, and oat flour in a bowl.
4. Blend coconut milk with vanilla and pitted fates in a blender until creamy.
5. Stir in oats mixture and mix evenly.
6. Spread ⅔ of the oats mixture in the prepared baking pan.
7. Add raspberry chia jam over the oats mixture and spread the remaining oats mixture on top.
8. Bake the flapjacks for 30 minutes in the preheated oven.
9. Cut into bars and serve.

Chapter 02: Breakfast Recipes

Chocolate Baked Oatmeal

SERVINGS	PREPARATION TIME	COOKING TIME
6	15 minutes	35 minutes

Nutritional Values Per Serving	
Calories	188
Total Fat	10g
Saturated Fat	7.6g
Cholesterol	0mg
Sodium	12mg
Total Carbohydrate	24.7g
Dietary Fiber	2.7g
Total Sugars	10.7g
Protein	3.5g

Meal Prep Suggestion:
Enjoy the oatmeal with some chocolate sauce on top.

Ingredients:
- 2 cups quick-cooking rolled oats
- 3 tablespoons cocoa powder, unsweetened
- 2 tablespoons ground chia seeds
- 6 tablespoons of water
- 1 cup coconut milk
- ⅓ cup of pure maple syrup
- ½ teaspoon of cinnamon
- ⅛ teaspoon of salt
- 1 teaspoon of baking powder

Instructions:
1. At 350 degrees F, preheat your oven.
2. Layer an 8x8 inches baking pan with parchment paper and grease with cooking oil.
3. Grind chia seeds in a spice grinder.
4. Mix this ground with water in a bowl and leave for 5 minutes.
5. Stir in oats, cocoa powder, and the rest of the ingredients, then mix evenly.
6. Spread this batter in the prepared pan and drizzle chocolate chips on top.
7. Bake for 30 minutes in the preheated oven.
8. Cut the meal into 8 bars of equal sizes.
9. Serve.

Chapter 02: Breakfast Recipes

Zucchini Bread

SERVINGS
8

PREPARATION TIME
15 minutes

COOKING TIME
45 minutes

Nutritional Values Per Serving	
Calories	272
Total Fat	14.8g
Saturated Fat	6.6g
Cholesterol	0mg
Sodium	392mg
Total Carbohydrate	32.4g
Dietary Fiber	1.6g
Total Sugars	10.3g
Protein	3.6g

Meal Prep Suggestion:

Keep the sliced bread in a loaf pan with wrap with a plastic sheet before refrigeration.

Ingredients:

- 1¾ cups all-purpose flour
- ¾ teaspoon baking powder
- ½ teaspoon baking soda
- 1 teaspoon salt
- ¾ teaspoon ground cinnamon
- ¾ cup almond milk
- 1 tablespoon lemon juice
- ½ cup cane sugar
- ½ cup brown sugar
- ⅓ cup vegetable oil
- 1½ cups grated zucchini, pressed

Instructions:

1. At 350 degrees F, preheat your oven.
2. Mix flour with cinnamon, salt, baking soda, powder, lemon juice, sugars and oil in a bowl until smooth.
3. Fold in zucchini and mix evenly.
4. Divide this batter in a greased loaf pan.
5. Bake this zucchini loaf for 45 minutes in the preheated oven.
6. Slice and serve.

Chapter 02: Breakfast Recipes

Apple Cinnamon Waffles

SERVINGS	PREPARATION TIME	COOKING TIME
6	10 minutes	10 minutes

Nutritional Values Per Serving

Calories	246
Total Fat	15.4g
Saturated Fat	10.5g
Cholesterol	0mg
Sodium	129mg
Total Carbohydrate	25.6g
Dietary Fiber	3.7g
Total Sugars	8.7g
Protein	3.5g

Meal Prep Suggestion:

Enjoy the waffles with peanut butter spread on top.

Ingredients:

- 1¼ cup oat flour
- 2 teaspoon baking powder
- ¼ teaspoon sea salt
- 3 teaspoon cinnamon
- 1 cup almond milk
- 3 tablespoons melted coconut oil
- 1 teaspoon vanilla extract
- 3 tablespoons maple syrup
- ⅓ cup grated apple

Instructions:

1. Mix oat flour, baking powder, sea salt, cinnamon, milk, oil, vanilla and maple syrup in a bowl until smooth.
2. Fold in the grated apple, then mix evenly.
3. Set a waffle iron on medium heat.
4. Pour a dollop of the apple batter into the waffle iron.
5. Cook the waffle as per the package's instructions.
6. Continue cooking more waffles in the same way.
7. Serve.

CHAPTER 03

LUNCH RECIPES

Chapter 03: Lunch Recipes

Mushroom Broccoli Stir Fry

SERVINGS 6   **PREPARATION TIME** 10 minutes   **COOKING TIME** 15 minutes

Nutritional Values Per Serving	
Calories	172
Total Fat	6.6g
Saturated Fat	0.8g
Cholesterol	0mg
Sodium	798mg
Total Carbohydrate	18.3g
Dietary Fiber	5.1g
Total Sugars	8.6g
Protein	11.3g

Meal Prep Suggestion:

Try the stir fry with boiled white rice.

Ingredients:

Teriyaki Sauce

- 5 tablespoons soy sauce
- 3 tablespoons maple syrup
- 3 tablespoons water
- 1 tablespoon mirin
- 1 teaspoon sesame oil
- ½ teaspoon red pepper flakes
- 1 tablespoon ginger grated
- 2 cloves garlic minced
- 1 tablespoon cornstarch

Stir Fry

- 1 tablespoon olive oil
- 2 cups broccoli florets
- 1 cup snap peas
- 2 cups fresh mushrooms sliced

Instructions:

1. Mix cornstarch, ginger, garlic, mirin, red pepper flakes, sesame oil, water, maple syrup and soy sauce in a bowl.
2. Sauté mushrooms and vegetables with oil in a deep pan for 7-10 minutes.
3. Stir in the prepared sauce and cook this mixture until it thickens.
4. Cook for 2 minutes.
5. Serve warm.

Chapter 03: Lunch Recipes

Green Bean Curry

SERVINGS
6

PREPARATION TIME
15 minutes

COOKING TIME
20 minutes

Nutritional Values Per Serving	
Calories	290
Total Fat	22g
Saturated Fat	14.3g
Cholesterol	0mg
Sodium	954mg
Total Carbohydrate	22.1g
Dietary Fiber	5.5g
Total Sugars	5.5g
Protein	5.5g

Meal Prep Suggestion:

Try the curry with bread slices.

Ingredients:

- 6 ounces green beans, pre-cooked
- 2 potatoes, boiled and quartered
- 1 block tofu, diced
- 1 onion, chopped
- 3 garlic cloves
- 1 (13 ½ oz) can coconut milk
- 2 ounces tomato paste
- 4 teaspoon curry powder
- 1 tablespoon soy sauce
- 2 ½ tablespoon sunflower oil
- 2 teaspoon salt
- ½ teaspoon black pepper

Instructions:

1. Sauté the potato with 1 tablespoon oil and ½ teaspoon salt in a skillet until golden brown.
2. Dice the tofu into cubes and sauté them with 1 tablespoon oil and ½ teaspoon salt in the same skillet until golden brown.
3. Sauté onion with garlic, 1 teaspoon curry powder and ½ tbsp. oil in a skillet for 1 minute.
4. Stir in ½ teaspoon black pepper, 1 teaspoon salt, 1 tablespoon soy sauce, 3 teaspoon curry powder, tomato paste and coconut milk.
5. Cook for 2 minutes, then add green beans and cook for 5 minutes on a simmer.
6. Add the sauteed potatoes, and tofu then cook for 2-3 minutes.
7. Serve warm.

Chapter 03: Lunch Recipes

Mediterranean Vegan Bowls

SERVINGS: 4 PREPARATION TIME: 10 minutes COOKING TIME: 10 minutes

Nutritional Values Per Serving	
Calories	204
Total Fat	2.7g
Saturated Fat	0.3g
Cholesterol	0mg
Sodium	184mg
Total Carbohydrate	37.5g
Dietary Fiber	6.2g
Total Sugars	0.8g
Protein	7.7g

Meal Prep Suggestion:

Enjoy the quinoa mixture with sauteed asparagus.

Ingredients:

- ¾ cup uncooked quinoa
- 1 (19 fluid ounce) can chickpeas drained
- 2 Persian cucumbers, sliced
- Handful little tomatoes halved
- 2 tablespoons red onions chopped
- Kalamata olives to taste
- Hummus to taste
- Salt and black pepper to taste
- Olive oil to taste
- Lemon juice to taste

Instructions:

1. Add quinoa and water to a suitable cooking pot and cook as per the package's directions.
2. Mix chickpeas with cucumber, tomatoes, red onion, olives, hummus, black pepper, salt, olive oil and lemon juice in a bowl.
3. Divide this mixture into the serving bowls.
4. Add quinoa on top and serve.

Chapter 03: Lunch Recipes

Tempeh Vegetable Quinoa Bowls

SERVINGS
8

PREPARATION TIME
10 minutes

COOKING TIME
30 minutes

Nutritional Values Per Serving	
Calories	469
Total Fat	13.7g
Saturated Fat	2.2g
Cholesterol	1mg
Sodium	191mg
Total Carbohydrate	65.7g
Dietary Fiber	7.8g
Total Sugars	3g
Protein	23.9g

Meal Prep Suggestion:
Try the quinoa bowls with fresh herbs on top.

Ingredients:

- 3 tablespoons balsamic vinegar
- 1 tablespoon olive oil
- 1 tablespoon Italian seasoning
- ½ teaspoon salt
- ½ teaspoon black pepper
- 1 package button mushrooms sliced
- 2 medium zucchinis, chopped
- 2 carrots quarter and chopped
- 2 red bell peppers chopped
- 1 large shallot, chopped
- 2 (8 oz) packages of tempeh
- 4 cups cooked quinoa

Instructions:

1. At 425 degrees F, preheat your oven.
2. Layer a baking sheet with parchment paper.
3. Mix spices with oil and vinegar in a large bowl.
4. Toss in tempeh and vegetables, then mix well.
5. Spread this mixture on a baking sheet, then roast for 30 minutes in the oven.
6. Toss in quinoa and serve.

Chapter 03: Lunch Recipes

Lunch Wrap

SERVINGS 4   **PREPARATION TIME** 10 minutes   **COOKING TIME** 0 minutes

Nutritional Values Per Serving	
Calories	442
Total Fat	17.4g
Saturated Fat	2.8g
Cholesterol	0mg
Sodium	2383mg
Total Carbohydrate	61.1g
Dietary Fiber	14.8g
Total Sugars	3.4g
Protein	16.3g

Meal Prep Suggestion:

Enjoy the lunch wrap with a tomato sauce.

Ingredients:

- 4 (whole wheat) tortilla wraps
- ½ cup hummus
- 4 cups baby spinach
- ½ cup canned black beans
- 4 tomato, chopped
- 16 green olives, halved
- 16 black olives, halved
- Salt, to taste
- Black pepper, to taste

Instructions:

1. Spread the tortilla wraps on the working surface.
2. Divide hummus and baby spinach on top of each tortilla.
3. Spread beans, spices, tomatoes, olives, salt and black pepper over the hummus.
4. Roll the tortillas into a burrito.
5. Serve.

Chapter 03: Lunch Recipes

Mushroom Cauliflower Rice

SERVINGS **4**   PREPARATION TIME **10 minutes**   COOKING TIME **10 minutes**

Nutritional Values Per Serving

Calories	144
Total Fat	7.2g
Saturated Fat	1.4g
Cholesterol	0mg
Sodium	887mg
Total Carbohydrate	14.9g
Dietary Fiber	1.6g
Total Sugars	7.1g
Protein	7.1g

Meal Prep Suggestion:

Store the cauliflower rice in a meal box along with sauteed carrots and broccoli for serving.

Ingredients:

- 1 ½ tablespoon sesame oil
- 6 garlic cloves, chopped
- 5 stalks green onion, chopped
- 1 red pepper, chopped
- 8 ounces white mushrooms, sliced
- 2 tablespoons soy sauce
- 2 teaspoons sriracha
- 2 teaspoons rice vinegar
- 16 ounces cauliflower rice
- ¼ teaspoon black pepper
- ½ teaspoon salt

Instructions:

1. Sauté garlic with sesame oil in a wok for 1 minute on medium-high heat.
2. Stir in mushrooms, bell pepper and green onion whites.
3. Cook for 3 minutes until golden brown.
4. Add sriracha, rice vinegar and soy sauce, then cook on low heat.
5. Stir in cauliflower rice, black pepper, and salt, then cover and cook for 6 minutes.
6. Garnish with green spring onion.
7. Serve warm.

Chapter 03: Lunch Recipes

Vegan Bowl With Cashew Pesto

SERVINGS	PREPARATION TIME	COOKING TIME
4	10 minutes	13 minutes

Nutritional Values Per Serving

Calories	243
Total Fat	11.9g
Saturated Fat	2.2g
Cholesterol	0mg
Sodium	181mg
Total Carbohydrate	28.2g
Dietary Fiber	3.1g
Total Sugars	1.9g
Protein	7.8g

Meal Prep Suggestion:

Enjoy these bowls with tofu skewers.

Ingredients:

Parsley Cashew Pesto

- 1 cup raw cashews
- ½ cup water
- 4 cups Italian parsley
- 4 cloves garlic
- 4 tablespoons lemon juice
- ½ teaspoon kosher salt
- Black pepper to taste

Assemble

- 1 cup uncooked Israeli couscous
- 2-pints cremini mushrooms, chopped
- 2 tablespoons olive oil
- 2 bunches of lacinto kale, chopped
- Tomato wedges to garnish
- Parsley to garnish

Instructions:

1. Soak cashews in water in a bowl for 1 hour, then drain.
2. Blend cashews with parsley, black pepper, salt, lemon juice and garlic in a blender until smooth.
3. Adjust seasoning with black pepper and salt.
4. Boil couscous with ¾ cup water in a suitable saucepan for 10 minutes.
5. Sauté mushrooms with 1 tablespoon oil, black pepper and salt in a large skillet for 10 minutes.
6. Stir in kale leaves and sauté for 3 minutes.
7. Adjust seasoning with black pepper and salt.
8. Stir in quinoa and rest of the ingredients then mix well.
9. Divide this mixture in four serving bowls.
10. Garnish with tomato wedges and parsley.
11. Enjoy.

Chapter 03: Lunch Recipes

Bbq Tofu Wraps

SERVINGS 4
PREPARATION TIME 35 minutes
COOKING TIME 10 minutes

Nutritional Values Per Serving

Calories	231
Total Fat	15.9g
Saturated Fat	3g
Cholesterol	0mg
Sodium	194mg
Total Carbohydrate	19.1g
Dietary Fiber	5.6g
Total Sugars	6.5g
Protein	6.3g

Meal Prep Suggestion:

Enjoy these wraps with a refreshing quinoa salad.

Ingredients:

BBQ Tofu Bacon

- 8 tablespoons BBQ sauce
- 4 tablespoons water
- 14 ounces extra firm tofu
- 1 tablespoon oil

Assemble

- 4 large flour tortillas
- 8 baby gem lettuce leaves
- 4 tomatoes, chopped

Avocado Mayonnaise

- 4 sprigs fresh coriander, chopped
- 1 small spring onion, chopped
- 2 small avocados, peeled
- 1 tablespoon olive oil
- 4 tablespoons water

Instructions:

1. Mix bbq sauce with some water in a bowl.
2. Add this sauce to the tofu slices in a bowl.
3. Cover and refrigerate the tofu for 30 minutes.
4. Sear the tofu slices in a frying pan with oil for 5 minutes per side.
5. Blend avocado with oil, ½ spring onion and coriander in a blender until smooth.
6. Spread the avocado mixture over the two tortillas and top it with tofu, tomatoes, and lettuce, then roll them tightly.
7. Serve.

Chapter 03: Lunch Recipes

Tofu With Zucchini Noodles

SERVINGS	PREPARATION TIME	COOKING TIME
6	10 minutes	10 minutes

Nutritional Values Per Serving	
Calories	258
Total Fat	20g
Saturated Fat	3.7g
Cholesterol	0mg
Sodium	706mg
Total Carbohydrate	11g
Dietary Fiber	1.9g
Total Sugars	6.5g
Protein	10.8g

Meal Prep Suggestion:

Store the tofu slices in a meal box then serve with freshly spiralized zucchini noodles.

Ingredients:

Sesame Peanut Sauce

- ½ cup peanut butter
- 2 tablespoons sesame oil
- ¼ cup soy sauce
- ¼ cup rice vinegar
- 1 teaspoon chilli flakes
- 2 tablespoons maple syrup
- 3 garlic cloves, chopped
- 1 knob ginger, peeled and chopped

Other Ingredients

- 1 tablespoon oil
- 12 ounces firm tofu, sliced or diced
- Zucchinis spiralized to serve

Instructions:

1. Blend all the peanut butter sauce ingredients in a blender until smooth.
2. Sauté tofu with oil in a skillet for 5 minutes.
3. Pour in the prepared peanut sauce and cook until the sauce thickens.
4. Serve the tofu on top of the zucchini noodles.
5. Enjoy.

Chapter 03: Lunch Recipes

Korean Barbeque Tofu

SERVINGS 4
PREPARATION TIME 20 minutes
COOKING TIME 18 minutes

Nutritional Values Per Serving	
Calories	267
Total Fat	10.9g
Saturated Fat	1.3g
Cholesterol	0mg
Sodium	1364mg
Total Carbohydrate	28.1g
Dietary Fiber	3.7g
Total Sugars	19.2g
Protein	15.4g

Meal Prep Suggestion:

Serve the tofu mixture with white rice or noodles.

Ingredients:

Sauce

- ½ cup ketchup
- ½ cup rice vinegar
- ¼ cup tamari
- 1 ½ tablespoons sugar
- 1 tablespoon sesame seeds
- 1 tablespoon Gochujang
- ¼ teaspoon black pepper
- 2 green onions, sliced
- 1 garlic clove, minced
- 1 1-inch piece ginger, grated
- 2 teaspoons toasted sesame oil

Bowls

- 2 tablespoons avocado oil
- 1 tablespoon water
- 1 medium zucchini, julienned
- 1 green bell pepper, julienned
- 2 red bell peppers, julienned
- 1 tablespoon tamari
- 1 (15-ounces) package extra-firm tofu, pressed and cubed

Instructions:

1. Mix ginger, garlic, onion, black pepper, gochujang, sesame seeds, sugar, tamari, vinegar and ketchup in a saucepan.
2. Cook this sauce on a simmer on medium-low heat for 15 minutes with occasional stirring.
3. Add sesame oil, then mix well and keep it aside.
4. Sauté tofu with oil in a skillet for 10 minutes.
5. Add ½ cup bbq sauce and cook for 2 minutes then keep it aside.
6. Sauté peppers and zucchini with 1 tablespoon avocado oil in a large skillet for 1 minute.
7. Stir in soy sauce.
8. Cook for 5 minutes, then toss in tofu, quinoa and cabbage
9. Pour the prepared sauce on top.
10. Serve warm.

Chapter 03: Lunch Recipes

Jerk Spiced Tofu

SERVINGS 4 **PREPARATION TIME** 10 minutes **COOKING TIME** 12 minutes

Nutritional Values Per Serving	
Calories	244
Total Fat	16.5g
Saturated Fat	3.3g
Cholesterol	0mg
Sodium	53mg
Total Carbohydrate	11.4g
Dietary Fiber	2.7g
Total Sugars	7.6g
Protein	17.4g

Meal Prep Suggestion:

Enjoy the tofu with fried cauliflower rice.

Ingredients:

Crispy Tofu

- 2 tablespoons vegetable oil
- 1 tablespoon jerk seasoning
- 10-ounce block of firm tofu, drained and diced

Broccoli

- 1 bunch tender stem broccoli
- 1 teaspoon olive oil
- Sea salt, to taste

Salsa

- ½ pineapple chopped
- 1 small red chilli diced
- zest and juice of 1 lime
- Salt to taste

Instructions:

1. Sauté tofu cubes with 1 tablespoon oil in a skillet for 1 minute per side.
2. Toss broccoli with remaining olive oil on a baking sheet.
3. Roast the broccoli for 10 minutes in the oven at 350 degrees F.
4. Toss all the salsa ingredients in a bowl.
5. Top this salsa with tofu and roasted broccoli.
6. Serve.

Chapter 03: Lunch Recipes

Curried Chickpea Bowls

SERVINGS 6 **PREPARATION TIME** 15 minutes **COOKING TIME** 12 minutes

Nutritional Values Per Serving	
Calories	285
Total Fat	4.7g
Saturated Fat	0.5g
Cholesterol	0mg
Sodium	121mg
Total Carbohydrate	48.5g
Dietary Fiber	14.1g
Total Sugars	9.4g
Protein	15.2g

Meal Prep Suggestion:
Add the fresh herbs or bean sprouts on top before serving.

Ingredients:

Curried Chickpeas

- 2 teaspoons avocado oil
- 2 garlic cloves, minced
- 1 large onion, chopped
- 1 (15 ounces) can chickpeas, rinsed
- 2 teaspoons curry
- 1 teaspoon cumin
- ½ teaspoon cinnamon
- 2 tablespoons tomato paste
- 3 tablespoons water
- ½ teaspoon sea salt
- ½ teaspoon pepper
- Fresh cilantro, chopped, for topping
- green onion, chopped, for topping
- 3 cups cooked brown rice

Garlicky Spinach

- 1 teaspoon avocado oil
- 3 cloves garlic, minced
- 5 ounces baby spinach
- ¼ teaspoon sea salt
- ½ lemon juiced

Instructions:

1. For garlicky spinach, sauté garlic with 1 teaspoon oil in a large skillet for 1 minute.
2. Stir spinach and cook for 3 minutes.
3. Add salt and lemon juice, then mix well.
4. Sauté garlic and onion with 2 teaspoon oil in a skillet for 5 minutes.
5. Stir in spices, chickpeas, tomato paste, black pepper and salt.
6. Cook for almost 3 minutes, then remove from the heat.
7. Divide the rice, chickpeas and spinach in the serving bowls.
8. Garnish with cilantro and green onion.
9. Serve.

Greek Couscous Salad

SERVINGS 8   **PREPARATION TIME** 10 minutes   **COOKING TIME** 10 minutes

Nutritional Values Per Serving	
Calories	376
Total Fat	16.1g
Saturated Fat	2.2g
Cholesterol	0mg
Sodium	22mg
Total Carbohydrate	48.6g
Dietary Fiber	10.3g
Total Sugars	9.4g
Protein	12.6g

Meal Prep Suggestion:

Add sauteed mushroom or tofu to the salad before serving.

Ingredients:

- 2 packages (5 ounces) Pearled Couscous Mix
- 1 English cucumber, chopped
- 3 bell peppers, chopped
- ½ red onion, chopped
- 1 cup cherry tomatoes, halved
- ½ cup Italian parsley, chopped
- 2 cans (15 ounces) chickpeas
- 1 lemon, cut into wedges

Salad Dressing

- ¼ cup red wine vinegar
- ½ cup olive oil
- 1 tablespoon lemon juice
- 1 teaspoon garlic, minced
- 1 teaspoon dried oregano
- ½ teaspoon Dijon mustard
- Sea salt and black pepper, to taste

Instructions:

1. Boil couscous as per the cooking instructions in a cooking pot.
2. Drain and keep the couscous aside.
3. Mix the mustard dressing ingredients in a salad bowl.
4. Toss in couscous and rest of the ingredients, then mix well.
5. Serve.

Chapter 03: Lunch Recipes

Thai Quinoa Salad

SERVINGS
8

PREPARATION TIME
10 minutes

COOKING TIME
10 minutes

Nutritional Values Per Serving	
Calories	203
Total Fat	8.8g
Saturated Fat	1.5g
Cholesterol	0mg
Sodium	281mg
Total Carbohydrate	23.9g
Dietary Fiber	4.2g
Total Sugars	4.6g
Protein	9.1g

Meal Prep Suggestion:

Enjoy this salad with colorful tofu skewers.

Ingredients:

- 1 cup uncooked quinoa
- 1 ½ cup red cabbage, sliced
- 1 large red bell pepper, diced
- ⅓ cup red onion, diced
- 1 cup carrots, shredded
- ½ cup edamame
- ½ cup cilantro, chopped
- 1-2 green onions, chopped
- ¼ cup peanuts, chopped, for garnish

Dressing

- ¼ cup peanut butter
- 1-2 teaspoon ginger, grated
- 1 garlic clove, minced
- 2 tablespoons soy sauce
- 1 tablespoon maple syrup
- 1 tablespoon rice vinegar
- 4 tablespoons warm water
- Juice from ½ lime

Instructions:

1. Boil quinoa in a pot filled with water as per the cooking instructions.
2. Drain and keep the quinoa aside.
3. Mix peanut butter dressing ingredients in a large salad bowl.
4. Toss in quinoa and the rest of the ingredients, then mix well.
5. Serve.

Chapter 03: Lunch Recipes

Tempeh Stir Fry

SERVINGS 4 **PREPARATION TIME** 10 minutes **COOKING TIME** 21 minutes

Nutritional Values Per Serving

Calories	385
Total Fat	22.3g
Saturated Fat	4.6g
Cholesterol	1mg
Sodium	991mg
Total Carbohydrate	36.3g
Dietary Fiber	4.3g
Total Sugars	13.1g
Protein	16g

Meal Prep Suggestion:

Keep this stir fry with white boiled rice in a meal box for complete serving.

Ingredients:

- 8 ounces of tempeh, cut into chunks
- 2 tablespoons ginger paste
- 2 tablespoons garlic paste
- 1 tablespoon sesame oil
- 1 tablespoon rice vinegar
- 4 tablespoons soy sauce
- 3 tablespoons maple syrup
- 1 tablespoon cornstarch
- 1 tablespoon nut butter
- 3 tablespoons olive oil
- 2 cups of green beans, ends trimmed
- 2 cups of carrots, sliced
- Sesame seeds, to garnish

Instructions:

1. Blend nut butter, cornstarch, maple syrup, soy sauce, rice vinegar, sesame oil, garlic and ginger in a blender.
2. Sauté tempeh with 2 tablespoons of oil in a skillet over medium heat for 8 minutes.
3. Stir in 2 tablespoons sauce and cook until tempeh is caramelized, then transfer to a plate.
4. Sauté carrots with green beans and remaining oil in the same skillet for 5 minutes.
5. Stir in a splash of water, cover and steam for 5 minutes.
6. Toss in tempeh and remaining sauce, then cook for 3 minutes.
7. Garnish with sesame seeds.
8. Serve warm.

Chapter 03: Lunch Recipes

Vermicelli Soup

SERVINGS 4
PREPARATION TIME 20 minutes
COOKING TIME 15 minutes

Nutritional Values Per Serving	
Calories	295
Total Fat	8g
Saturated Fat	1.4g
Cholesterol	0mg
Sodium	47mg
Total Carbohydrate	46.6g
Dietary Fiber	3.3g
Total Sugars	5.4g
Protein	8g

Meal Prep Suggestion:

Reheat the soup for delayed serving in the microwave for 2 minutes on medium-low heat.

Ingredients:

- 12 ounces vermicelli pasta
- 2 tablespoons vegetable oil
- 2 cups water
- ¼ yellow onion
- 2 tomatoes, chopped
- 1 garlic clove, minced
- 1 cup bell pepper, chopped
- salt to taste
- ¼ cup cilantro, chopped

Instructions:

1. Sauté vermicelli with oil in a deep frying pan until golden brown.
2. Blend tomatoes, salt, and garlic in a food processor and strain.
3. Add this mixture to the vermicelli and cook to a boil.
4. Stir in bell pepper and cook for 5 minutes.
5. Add cilantro and serve warm.

The Plant Based Vegan Diet Meal Prep Cookbook
200+ Easy And Simple Recipes To Eat Healthy At Work, Home And On The Go With 7 Weekly Meal Plans

Chapter 03: Lunch Recipes

Broccoli, Carrot And Potato Soup

SERVINGS	PREPARATION TIME	COOKING TIME
4	10 minutes	17 minutes

Nutritional Values Per Serving	
Calories	373
Total Fat	10.7g
Saturated Fat	1.5g
Cholesterol	0mg
Sodium	112mg
Total Carbohydrate	59.7g
Dietary Fiber	14.4g
Total Sugars	14.2g
Protein	15.2g

Meal Prep Suggestion:

Add baked croutons on top of the soup before serving.

Ingredients:

- 2 tablespoons olive oil
- 1 cup chopped onion
- 1 tablespoon minced garlic
- ¾ cup diced carrot
- ½ cup diced celery
- Kosher salt, to taste
- 1 teaspoon dried oregano
- 2 cups peeled potatoes, diced
- 2 cups broccoli, chopped
- 8 cups vegetable broth
- Fresh herbs for serving

Instructions:

1. Sauté celery, carrot, garlic and onion with oil in a deep pot for 5 minutes.
2. Stir in salt and cook for 2 minutes.
3. Add oregano and broccoli, then cook for 5 minutes.
4. Stir in broth, and vegetables then cook to a boil.
5. Then reduce its heat to a simmer, then cook for 5 minutes.
6. Garnish with herbs.
7. Serve warm.

Chapter 03: Lunch Recipes

Vegan Borsch Soup

SERVINGS 6
PREPARATION TIME 15 minutes
COOKING TIME 27 minutes

Nutritional Values Per Serving	
Calories	325
Total Fat	4.5g
Saturated Fat	1.1g
Cholesterol	0mg
Sodium	1734mg
Total Carbohydrate	55.6g
Dietary Fiber	10.2g
Total Sugars	22.5g
Protein	18.4g

Meal Prep Suggestion:

Serve this soup with toasted bread and quinoa salad.

Ingredients:

- 2 tablespoons avocado oil
- 1 bay leaf
- 8 cups vegetable broth
- 1 ¾ pounds beets, scrubbed and sliced
- 1 cup broccoli florets
- 4 medium carrots, chopped
- 3 large celery ribs, diced
- 1 large onion, chopped
- 1 large potato, scrubbed and chopped
- ½ pound cabbage, sliced
- 4 large garlic cloves, minced
- ½ teaspoon salt
- ¼ teaspoon black pepper
- ¼ teaspoon allspice
- 3 tablespoons tomato paste
- 6 tablespoons red wine vinegar
- ¼ cup chopped fresh dill

Instructions:

1. Sauté onion with oil in a deep pot for 5 minutes.
2. Stir in potatoes and beets, then sauté for 2 minutes.
3. Add broth, and cook for 15 minutes until potatoes are soft.
4. Stir in the rest of the ingredients and cook for 5 minutes.
5. Serve warm.

Chapter 03: Lunch Recipes

Cream Of Broccoli Soup

SERVINGS 4   **PREPARATION TIME** 10 minutes   **COOKING TIME** 39 minutes

Nutritional Values Per Serving	
Calories	161
Total Fat	6.1g
Saturated Fat	3.6g
Cholesterol	0mg
Sodium	805mg
Total Carbohydrate	18.7g
Dietary Fiber	4.4g
Total Sugars	4.4g
Protein	9.8g

Meal Prep Suggestion:

Add this soup to a sealable container, then refrigerate it for storage.

Ingredients:

- ¼ cup almond butter
- 1 yellow onion, diced small
- ¼ cup all-purpose flour
- 2 teaspoons turmeric powder
- 4 cups vegetable broth
- 1 pound broccoli, cut into florets
- ¼ cup coconut cream
- Salt and black pepper, to taste

Instructions:

1. Sauté onion with butter in a medium pot for 8 minutes.
2. Stir in flour, then cook for 1 minute.
3. Add 1 cup water and cook to a boil while mixing well.
4. Reduce its heat and cook for 10 minutes on a simmer with occasional stirring.
5. Stir in broccoli, turmeric powder, black pepper, and salt, then cook for 20 minutes on a simmer.
6. Puree this soup until smooth using a hand blender.
7. Stir in coconut cream, and cook until warm.
8. Garish with broccoli floret and serve.

Chapter 03: Lunch Recipes

Greens Soup

SERVINGS 6 **PREPARATION TIME** 13 minutes **COOKING TIME** 27 minutes

Nutritional Values Per Serving

Calories	197
Total Fat	9.4g
Saturated Fat	1.7g
Cholesterol	0mg
Sodium	1498mg
Total Carbohydrate	19.3g
Dietary Fiber	6.7g
Total Sugars	9.5g
Protein	11.2g

Meal Prep Suggestion:

Serve this soup with boiled rice.

Ingredients:

- 2 tablespoons olive oil
- 1 cup onions, chopped
- ½ cup carrot, chopped
- ½ cup celery, chopped
- 4 teaspoons garlic, chopped
- ½ teaspoon salt
- ½ teaspoon dried thyme leaves
- ¼ teaspoon dried rosemary leaves
- ¼ teaspoon dried sage leaves
- ¼ teaspoon black pepper
- 1 cup broccoli florets
- 6 cups vegetable broth
- 1 container (5 oz) mixed baby hearty greens
- 1 purple cabbage, shredded

Instructions:

1. Sauté onions, celery and carrot with oil in a Dutch oven for 12 minutes.
2. Stir in black pepper and the rest of the ingredients, then cook for 15 minutes.
3. Serve warm.

Chapter 03: Lunch Recipes

Soup of Broccoli And Spinach

SERVINGS	PREPARATION TIME	COOKING TIME
4	10 minutes	15 minutes

Nutritional Values Per Serving

Calories	129
Total Fat	1.4g
Saturated Fat	0.2g
Cholesterol	0mg
Sodium	248mg
Total Carbohydrate	25.1g
Dietary Fiber	9.6g
Total Sugars	8g
Protein	9.7g

Meal Prep Suggestion:

Add this soup to a plastic bag, seal and refrigerate it for longer storage.

Ingredients:

- 17 ½ oz broccoli, florets
- 3 ½ oz. spinach
- 2 garlic cloves, chopped
- 1 onion, chopped
- 2 tablespoons olive oil
- 3 cups vegetable stock
- Black pepper to taste

Instructions:

1. Sauté garlic and onion with oil in a deep pot for 5 minutes.
2. Stir in broccoli, spinach, black pepper and vegetable stock.
3. Cook the soup for 10 minutes on a simmer.
4. Puree this mixture with a hand blender until smooth.
5. Serve.

Chapter 03: Lunch Recipes

Chickpeas Creme Soup

SERVINGS 4   **PREPARATION TIME** 10 minutes   **COOKING TIME** 26 minutes

Nutritional Values Per Serving

Calories	317
Total Fat	6.5g
Saturated Fat	0.8g
Cholesterol	0mg
Sodium	113mg
Total Carbohydrate	51.9g
Dietary Fiber	13.2g
Total Sugars	7.7g
Protein	14.8g

Meal Prep Suggestion:

Serve this crème soup with roasted broccoli and carrots.

Ingredients:

- 1 tablespoon olive oil
- 3 large garlic cloves, minced
- 1 teaspoon paprika
- 1 teaspoon dried rosemary
- ½ teaspoon dried thyme
- ¼ teaspoon chilli flakes
- 2 cans (15 oz) chickpeas
- 1 (6 oz) large potato, diced
- 2 cups vegetable broth
- Salt and black pepper, to taste

Instructions:

1. Sauté garlic with oil in a deep pot for 1 minute.
2. Stir in cracker pepper, chilli flakes, thyme, rosemary, paprika, potato and chickpeas.
3. Cover and cook for 25 minutes on a simmer with occasional stirring.
4. Puree this soup using a hand blender.
5. Garnish with canned chickpeas and serve.

Chapter 03: Lunch Recipes

Italian Chickpea Soup

SERVINGS	PREPARATION TIME	COOKING TIME
6	10 minutes	44 minutes

Nutritional Values Per Serving

Calories	342
Total Fat	9.8g
Saturated Fat	1.5g
Cholesterol	2mg
Sodium	1159mg
Total Carbohydrate	51.6g
Dietary Fiber	13.5g
Total Sugars	15.4g
Protein	14.2g

Meal Prep Suggestion:

Serve the chickpeas with whole wheat bread slices.

Ingredients:

- 2 tablespoons olive oil
- 1 Vidalia onion, chopped
- 2 carrots, peeled and sliced
- 2 stalks celery, sliced
- 2 garlic cloves, minced
- 2 tablespoons tomato paste
- 1 (28-oz) can crush fire-roasted tomatoes
- 4 cups vegetable broth
- 2 (14-oz) can chickpeas, rinsed and drained
- 2 teaspoon Italian seasoning
- ½ teaspoon salt
- ½ teaspoon black pepper, to taste
- Fresh basil, torn, for serving

Instructions:

1. Sauté celery, carrots and onion with oil in a Dutch oven for 10 minutes.
2. Stir in garlic, then cook for 1 minute.
3. Add 2 tablespoons tomato paste, then continue cooking for 3 minutes.
4. Stir in tomatoes, black pepper, salt, Italian seasoning 2 cups broth, and chickpeas.
5. Cook this chickpeas mixture for 30 minutes on a slow simmer.
6. Serve warm.

Chapter 03: Lunch Recipes

Lentil Soup

SERVINGS
4

PREPARATION TIME
10 minutes

COOKING TIME
21 minutes

Nutritional Values Per Serving	
Calories	338
Total Fat	4.9g
Saturated Fat	0.6g
Cholesterol	0mg
Sodium	106mg
Total Carbohydrate	54g
Dietary Fiber	24.9g
Total Sugars	6.4g
Protein	20.6g

Meal Prep Suggestion:

Reheat the soup covered in a sealable container in the microwave for 3-5 minutes before serving.

Ingredients:

- 1 tablespoon olive oil
- 1 white onion, peeled and diced
- 2 carrots, diced
- 5 garlic cloves, peeled and minced
- 6 cups vegetable stock
- 1 ½ cups red lentils, rinsed
- ⅔ cup whole-kernel corn
- 2 teaspoons ground cumin
- 1 teaspoon curry powder
- 1 pinch saffron
- 1 pinch cayenne powder
- zest and juice of 1 small lemon

Instructions:

1. Sauté carrot and onion with oil in a stockpot for 5 minutes.
2. Stir in garlic and sauté for 1 minute.
3. Add curry powder, cumin, corn, lentils, and vegetable stock, then cook for 15 minutes on a simmer.
4. Puree this soup using a hand blender until smooth.
5. Stir in lemon juice and zest, black pepper and salt.
6. Serve warm.

Lentil Soup With Mixed Veggies

SERVINGS	PREPARATION TIME	COOKING TIME
4	10 minutes	45 minutes

Nutritional Values Per Serving

Calories	355
Total Fat	14.9g
Saturated Fat	2.3g
Cholesterol	0mg
Sodium	1440mg
Total Carbohydrate	38.3g
Dietary Fiber	17.2g
Total Sugars	5.4g
Protein	18.6g

Meal Prep Suggestion:

Enjoy this soup with toasted bread slices.

Ingredients:

- ¼ cup olive oil
- 1 medium yellow onion, chopped
- 2 carrots, peeled and chopped
- 4 garlic cloves, pressed or minced
- 2 teaspoons ground cumin
- 1 teaspoon curry powder
- ½ teaspoon dried thyme
- 1 (28 ounces) can diced tomatoes, drained
- 1 cup lentils, rinsed
- 4 cups vegetable broth
- 2 cups water
- 1 teaspoon salt, more to taste
- Pinch of red pepper flakes
- Freshly ground black pepper, to taste
- 1 cup collard greens, chopped
- 1 tablespoon lemon juice

Instructions:

1. Sauté carrot and onion within a deep pot for 5 minutes.
2. Stir in thyme, curry powder, cumin and garlic, then sauté for 30 seconds.
3. Add tomatoes and cook for 4 minutes.
4. Stir in water, broth, lentils, red pepper flakes, black pepper and 1 teaspoon salt.
5. Cook to a boil first, then reduce the heat and cook for 30 minutes on a simmer.
6. Puree half of the lentil soup in a blender and transfer it to a soup pot.
7. Stir in chopped greens and cook for almost 5 minutes.
8. Add the rest of the ingredients and mix well.
9. Serve warm.

Chapter 03: Lunch Recipes

Penne Pasta With Pesto Sauce

SERVINGS **2** | PREPARATION TIME **10 minutes** | COOKING TIME **10 minutes**

Nutritional Values Per Serving	
Calories	305
Total Fat	8.4g
Saturated Fat	1g
Cholesterol	55mg
Sodium	118mg
Total Carbohydrate	46.4g
Dietary Fiber	1.4g
Total Sugars	2.2g
Protein	11.9g

Meal Prep Suggestion:

Pack the pasta with sauteed tofu in the meal box for a complete serving.

Ingredients:

- 3 ½ oz. broccoli, cooked
- 1 garlic clove, chopped
- 6 fresh basil leaves
- Olive oil, to taste
- 3 tablespoons vegan parmesan
- ¼ cup frozen peas, thawed
- Salt, to taste
- 10 ½ oz. penne pasta
- 2 zucchini, sliced
- ¼ cup dried tomatoes
- grated vegan Parmesan to serve

Instructions:

1. Boil pasta as per the package's instructions, then drain.
2. Puree basil, salt, Parmesan, garlic, peas and broccoli in a blender.
3. Mix pasta with pesto in a bowl.
4. Stir in broccoli, peas, and zucchini, then mix well.
5. Garnish with vegan Parmesan.
6. Serve.

Chapter 03: Lunch Recipes

Pasta Salad With Tomato And Broccoli

SERVINGS	PREPARATION TIME	COOKING TIME
4	10 minutes	10 minutes

Nutritional Values Per Serving

Calories	279
Total Fat	3.5g
Saturated Fat	1.2g
Cholesterol	61mg
Sodium	133mg
Total Carbohydrate	50.2g
Dietary Fiber	2.8g
Total Sugars	3.7g
Protein	11.9g

Meal Prep Suggestion:

Enjoy this pasta bowl with roasted asparagus salad.

Ingredients:

- 1 pound rotini pasta
- 4 cups broccoli florets, diced
- 1½ cups cherry tomatoes, cut in half
- 1 cup green bell pepper, diced
- ½ cup red onion, diced
- ½ cup kalamata olives, sliced

Dressing

- ½ cup red wine vinegar
- 2 teaspoons Dijon mustard
- 2 teaspoons honey
- 2 teaspoons minced garlic
- 1 teaspoon dried oregano
- 1 teaspoon kosher salt
- ½ teaspoon black pepper
- ½ cup olive oil

Instructions:

1. Boil pasta as per the package's instructions, then drain.
2. Toss broccoli with the rest of the veggies in a salad bowl.
3. Mix the dressing ingredients in a small bowl and pour into the salad.
4. Toss well and serve.

Chapter 03: Lunch Recipes

Pasta With Lentil Sauce

SERVINGS 4
PREPARATION TIME 10 minutes
COOKING TIME 31 minutes

Nutritional Values Per Serving	
Calories	366
Total Fat	9g
Saturated Fat	1.3g
Cholesterol	2mg
Sodium	787mg
Total Carbohydrate	51.9g
Dietary Fiber	19.2g
Total Sugars	12.9g
Protein	17.2g

Meal Prep Suggestion:

Store the lentil sauce and the pasta separately to store in the refrigerator.

Ingredients:

- 2 tablespoons olive oil
- 1 large onion, dice
- 1 green bell pepper, seeded and diced
- 2 medium carrots, peeled and diced
- 6 garlic cloves, minced
- 1 tablespoon Italian seasoning
- 1 teaspoon salt
- ¼ teaspoon black pepper
- 1 (28-ounces) can fire-roasted tomatoes
- 16-ounce can tomato paste
- 2 cups vegetable broth
- ½ cup red wine
- 1 cup red lentils
- ½ cup minced fresh parsley
- 2 cups penne pasta, boiled

Instructions:

1. Sauté carrots, green peppers and onions with oil in a large pot for 5 minutes.
2. Stir in black pepper, salt, Italian seasoning, and garlic, then cook for 1 minute.
3. Add lentils, wine, broth, tomato paste and tomatoes, then cook for 25 minutes on a simmer.
4. Add black pepper, salt and parsley.
5. Serve warm over boiled pasta.

Chapter 03: Lunch Recipes

Sauteed Zoodles

SERVINGS: 4
PREPARATION TIME: 10 minutes
COOKING TIME: 8 minutes

Nutritional Values Per Serving	
Calories	111
Total Fat	7.4g
Saturated Fat	1.1g
Cholesterol	0mg
Sodium	85mg
Total Carbohydrate	8.6g
Dietary Fiber	2.2g
Total Sugars	3.4g
Protein	4.6g

Meal Prep Suggestion:

Enjoy these noodles with roasted tofu steaks.

Ingredients:

- 2 tablespoons olive oil
- 4 garlic cloves, minced
- 1 cup purple cabbage, shredded
- 2 cups noodles, boiled
- 1 teaspoon soy sauce
- ½ cup lettuce leaves, chopped
- Salt and black pepper, to taste

Instructions:

1. Sauté garlic with oil in a deep pan for 30 seconds.
2. Stir in noodles, lettuce leaves and cabbage, then cook for 7 minutes.
3. Season the veggie with soy sauce, black pepper and salt.
4. Serve.

Chapter 03: Lunch Recipes

Penne Pasta With Tomato Sauce

SERVINGS	PREPARATION TIME	COOKING TIME
4	15 minutes	47 minutes

Nutritional Values Per Serving	
Calories	342
Total Fat	9.3g
Saturated Fat	1.3g
Cholesterol	41mg
Sodium	806mg
Total Carbohydrate	58.1g
Dietary Fiber	7g
Total Sugars	0.6g
Protein	12.4g

Meal Prep Suggestion:

Store the pasta and tomato sauce separately in the container for storage.

Ingredients:

- 4 tablespoons olive oil
- 1 medium onion, diced
- 1 teaspoon red chilli flakes
- 2 garlic cloves, minced
- 2 (14 oz.) can crushed tomato
- salt, to taste
- 1 lb/ penne pasta
- Coriander, chopped

Instructions:

1. Sauté onion with oil in a large sauté pan for 10 minutes.
2. Stir in garlic, and chile flakes, then cook for 2 minutes.
3. Add tomatoes and cook for 20-25 minutes on a simmer.
4. Meanwhile, boil pasta as per the package's instructions, then drain; keep ½ cup of the cooking water aside.
5. Mix the drained pasta with the prepared tomato sauce in a bowl.
6. Garnish with coriander.
7. Serve warm.

Chapter 03: Lunch Recipes

Three Colors Pasta

SERVINGS | PREPARATION TIME | COOKING TIME
4 | 15 minutes | 10 minutes

Nutritional Values Per Serving	
Calories	233
Total Fat	10.9g
Saturated Fat	1.6g
Cholesterol	20mg
Sodium	156mg
Total Carbohydrate	30.1g
Dietary Fiber	2.7g
Total Sugars	6.7g
Protein	4.3g

Meal Prep Suggestion:

Store the pasta in a meal box, seal the lid and refrigerate.

Ingredients:

- 24 oz box tri-colour rotini pasta
- 1 cup Italian salad dressing
- 6 stalks of celery, chopped
- 2 pints cherry tomatoes halved
- 1 cup sliced black olives
- 2 tablespoons dried basil
- 2 tablespoons dried oregano

Instructions:

1. Boil pasta as per the package's instructions, then drain.
2. Mix oregano, basil, olives, tomatoes, celery and salad dressing in a bowl.
3. Stir in pasta and the rest of the ingredients.
4. Serve.

Chapter 03: Lunch Recipes

Vegan Poke Bowl

SERVINGS 4 | **PREPARATION TIME** 15 minutes | **COOKING TIME** 18 minutes

Nutritional Values Per Serving	
Calories	329
Total Fat	2g
Saturated Fat	0.4g
Cholesterol	0mg
Sodium	1039mg
Total Carbohydrate	67.4g
Dietary Fiber	5.2g
Total Sugars	6.5g
Protein	10.4g

Meal Prep Suggestion:

Store all the ingredients in the bowl in separate portions of the meal box in the refrigerator for better storage.

Ingredients:

Tofu Poke

- ⅔ cup tamari
- 2 tablespoons rice vinegar
- 1 tablespoon sambal oelek
- 2 teaspoons sesame oil
- 4 garlic cloves, smashed
- 2-inches piece ginger, peeled and chopped
- 1 small sweet onion, julienned
- 28 oz block tofu, cut into ½ inch cubes

Bowl Filling

- 1 bundle asparagus
- ½ avocado, sliced
- 2 tablespoons bean sprouts
- ½ cup pineapple, cubed
- 6 small baby carrots, shredded
- 3 cups cooked quinoa
- ½ cup edamame beans
- ½ cup purple cabbage, shredded

To Serve

- 2 teaspoons sesame seeds

Instructions:

1. Mix tofu with tamari and the rest of the tofu ingredients in a bowl.
2. Cover and marinate the tofu for 20 minutes.
3. Set a skillet greased with cooking oil over medium heat.
4. Sear the tofu cubes for 2-3 minutes per side, then transfer to a plate.
5. Sear the carrots in the same pan for 2-3 minutes per side.
6. Transfer the carrots to the tofu cubes.
7. Sear the tomatoes in the same pan and cook for 3 minutes per side.
8. To assemble, add quinoa to a serving bowl.
9. Add asparagus, cabbage and the rest of the bowl ingredients on top of the quinoa
10. Spread seared tofu cubes on top and garnish with sesame seeds.
11. Serve.

Rice With Vegetables

SERVINGS	PREPARATION TIME	COOKING TIME
4	10 minutes	29 minutes

Nutritional Values Per Serving

Calories	173
Total Fat	3.2g
Saturated Fat	0.6g
Cholesterol	0mg
Sodium	683mg
Total Carbohydrate	33g
Dietary Fiber	8.1g
Total Sugars	19.1g
Protein	9.7g

Meal Prep Suggestion:

Enjoy the rice with a bowl of tomato soup.

Ingredients:

- 4 teaspoons olive oil
- 1 onion, diced
- 2 cups white long-grain rice, uncooked
- 1 teaspoon garlic salt
- 1 teaspoon basil leaves, chopped
- 1 teaspoon ground turmeric
- 4 cups vegetable broth
- 2 cups peas and carrots mix, chopped

Instructions:

1. Sauté onion with oil in a suitable skillet for 3 minutes.
2. Stir in rice, turmeric, basil and garlic salt, then sauté for 1 minute.
3. Add broth, then cook for 15 minutes on a simmer.
4. Stir in carrots and peas, then cook for another 10 minutes.
5. Serve warm.

Chapter 03: Lunch Recipes

Rice With Chopped Carrots

SERVINGS 4
PREPARATION TIME 10 minutes
COOKING TIME 39 minutes

Nutritional Values Per Serving

Calories	253
Total Fat	14.3g
Saturated Fat	2g
Cholesterol	0mg
Sodium	519mg
Total Carbohydrate	30.6g
Dietary Fiber	3.2g
Total Sugars	8.3g
Protein	2.6g

Meal Prep Suggestion:

Serve this rice meal with grilled eggplant steaks.

Ingredients:

- 4 cups of water
- 4 tablespoons olive oil
- 2 medium onions, peeled and chopped
- 4 carrots, peeled, trimmed, and chopped
- 1 tablespoon sugar
- 2 cups basmati rice, rinsed
- 1 teaspoon kosher salt

Instructions:

1. Sauté onion with oil in a Dutch oven for 4 minutes.
2. Stir in carrot and cook for 5 minutes.
3. Add sugar, rice, salt and the rest of the ingredients.
4. Cover and cook the rice for 25 minutes on a simmer.
5. Steam the rice for 5 minutes, then serve.

Chapter 03: Lunch Recipes

Black Rice Meal

SERVINGS: 4 PREPARATION TIME: 10 minutes COOKING TIME: 40 minutes

Nutritional Values Per Serving

Calories	244
Total Fat	18g
Saturated Fat	7.7g
Cholesterol	31mg
Sodium	84mg
Total Carbohydrate	17.9g
Dietary Fiber	2.3g
Total Sugars	1.1g
Protein	4.3g

Meal Prep Suggestion:

Store the rice in a meal box with fresh vegetables.

Ingredients:

- 4 tablespoons almond butter
- 2 cups black rice
- ½ cup onion, chopped
- ½ cup almonds, chopped
- 3 cups vegetable broth

Serve

- Boiled baby corn cobs
- Steamed green beans
- Boil baby carrots

Instructions:

1. Sauté black rice, almonds, and onion with butter in a saucepan for 10 minutes.
2. Stir in vegetable broth and cook on a simmer for 30 minutes with occasional stirring.
3. Serve with boiled baby corn cobs, green peas and carrots.

CHAPTER 04

DINNER RECIPES

Chapter 04: Dinner Recipes

Stuffed Aubergine Rolls

SERVINGS	PREPARATION TIME	COOKING TIME
4	15 minutes	11 minutes

Nutritional Values Per Serving	
Calories	290
Total Fat	21.2g
Saturated Fat	3g
Cholesterol	0mg
Sodium	14mg
Total Carbohydrate	27g
Dietary Fiber	12.3g
Total Sugars	14.2g
Protein	4.7g

Meal Prep Suggestion:

Serve the rolls with tomato salsa.

Ingredients:

Filling

- 1 ½ cups bell peppers, julienned
- 1 tablespoon lemon juice
- 1 tablespoon fresh oregano, minced
- 1 tablespoon cooking oil
- 1 teaspoon fresh mint, minced
- 1 teaspoon fresh dill, minced
- 1 teaspoon garlic, minced
- Salt and black pepper, to taste

Eggplant Rolls

- 2 large eggplants, sliced
- ⅓ cup olive oil
- 3 Roma tomatoes, sliced
- 1 English cucumber, julienned
- Salt and black pepper, to taste

Instructions:

1. Sauté bell peppers with oil, oregano, mint, dill, garlic, black pepper, and salt in a skillet for 5 minutes.
2. Transfer this filling to a plate.
3. Sear the eggplant slices with more olive oil in the same skillet for 2-3 minutes per side.
4. Spread the eggplant slices on the working surface.
5. Divide the bell pepper filling, cucumber and tomatoes on top of the eggplant slices.
6. Roll the slices and Serve.

Chapter 04: Dinner Recipes

Tofu And Rice Platter

SERVINGS 4 **PREPARATION TIME** 15 minutes **COOKING TIME** 22 minutes

Nutritional Values Per Serving	
Calories	329
Total Fat	2g
Saturated Fat	0.4g
Cholesterol	0mg
Sodium	1039mg
Total Carbohydrate	67.4g
Dietary Fiber	5.2g
Total Sugars	6.5g
Protein	10.4g

Meal Prep Suggestion:

For storage, keep all the cooked ingredients of the platter in different portions of the meal box, then refrigerate.

Ingredients:

Tofu Poke

- ⅔ cup tamari
- 2 tablespoons rice vinegar
- 1 tablespoon sambal oelek
- 2 teaspoons sesame oil
- 4 garlic cloves, smashed
- 2-inches piece ginger, peeled and chopped
- 1 small sweet onion, julienned
- 28 oz block tofu, cut into ½ inch cubes

Bowl Filling

- 1 bundle asparagus
- 8 cherry tomatoes
- 6 small baby carrots
- 3 cups cooked rice
- To Serve
- 2 teaspoons sesame seeds

Instructions:

1. Mix tofu with tamari and the rest of the tofu ingredients in a bowl.
2. Cover and marinate the tofu for 20 minutes.
3. Set a skillet greased with cooking oil over medium heat.
4. Sear the tofu cubes for 2-3 minutes per side, then transfer to a plate.
5. Sear the carrots in the same pan for 2-3 minutes per side.
6. Transfer the carrots to the tofu cubes.
7. Sear the tomatoes in the same pan and cook for 3 minutes per side.
8. Transfer the tomatoes to the tofu plate.
9. Sauté asparagus sticks in the same pan for 5 minutes.
10. Transfer the asparagus to the tofu.
11. Add boiled rice to the tofu and garnish with sesame seeds.
12. Serve.

Chapter 04: Dinner Recipes

Vegetable Meatballs With Zucchini Noodles

SERVINGS 4 | **PREPARATION TIME** 15 minutes | **COOKING TIME** 35 minutes

Nutritional Values Per Serving

Calories	235
Total Fat	10.4g
Saturated Fat	0.9g
Cholesterol	0mg
Sodium	154mg
Total Carbohydrate	28.8g
Dietary Fiber	7g
Total Sugars	5.1g
Protein	8.9g

Meal Prep Suggestion:

For storage, freeze the unbaked meatballs in a sealable container in the freezer then cook before serving.

Ingredients:

- 3 garlic cloves, minced

Tomato Zucchini

- 2 large tomatoes, chopped
- 1 teaspoon tomato purée
- 1 teaspoon balsamic vinegar
- 2 zucchinis, cut into 'noodles.'
- ¼ cup frozen peas, thawed

Veggie Meatballs

- 2 teaspoon rapeseed oil
- 1 small onion, chopped
- 2 teaspoon balsamic vinegar
- 3 ½ oz. canned red kidney beans
- 1 tablespoon flaxseed egg
- 1 teaspoon tomato purée
- 1 teaspoon chilli powder
- ½ teaspoon ground coriander
- 1 teaspoon ground almonds
- 1 oz. cooked sweetcorn
- 2 teaspoon chopped thyme leaves

Instructions:

1. Sauté onion with oil in a deep pan for 8 minutes.
2. Stir in vinegar and cook for 2 minutes.
3. Mix beans with spices, tomato puree and flaxseed egg in a bowl.
4. Mash with a fork and stir in almonds, corn, onions and garlic.
5. Mix well and make 8 balls out of this mixture.
6. Place these balls in a greased baking sheet.
7. At 425 degrees F, preheat your oven.
8. Bake the veggies meatballs for 15 minutes in the oven.
9. Meanwhile, mix tomato puree, tomatoes and vinegar in a pan.
10. Cook the tomatoes until soft then mash the ingredients together.
11. Stir in garlic and mix well.
12. Top the zucchini noodles with the tomato sauce, vegetable meatballs.
13. Garnish with peas and serve.

Chapter 04: Dinner Recipes

Noodles With Tofu

SERVINGS 4
PREPARATION TIME 15 minutes
COOKING TIME 15 minutes

Nutritional Values Per Serving	
Calories	270
Total Fat	17g
Saturated Fat	2.4g
Cholesterol	0mg
Sodium	1881mg
Total Carbohydrate	22.3g
Dietary Fiber	5.1g
Total Sugars	9.2g
Protein	10.4g

Meal Prep Suggestion:

Try the noodles with roasted broccoli salad.

Ingredients:

- 4 tablespoons olive oil
- 12 oz. onion, sliced
- 13 oz carrot, shredded
- 1 mild red chilli, chopped
- 6 garlic cloves, minced
- 1 teaspoon puréed ginger
- 11 oz tofu, pressed and diced
- 28 oz fresh egg noodles, boiled
- 8 tablespoons soy sauce
- ½ teaspoon Chinese five spice
- Black pepper, to taste

Instructions:

1. Sauté onion with oil, ginger, chilli and garlic in a deep wok for 5 minutes.
2. Stir in tofu and sear until golden brown.
3. Add noodles, soy sauce and the rest of the ingredients.
4. Sauté these noodles for 5 minutes.
5. Serve warm.

The Plant Based Vegan Diet Meal Prep Cookbook
200+ Easy And Simple Recipes To Eat Healthy At Work, Home And On The Go With 7 Weekly Meal Plans

Chapter 04: Dinner Recipes

Eggplant Casserole

SERVINGS
4

PREPARATION TIME
15 minutes

COOKING TIME
25 minutes

Nutritional Values Per Serving	
Calories	316
Total Fat	18.4g
Saturated Fat	3.9g
Cholesterol	8mg
Sodium	410mg
Total Carbohydrate	31g
Dietary Fiber	4.6g
Total Sugars	8g
Protein	9.6g

Meal Prep Suggestion:

Enjoy the casserole with flatbread and fresh greens salad.

Ingredients:

- 1 large eggplant, sliced
- 2 tablespoons olive oil
- 4 medium tomatoes, sliced
- 1 pound vegan mozzarella cheese, sliced
- ½ cup fresh basil, chopped
- 2 tablespoons fresh thyme, chopped
- Salt and black pepper, to taste
- ¼ cup bread crumbs
- ½ cup vegan Parmesan cheese, grated

Instructions:

1. At 400 degrees F, preheat your oven.
2. Take a round casserole dish and arrange the eggplant slices, tomato and mozzarella slices in it alternatively in a circle.
3. Drizzle oil, thyme, black pepper, salt, breadcrumbs and vegan Parmesan on top.
4. Bake the casserole for 25 minutes in the preheated oven.
5. Serve warm.

Chapter 04: Dinner Recipes

Vegetarian Eggplants Stew

SERVINGS 4

PREPARATION TIME 15 minutes

COOKING TIME 53 minutes

Nutritional Values Per Serving	
Calories	280
Total Fat	13.6g
Saturated Fat	1.9g
Cholesterol	0mg
Sodium	22mg
Total Carbohydrate	29.4g
Dietary Fiber	12.6g
Total Sugars	14.7g
Protein	5.2

Meal Prep Suggestion:

Enjoy this eggplant stew with white boiled rice.

Ingredients:

- 2 eggplants, diced
- ¼ cup olive oil
- 1 cup onion, chopped
- 5 garlic cloves, chopped
- 1 zucchini, chopped
- 1 large red bell pepper, chopped
- 3 fresh tomatoes, diced
- 1 cup Marsala wine
- 1½ cups water
- ½ teaspoon salt, or to taste
- ¼ teaspoon red pepper flakes
- ¼ cup chopped fresh basil
- ¼ cup chopped fresh parsley
- 1 sprig fresh rosemary, chopped

Instructions:

1. Add eggplant to a colander and drizzle salt over the eggplant, then leave for 5 minutes.
2. Sauté onion with oil in a Dutch oven until golden brown.
3. Stir in garlic, then sauté for 3 minutes.
4. Add red pepper flakes, salt, wine, water, tomatoes, red bell pepper, and zucchini, then cook to a boil.
5. Reduce its heat and cook to a simmer 45 minutes.
6. Stir in parsley, rosemary, and basil.
7. Serve warm.

Chapter 04: Dinner Recipes

Pasta With Vegetables And Chickpeas

SERVINGS	PREPARATION TIME	COOKING TIME
4	15 minutes	60 minutes

Nutritional Values Per Serving

Calories	358
Total Fat	7.1g
Saturated Fat	0.9g
Cholesterol	0mg
Sodium	22mg
Total Carbohydrate	60.6g
Dietary Fiber	14.4g
Total Sugars	14.3g
Protein	16g

Meal Prep Suggestion:

Serve the pasta with roasted asparagus.

Ingredients:

- 1 (15 ½ oz.) can chickpeas, rinsed and drained
- 1 pint tomatoes, halved
- ¼ cup raisins
- 4 garlic cloves, minced
- 5 tablespoons olive oil
- 2 cups tomato sauce
- 1 box gluten-free pasta

Instructions:

1. At 400 degrees F, preheat your oven.
2. Mix chickpeas with black pepper, oil and salt on a baking sheet.
3. Roast the chickpeas for 15 minutes.
4. Toss tomatoes with oil, black pepper and oil on a baking sheet.
5. Roast the tomatoes for 45 minutes at 400 degrees F in the oven
6. Boil pasta as per the package's instructions, then drain.
7. Toss pasta with tomatoes and the rest of the ingredients in a bowl.
8. Serve.

Chapter 04: Dinner Recipes

Salad With Roasted Eggplant And Kale

SERVINGS 4

PREPARATION TIME 10 minutes

COOKING TIME 13 minutes

Nutritional Values Per Serving	
Calories	259
Total Fat	14.8g
Saturated Fat	2.1g
Cholesterol	0mg
Sodium	335mg
Total Carbohydrate	31.6g
Dietary Fiber	12.4g
Total Sugars	13.9g
Protein	6.1g

Meal Prep Suggestion:

Serve this salad with grilled tofu.

Ingredients:

- 4 tablespoons olive oil
- 2 garlic cloves, minced
- 1 teaspoon dried Italian herbs

Salad

- 2 large eggplants, sliced
- 17 oz roasted red peppers, drained
- 4 cups kale, sliced
- 4 tablespoons parsley, chopped

Dressing

- 12 tablespoons tahini sesame paste
- 4 teaspoons lemon juice
- 4 teaspoons Erythritol
- 2 tablespoons water
- Salt and black pepper, to taste

Instructions:

1. Mix the tahini paste with the rest of the dressing ingredients in a bowl.
2. Season eggplants with oil, garlic, and herbs.
3. Set a grill pan over medium heat.
4. Grill the eggplants for 3-5 minutes per side.
5. Sauté red peppers, kale and parsley in the grill pan and sauté for 3 minutes.
6. Toss in eggplants and the rest of the tahini dressing.
7. Mix well and serve.

Chapter 04: Dinner Recipes

Farfalle Pasta With Chickpeas

SERVINGS: 4
PREPARATION TIME: 15 minutes
COOKING TIME: 35 minutes

Nutritional Values Per Serving

Calories	372
Total Fat	18.6g
Saturated Fat	13.3g
Cholesterol	0mg
Sodium	164mg
Total Carbohydrate	44.4g
Dietary Fiber	5.3g
Total Sugars	8.2g
Protein	9.5g

Meal Prep Suggestion:

Serve this pasta with roasted cauliflower salad.

Ingredients:

Chickpeas
- 1 tablespoon olive oil
- 1 cup canned chickpeas, drained
- ¼ teaspoon salt
- 1 tablespoon black pepper

Pasta
- 8 oz farfalle pasta
- Spinach leaves, to serve

Green Pasta Sauce
- 1 tablespoon olive oil
- 10 oz mushrooms, sliced
- 12 oz spinach, chopped
- 1 cup coconut cream
- ¼ teaspoon salt

Instructions:

1. Toss the chickpeas with oil, black pepper, and salt on a baking sheet.
2. Roast the chickpeas for 15 minutes in the oven at 350 degrees F.
3. Boil the pasta as per the package's instructions, then drain.
4. Sauté mushrooms with oil in a skillet for 5 minutes.
5. Stir in spinach, and salt then cook for 3 minutes.
6. Add coconut cream and blend this mixture until pureed.
7. Add pasta to the spinach mushroom sauce.
8. Mix well and serve with roasted chickpeas on top.
9. Garnish with spinach leaves.
10. Enjoy.

Chapter 04: Dinner Recipes

Spicy Tomato Soup

SERVINGS
4

PREPARATION TIME
15 minutes

COOKING TIME
48 minutes

Nutritional Values Per Serving	
Calories	138
Total Fat	10.4g
Saturated Fat	1.5g
Cholesterol	0mg
Sodium	600mg
Total Carbohydrate	6.9g
Dietary Fiber	1.5g
Total Sugars	3.9g
Protein	5.3g

Meal Prep Suggestion:

Serve the tomato soup with toasted croutons on top.

Ingredients:

- 2 tablespoons olive oil
- 1 tablespoon almond butter
- 1 white onion, chopped
- 1 garlic clove, smashed and peeled
- 2 tablespoons all-purpose flour
- 3 cups vegetable broth
- 1 (28-oz.) can plum tomatoes, puréed
- 1-½ teaspoon coconut sugar
- 1 sprig of fresh thyme
- Kosher salt and black pepper, to taste
- 3 tablespoons fresh basil, sliced
- A drizzle of coconut cream to garnish

Instructions:

1. Sauté garlic and onion with oil and butter in a Dutch oven for 8 minutes.
2. Stir in flour and mix well.
3. Add black pepper, salt, thyme, sugar, tomatoes and broth, then cook on a simmer for 40 minutes.
4. Then puree the cooked soup with a hand blender until smooth.
5. Garnish with coconut cream and herbs.
6. Serve.

Chapter 04: Dinner Recipes

Rustic Gnocchi Pasta

SERVINGS	PREPARATION TIME	COOKING TIME
4	15 minutes	39 minutes

Nutritional Values Per Serving

Calories	226
Total Fat	4.2g
Saturated Fat	0.5g
Cholesterol	0mg
Sodium	498mg
Total Carbohydrate	37.1g
Dietary Fiber	1.4g
Total Sugars	3.5g
Protein	8.2g

Meal Prep Suggestion:

Serve the pasta with roasted asparagus.

Ingredients:

- 1 tablespoon olive oil
- 1 small onion, finely chopped
- 3 garlic cloves, minced
- ¼ cup kale, chopped
- ¼ cup dry white wine
- 1 can (28 ounces) whole plum tomatoes, crushed
- 1 can (14 ½ ounces) tomato sauce
- 2 sprigs basil
- ¼ teaspoon crushed red pepper
- Coarse salt and black pepper, to taste
- 1 package basic potato gnocchi

Instructions:

1. Sauté garlic and onion with oil in a saucepan for 7 minutes.
2. Stir in wine and cook until the liquid is evaporated.
3. Add tomatoes, kale, tomato juice, red pepper flakes, basil and tomato sauce.
4. Cook the mixture for 30 minutes on a simmer with occasional stirring.
5. Stir in black pepper and salt.
6. Boil gnocchi with salted water in a cooking pot for 2 minutes.
7. Transfer the gnocchi to the sauce using a slotted spoon.
8. Mix well and serve.

Chapter 04: Dinner Recipes

Mushroom Soup

SERVINGS
4

PREPARATION TIME
10 minutes

COOKING TIME
34 minutes

Nutritional Values Per Serving

Calories	260
Total Fat	15.7g
Saturated Fat	4.3g
Cholesterol	21mg
Sodium	790mg
Total Carbohydrate	16.7g
Dietary Fiber	3.7g
Total Sugars	4.9g
Protein	10.6g

Meal Prep Suggestion:

Keep the soup in a sealable container in the refrigerator for delayed serving.

Ingredients:

- 4 tablespoons almond butter
- 1 ½ lb. mushrooms, sliced
- Salt and black pepper, to taste
- 1 medium onion, diced
- ¾ cup dry white wine
- 2 stalks celery, sliced
- 4 garlic cloves, chopped
- 2 sprigs thyme leaves, fresh
- 3 tablespoons all-purpose flour
- 4 cups vegetable stock
- ½ cup coconut cream
- 2 teaspoon balsamic vinegar
- Chopped fresh parsley for serving

Instructions:

1. Sauté mushrooms with butter in a deep pan for 5 minutes.
2. Stir in black pepper and salt, then transfer to a plate.
3. Sauté mushrooms with thyme, celery and onion in the same pan for 6 minutes.
4. Drizzle flour, black pepper and salt over the vegetables.
5. Sauté for 3 minutes, then pour in the wine and mix well.
6. Pour in stock and cream, then cook on a simmer for 20 minutes with occasional stirring.
7. Puree this soup with a hand blender until smooth.
8. Serve warm.

The Plant Based Vegan Diet Meal Prep Cookbook
200+ Easy And Simple Recipes To Eat Healthy At Work, Home And On The Go With 7 Weekly Meal Plans

Chapter 04: Dinner Recipes

Lentil Soup With Mushrooms

SERVINGS 6   **PREPARATION TIME** 15 minutes   **COOKING TIME** 50 minutes

Nutritional Values Per Serving	
Calories	439
Total Fat	15.1g
Saturated Fat	2.1g
Cholesterol	0mg
Sodium	1216mg
Total Carbohydrate	58.7g
Dietary Fiber	23.1g
Total Sugars	10.4g
Protein	21.2g

Meal Prep Suggestion:

Enjoy the lentils with boiled rice.

Ingredients:

- 4 tablespoons olive oil
- 2 onions, chopped
- 2 ribs celery, chopped
- 3 garlic cloves, minced
- 1 ⅔ cups brown lentils
- 3 tablespoons chopped fresh parsley
- 9 cups water
- ½ teaspoon dried thyme
- 1 bay leaf
- 2 teaspoons salt
- 1 pound portobello mushrooms, diced
- 6 tablespoons pomegranate arils
- ¼ teaspoon fresh-ground black pepper

Instructions:

1. Sauté garlic, celery, and onions with 2 tablespoons oil in a large pot for 5 minutes.
2. Stir in bay leaf, thyme, water, parsley and lentils.
3. Cover and cook for 35 minutes on a simmer.
4. Add 1 ¾ teaspoon salt, then cook for 5 minutes.
5. Discard the bay leaf, then add mushrooms.
6. Cook for 5 minutes, then garnish with pomegranate arils.
7. Serve.

Chapter 04: Dinner Recipes

Mushroom Soup With Green Vegetables

SERVINGS
6

PREPARATION TIME
15 minutes

COOKING TIME
33 minutes

Nutritional Values Per Serving	
Calories	332
Total Fat	11g
Saturated Fat	1.4g
Cholesterol	0mg
Sodium	739mg
Total Carbohydrate	47.4g
Dietary Fiber	6.6g
Total Sugars	9g
Protein	13.5g

Meal Prep Suggestion:
Serve the soup with crispy bread slices.

Ingredients:
- 1 tablespoon vegetable oil
- 1 medium onion, halved and sliced
- 3 cups vegetable broth
- ½ teaspoon black pepper
- Salt, to taste
- 12 ounces Yukon gold potatoes, diced
- 2 tablespoons almond butter
- 4 cups fresh mushrooms, sliced
- 2 cups almond milk
- 2 cups fresh Italian parsley leaves, chopped

Instructions:
1. Sauté onion with oil in a saucepan for 5 minutes.
2. Stir in salt, black pepper and broth, then cook to a boil.
3. Add potatoes, cover and cook on a simmer for 10 minutes.
4. Sauté mushrooms with butter in a large skillet for 8 minutes.
5. Stir in the rest of the ingredients, then mix well and cook for 10 minutes.
6. Serve warm.

Chapter 04: Dinner Recipes

Miso Soup With Mushrooms

SERVINGS	PREPARATION TIME	COOKING TIME
6	10 minutes	10 minutes

Nutritional Values Per Serving	
Calories	213
Total Fat	0.7g
Saturated Fat	0.1g
Cholesterol	0mg
Sodium	3069mg
Total Carbohydrate	49.3g
Dietary Fiber	9.9g
Total Sugars	14.4g
Protein	4.7g

Meal Prep Suggestion:

Enjoy the soup with boiled somen noodles.

Ingredients:

- 4 cups vegetable broth
- 3 tablespoons red miso paste
- 3 cups portobello mushrooms, sliced
- 2 cups raw kale, sliced
- 1 teaspoon ginger root, grated
- 3 garlic cloves, sliced
- ½ cup green onions, chopped
- ¼ teaspoon red chilli flakes
- Sesame seeds, to garnish

Instructions:

1. Add broth to a cooking pot and cook for 5 minutes.
2. Stir in miso paste and rest of the ingredients, then cook for 5 minutes.
3. Garnish with sesame seeds.
4. Serve warm.

Cutlets Cauliflower

SERVINGS
4

PREPARATION TIME
10 minutes

COOKING TIME
11 minutes

Nutritional Values Per Serving	
Calories	169
Total Fat	1.1g
Saturated Fat	0.1g
Cholesterol	0mg
Sodium	156mg
Total Carbohydrate	36g
Dietary Fiber	9.9g
Total Sugars	9.2g
Protein	7.6g

Meal Prep Suggestion:

Try the cutlets with whole wheat buns, vegetable salad and tomato sauce.

Ingredients:

- 1 lb. cauliflower, riced
- ½ lb. potatoes, boiled and mashed
- 1 teaspoon mustard seeds
- 1 teaspoon cumin seeds
- 1 teaspoon aniseed
- 1 onion chopped
- 1 oz. gram flour
- Oil for frying
- Salt to taste

Instructions:

1. Sauté onions, aniseeds, cumin seeds and mustard seeds in a wok for 30 seconds.
2. Stir in cauliflower, salt, gram flour, and potatoes, then remove from the heat.
3. Mix well and make 4-6 cutlets out of this mixture.
4. Sear the cutlets in a greased skillet for 3-5 minutes per side.
5. Serve warm.

Chapter 04: Dinner Recipes

Mushroom Tofu Soup

SERVINGS 4 **PREPARATION TIME** 15 minutes **COOKING TIME** 25 minutes

Nutritional Values Per Serving	
Calories	133
Total Fat	2.7g
Saturated Fat	0.6g
Cholesterol	0mg
Sodium	1288mg
Total Carbohydrate	23.3g
Dietary Fiber	4.1g
Total Sugars	6.2g
Protein	8.2g

Meal Prep Suggestion:

Try the tofu soup with bread slices.

Ingredients:

- 1 cup dried shiitake mushrooms, soaked and drained
- 4 cups water
- 1 tablespoon soy sauce
- 1 cup seaweed, chopped
- ½ teaspoon rice wine vinegar
- 2 ounces firm tofu, diced

Instructions:

1. Add mushrooms, water, soy sauce, rice vinegar, tofu and seaweed to a cooking pot.
2. Cook the mushroom mixture for 25 minutes on a simmer.
3. Serve warm.

Chapter 04: Dinner Recipes

Chickpea Rice

SERVINGS 4
PREPARATION TIME 10 minutes
COOKING TIME 24 minutes

Nutritional Values Per Serving	
Calories	359
Total Fat	12.5g
Saturated Fat	1.5g
Cholesterol	0mg
Sodium	768mg
Total Carbohydrate	54.2g
Dietary Fiber	4.6g
Total Sugars	1.3g
Protein	8.3g

Meal Prep Suggestion:

Enjoy the chickpea rice with sauteed asparagus.

Ingredients:

- 1 (15 ounces) can chickpeas, drained
- 1 small onion, chopped
- 2 tablespoons almond butter
- 2 tablespoons olive oil
- 2 tablespoons tomatoes, chopped
- 1 teaspoon salt
- 1 teaspoon black pepper
- 1 cup basmati rice, rinsed
- 2 cups water

Instructions:

1. Sauté onion with oil and butter in a deep pan for 5 minutes.
2. Stir in rice, salt, black pepper and water, then cook the rice on a simmer for 14 minutes
3. Stir in chickpeas and tomatoes, then cook for 5 minutes.
4. Garnish with carrot and lemon slices.
5. Serve warm.

Chapter 04: Dinner Recipes

Stinky Tofu

SERVINGS 4 **PREPARATION TIME** 10 minutes **COOKING TIME** 12 minutes

Nutritional Values Per Serving

Calories	371
Total Fat	6g
Saturated Fat	0.9g
Cholesterol	0mg
Sodium	378mg
Total Carbohydrate	61.6g
Dietary Fiber	9.9g
Total Sugars	2.3g
Protein	14.9g

Meal Prep Suggestion:

Try the stinky tofu with fresh herbs on top.

Ingredients:

- 14 ounce block of firm tofu
- 4 Stinky fermented bean curd blocks, mashed
- 2 green onions, minced
- ½ teaspoon red chili peppers
- 2 teaspoons potato starch
- 2 teaspoons oyster sauce
- 1 teaspoon sugar
- 2 medium garlic cloves, minced
- 1 tablespoon parsley
- 1 teaspoon white spirit
- 1 teaspoon fennel powder
- 1 teaspoon vegetable oil
- Chopped chilies to serve

Instructions:

1. Mix white spirit, bean curd and water in a large sealable container.
2. Add tofu to the water, seal the lid and refrigerate for 24 hours.
3. Sear the tofu in a wok with cooking oil for 5 minutes per side, then transfer to a plate.
4. Stir in oyster sauce, fennel powder and ½ cup water, then cook for 2 minutes.
5. Stir in starch and parsley, then cook until it thickens.
6. Place the tofu in this sauce and mix well.
7. Garnish with sliced chilies.
8. Serve.

Chapter 04: Dinner Recipes

Steamed White Beans In Tomato Sauce

SERVINGS 4
PREPARATION TIME 10 minutes
COOKING TIME 43 minutes

Nutritional Values Per Serving	
Calories	198
Total Fat	14.2g
Saturated Fat	2.1g
Cholesterol	0mg
Sodium	940mg
Total Carbohydrate	14.1g
Dietary Fiber	6g
Total Sugars	1.6g
Protein	4.3g

Meal Prep Suggestion:

Enjoy the beans with flatbread.

Ingredients:

- 2 ½ cups dry cannellini beans
- 2 teaspoons baking soda
- 2 small carrots, chopped
- 4 rocket leaves, chopped
- 4 tablespoons olive oil
- 4 garlic cloves, peeled and crushed
- 2 sprigs fresh sage
- 3 cups tomato sauce
- salt and black pepper to taste

Instructions:

1. Soak beans in water for 12 hours drain.
2. Add these beans and water to a cooking pot and cook for 25 minutes until beans are soft.
3. Drain the beans and keep them aside.
4. Sauté sage and garlic with oil in the same pot for 2 minutes.
5. Stir in beans and carrots, then cook for 30 seconds.
6. Add tomato sauce and cook for almost 15 minutes.
7. Stir in black pepper and salt, then mix well.
8. Garnish with rocket leaves.
9. Serve warm.

Chapter 04: Dinner Recipes

Grilled Eggplant Rolls

SERVINGS 4   **PREPARATION TIME** 10 minutes   **COOKING TIME** 10 minutes

Nutritional Values Per Serving	
Calories	142
Total Fat	4.1g
Saturated Fat	0.4g
Cholesterol	0mg
Sodium	90mg
Total Carbohydrate	19.3g
Dietary Fiber	10.3g
Total Sugars	8.8g
Protein	5.2g

Meal Prep Suggestion:
Serve the rolls with sauteed carrots and broccoli.

Ingredients:
- 1 large eggplant
- ¼ cup pine nuts toasted
- 8 oz vegan cheese, crumbed
- 5 oz arugula, chopped
- 1 cup balsamic vinegar
- Kosher salt, to taste
- Olive oil, to cook

Instructions:
1. Cut the eggplant into a thin slices and brush them with olive oil.
2. Grill these slices for 5 minutes per side in a grill pan over medium heat.
3. Transfer the eggplant slices to a working surface.
4. Mix chopped arugula with vegan cheese, pine nuts, salt and vinegar in a bowl.
5. Divide this filling at the center of each eggplant slice.
6. Roll the eggplant slices and serve.

Chapter 04: Dinner Recipes

Mushroom Broccoli Stir Fry

SERVINGS **PREPARATION TIME** **COOKING TIME**
4   10 minutes   7 minutes

Nutritional Values Per Serving

Calories	216
Total Fat	10.8g
Saturated Fat	1.9g
Cholesterol	0mg
Sodium	960mg
Total Carbohydrate	22.5g
Dietary Fiber	5.3g
Total Sugars	6.2g
Protein	9.8g

Meal Prep Suggestion:

Enjoy this stir fry with boiled rice.

Ingredients:

- 4 cups broccoli cut into small florets
- ½ cup red onion, chopped
- 6 garlic cloves, minced
- 4 cups mushrooms, sliced
- ½ teaspoon crushed red pepper
- 4 teaspoons ginger fresh, grated
- ½ cup vegetable broth
- 1 cup carrot, shredded
- ½ cup red bell pepper, sliced
- 4 tablespoons rice wine vinegar
- 4 tablespoons soy sauce
- 2 tablespoons coconut sugar
- 2 tablespoons sesame seeds

Instructions:

1. Cook broccoli with mushrooms, water, ginger, red pepper, garlic and onion in a skillet for 5 minutes.
2. Stir in coconut sugar, soy sauce, vinegar, bell pepper and carrot, then cook for 2 minutes.
3. Garnish with sesame seeds, then serve warm.

Chapter 04: Dinner Recipes

Traditional Pizza

SERVINGS 4   **PREPARATION TIME** 35 minutes   **COOKING TIME** 7 minutes

Nutritional Values Per Serving

Calories	231
Total Fat	15.9g
Saturated Fat	3g
Cholesterol	0mg
Sodium	194mg
Total Carbohydrate	19.1g
Dietary Fiber	5.6g
Total Sugars	6.5g
Protein	6.3g

Meal Prep Suggestion:

Enjoy this pizza with a refreshing quinoa salad.

Ingredients:

- 5 cups all purpose flour
- 1 ½ teaspoon active dry yeast
- 1 ½ teaspoon sea salt
- 2 ¼ cups water
- 1 tbs olive oil

Topping

- 1 cup pizza sauce
- ¼ cup basil leaves
- 1 cup cherry tomatoes, cut into half
- 1 cup vegan mozzarella cheese, shredded

Instructions:

1. Mix all the pizza dough ingredients in a stand mixer with a dough hook for 10 minutes on low speed.
2. Knead the pizza dough for 5 minutes, cover and leave for 1 hour.
3. Roll out the pizza dough on the working surface into a 9 inch round.
4. Spread the pizza sauce at the center of the pizza dough leaving 1 inch on the side.
5. Drizzle vegan mozzarella cheese on top and bake for 7 minutes at 525 degrees F in the oven.
6. Top the pizza with tomatoes and basil.
7. Serve.

Chapter 04: Dinner Recipes

Stuffed Cabbage Rolls

SERVINGS
4

PREPARATION TIME
10 minutes

COOKING TIME
30 minutes

Nutritional Values Per Serving	
Calories	151
Total Fat	4.9g
Saturated Fat	1g
Cholesterol	0mg
Sodium	646mg
Total Carbohydrate	17.8g
Dietary Fiber	2.2g
Total Sugars	2.6g
Protein	11g

Meal Prep Suggestion:

Store the cabbage rolls in a meal box with tomato sauce for serving.

Ingredients:

- ⅔ cup water
- ⅓ cup uncooked white rice
- 8 cabbage leaves
- 1 pound tofu, crumbled
- ¼ cup chopped onion
- 1 flaxseed egg
- 1 teaspoon salt
- ¼ teaspoon ground black pepper
- 2 tablespoons condensed tomato soup
- Coriander, chopped

Instructions:

1. Add rice and water to a cooking pot and cook for 20 minutes on a simmer.
2. Meanwhile, boil salted water in a cooking pot.
3. Add cabbage leaves to this water and cook for 4 minutes, then drain.
4. Mix 2 tablespoons tomato soup, black pepper, salt, onion, 1 cup rice, tofu and flaxseed egg in a bowl.
5. Spread the cabbage leaves on the working surface.
6. Divide the tofu filling over the cabbage leaves.
7. Roll and secure the cabbage rolls with a toothpick.
8. Sear the cabbage rolls in a greased skillet for 2-3 minutes per side.
9. Garnish the rolls with coriander.
10. Serve.

Chapter 04: Dinner Recipes

Rice Stuffed Butternut Squash

SERVINGS 4 | **PREPARATION TIME** 20 minutes | **COOKING TIME** 45 minutes

Nutritional Values Per Serving	
Calories	272
Total Fat	9.4g
Saturated Fat	0.8g
Cholesterol	0mg
Sodium	352mg
Total Carbohydrate	45.8g
Dietary Fiber	5.2g
Total Sugars	13g
Protein	6.5g

Meal Prep Suggestion:
Serve the stuffed squash with grilled eggplant skewers.

Ingredients:
- 2 small butternut squash
- 1 ⅔ cup cooked long-grain rice
- 6 tablespoons mango chutney
- 2 green onions, chopped
- 1 ⅔ teaspoon curry powder
- ½ teaspoon salt
- ½ teaspoon black pepper
- 4 teaspoons almond butter
- Chopped coriander to garnish

Instructions:
1. Cut the small butternut squashes in half; remove and discard the seeds.
2. Place cut side down in a baking sheet.
3. Bake for almost 45 minutes at 350 degrees F in the oven.
4. Flip the butternut squash and cut crossed slits in the flesh.
5. Mix rice with mango chutney, onion, curry powder, black pepper, salt and almond butter in a bowl.
6. Stuff the butternut squash with the rice filling.
7. Garnish with coriander.
8. Serve warm.

Chapter 04: Dinner Recipes

Potato Kale Burger

SERVINGS 4 **PREPARATION TIME** 10 minutes **COOKING TIME** 10 minutes

Nutritional Values Per Serving

Calories	216
Total Fat	10.8g
Saturated Fat	1.9g
Cholesterol	0mg
Sodium	960mg
Total Carbohydrate	22.5g
Dietary Fiber	5.3g
Total Sugars	6.2g
Protein	9.8g

Meal Prep Suggestion:

Enjoy the burgers with tomato sauce and vegan mayo dip.

Ingredients:

- 4 baked potatoes, peeled
- 6 oz. kale, chopped
- 4 oz. red onions, chopped
- 1 teaspoon garlic
- ½ cup 1 tablespoon scallions, chopped
- 2 ½ oz. red peppers, chopped
- 1 ½ oz. jalapeños, chopped
- 1 teaspoon Kosher salt
- ½ teaspoon ground black pepper
- 4 oz. Rice Chex rice, crushed

Dressing

- 4-6 whole wheat buns
- Lettuce leaves
- Vegan mayo
- Yellow pepper slices.

Instructions:

1. Mash baked potatoes in a large bowl with a fork.
2. Stir in kale, garlic and the rest of the ingredients, then mix well.
3. Make 4-6 patties of this potato mixture.
4. Sear the patties in a greased skillet for 5 minutes per side.
5. Place a patty with lettuce leaves, vegan mayo and yellow pepper slices in between each bun halves.
6. Serve.

Chapter 04: Dinner Recipes

Broccoli Mushroom Quinoa Bowl

SERVINGS 4   **PREPARATION TIME** 15 minutes   **COOKING TIME** 19 minutes

Nutritional Values Per Serving	
Calories	262
Total Fat	9.8g
Saturated Fat	1.3g
Cholesterol	0mg
Sodium	353mg
Total Carbohydrate	35.9g
Dietary Fiber	6.2g
Total Sugars	2g
Protein	10.1g

Meal Prep Suggestion:
Add bean sprouts on top before serving.

Ingredients:

- 1-½ cups dry tricolor quinoa
- 2 tablespoons olive oil
- 1 small onion, chopped
- 2 garlic cloves, minced
- ½ teaspoon salt
- ½ teaspoon ground black pepper
- 2 dry pints mushrooms, sliced
- 2 small broccoli crowns, cut into florets
- 3-4 tablespoons fresh basil leaves

Instructions:

1. Boil quinoa as per the package's instruction, then drain.
2. Sauté quinoa with oil in a skillet for 2 minutes.
3. Stir in black pepper, salt, garlic, and onions, then sauté for 3 minutes.
4. Add mushrooms and cook for 3 minutes.
5. Stir in broccoli and cook for 30 seconds.
6. Add quinoa and basil, then mix well.
7. Serve.

Chapter 04: Dinner Recipes

Vegetarian Meal Salad

SERVINGS 4   **PREPARATION TIME** 10 minutes   **COOKING TIME** 15 minutes

Nutritional Values Per Serving	
Calories	144
Total Fat	7.1g
Saturated Fat	0.9g
Cholesterol	0mg
Sodium	1580mg
Total Carbohydrate	15.9g
Dietary Fiber	2.7g
Total Sugars	11.3g
Protein	5.5g

Meal Prep Suggestion:

Add sauteed mushrooms to the salad before serving.

Ingredients:

- 1 tablespoon sweet chilli sauce
- ½ teaspoon grated fresh ginger root
- 2 garlic cloves, crushed
- 1 tablespoon dark soy sauce
- 1 tablespoon sesame oil
- ½ (16 ounce) package tofu, diced
- 1 cup snow peas, trimmed
- 2 lettuce leaves, torn
- 1 red chilli, sliced
- 2 small carrots, grated
- 1 cup finely shredded red cabbage
- 2 tablespoons chopped nuts

Instructions:

1. Mix tofu with sesame oil, soy sauce, garlic, ginger, and chilli sauce in a large bowl. Cover and marinate for 1 hour.
2. Sear the tofu slices in a skillet for 3-5 minutes per side.
3. Stir in the rest of the ingredients, then mix well and cook for 5 minutes.
4. Serve.

Chapter 04: Dinner Recipes

Edamame Quinoa Salad

SERVINGS 4 | **PREPARATION TIME** 10 minutes | **COOKING TIME** 8 minutes

Nutritional Values Per Serving	
Calories	355
Total Fat	8.6g
Saturated Fat	1.1g
Cholesterol	0mg
Sodium	326mg
Total Carbohydrate	56.5g
Dietary Fiber	6.5g
Total Sugars	0.7g
Protein	13.8g

Meal Prep Suggestion:

Enjoy this salad with roasted mushroom skewers.

Ingredients:

- 1 tablespoon toasted sesame oil
- 2 garlic cloves minced
- 3 cups cooked quinoa chilled
- 1 cup edamame beans, boiled
- 1 16oz bag frozen veggies, chopped
- 1 block tofu, crumbled
- 3 tablespoons gluten-free soy sauce
- ½ teaspoon ground ginger

Instructions:

1. Sauté garlic with oil in a large skillet for 30 seconds.
2. Stir in vegetables, edamame beans and quinoa, then cook for 2 minutes.
3. Add the rest of the ingredients, then cook for 5 minutes.
4. Serve.

Chapter 04: Dinner Recipes

Rotini Pasta Salad With Arugula

SERVINGS 4 | **PREPARATION TIME** 10 minutes | **COOKING TIME** 0 minutes

Nutritional Values Per Serving

Calories	332
Total Fat	1.7g
Saturated Fat	0g
Cholesterol	0mg
Sodium	6mg
Total Carbohydrate	69.6g
Dietary Fiber	4.2g
Total Sugars	5.5g
Protein	10g

Meal Prep Suggestion:

Keep this pasta salad with grilled tofu in a meal box for complete serving.

Ingredients:

- 2 pints cherry tomatoes, halved
- 2 garlic cloves, minced
- Salt to taste
- 2 teaspoons balsamic vinegar
- 2 cups arugula leaves, chopped
- 2 tablespoons fresh basil, chopped
- 4 tablespoons olive oil
- 1 $\frac{2}{3}$ pound rotini pasta, boiled

Instructions:

1. Toss pasta with vinegar, arugula and the rest of the ingredients in a bowl.
2. Serve.

Chapter 04: Dinner Recipes

Rigatoni with Tomatoes and Zucchini

SERVINGS	PREPARATION TIME	COOKING TIME
4	15 minutes	46 minutes

Nutritional Values Per Serving

Calories	348
Total Fat	9.1g
Saturated Fat	1.7g
Cholesterol	6mg
Sodium	472mg
Total Carbohydrate	52.3g
Dietary Fiber	4.2g
Total Sugars	6.8g
Protein	9.7g

Meal Prep Suggestion:

Serve this pasta with mashed potatoes and roasted asparagus on the side.

Ingredients:

- ¾ lb rigatoni
- 3 tablespoons olive oil
- 1 large yellow onion, chopped
- ¼ teaspoon crushed red pepper flakes
- 1 lb yellow squash, peeled and sliced
- 5 garlic cloves, minced
- 3 tablespoons tomato paste
- 1 cup grape tomatoes
- 1 cup sun-dried tomatoes
- 1 cup white wine
- 2 small zucchini, diced
- 1 teaspoon salt
- ½ teaspoon black pepper

Instructions:

1. Boil rigatoni pasta in salted water as per the package's instructions then drain.
2. Sauté onion with red pepper and oil in a large pot for 10 minutes.
3. Stir in squash and cook for 10 minutes.
4. Add garlic and sauté for 1 minute.
5. Stir in tomato paste, tomatoes, black pepper and salt then cook for 10 minutes.
6. Add zucchini and cook for 5 minutes.
7. Add cooked rigatoni pasta and mix well.
8. Serve warm.
9. Serve.

Chapter 04: Dinner Recipes

Lemon Sauteed Cabbage

SERVINGS 4 **PREPARATION TIME** 15 minutes **COOKING TIME** 15 minutes

Nutritional Values Per Serving	
Calories	107
Total Fat	5.6g
Saturated Fat	0.9g
Cholesterol	0mg
Sodium	277mg
Total Carbohydrate	14g
Dietary Fiber	5.8g
Total Sugars	7.5g
Protein	3.1g

Meal Prep Suggestion:

Enjoy the cabbage meal with crispy breadcrumbs on top and a warming bowl of tomato soup on the side.

Ingredients:

- 2 pounds white cabbage, cored and shredded
- 1 ½ tablespoons olive oil
- 1 tablespoon garlic, minced
- Pinch crushed red pepper flakes
- ½ teaspoon sea salt
- 2 tablespoons lemon juice

Instructions:

1. Sauté cabbage with salt, red pepper flakes, garlic and oil in a deep pan for 15 minutes.
2. Stir in lemon juice, black pepper and salt.
3. Mix well and serve warm.

Chapter 04: Dinner Recipes

White Rice Cakes

SERVINGS 6   **PREPARATION TIME** 15 minutes   **COOKING TIME** 10 minutes

Nutritional Values Per Serving	
Calories	214
Total Fat	8.7g
Saturated Fat	4.5g
Cholesterol	0mg
Sodium	444mg
Total Carbohydrate	30.4g
Dietary Fiber	1.3g
Total Sugars	0.9g
Protein	4.5g

Meal Prep Suggestion:

These rice cakes can be served with soups and stews.

Ingredients:

- 3 cups white rice, cooked
- ½ cup coconut cream
- 1 cup vegan cheddar, grated
- 1 teaspoon salt
- ½ teaspoon black pepper
- 2 tablespoons almond butter

Instructions:

1. Blend rice with cream, cheddar and rest of the ingredients in a food processor for 1 minute.
2. Make 3 inch round cakes out of this mixture.
3. Set a greased pan over medium heat and sear the cakes for 5 minutes per side.
4. Serve.

Chapter 04: Dinner Recipes

Kimchi

SERVINGS
6

PREPARATION TIME
15 minutes

COOKING TIME
7 minutes

Nutritional Values Per Serving

Calories	263
Total Fat	2.3g
Saturated Fat	0.3g
Cholesterol	0mg
Sodium	22155mg
Total Carbohydrate	55.5g
Dietary Fiber	12.7g
Total Sugars	26.8g
Protein	15.4g

Meal Prep Suggestion:

Kimchi can be served with fried rice or boiled noodles on the side.

Ingredients:

- 10 pounds napa cabbage, shredded
- 1 cup kosher salt
- ½ cup sweet rice flour
- ¼ cup sugar
- Water, to soak
- 1 cup of crushed garlic
- 2 tablespoon ginger, minced
- 1 cup onion, minced
- 1 cup vegan fish sauce
- 2½ cups hot pepper flakes
- 2 cups leek, chopped
- 10 green onions, diagonally sliced
- ¼ cup of carrot, julienned
- 2 cups Korean radish, julienned

Instructions:

1. Cut the cabbage in quarters and remove their core.
2. Soak the cabbage in cold water in a large bowl.
3. Drizzle salt on top and leave for 1 hr. 30 minutes then drain.
4. Mix 3 cups water with sweet rice flour in a cooking pot for 5 minutes.
5. Stir in ¼ cup sugar and cook for 2 minutes then allow the mixture to cool.
6. Add cabbage and rest of the ingredients to the cooking pot.
7. Mix well and serve.

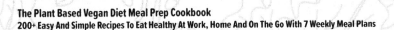

Chapter 04: Dinner Recipes

Herbed Couscous

SERVINGS — PREPARATION TIME — COOKING TIME
4 — 10 minutes — 15 minutes

Nutritional Values Per Serving	
Calories	210
Total Fat	4.1g
Saturated Fat	0.7g
Cholesterol	0mg
Sodium	237mg
Total Carbohydrate	35.3g
Dietary Fiber	2.7g
Total Sugars	0.7g
Protein	6.9g

Ingredients:

- 1 cup vegetable broth
- 1 tablespoons olive oil
- Kosher Salt, to taste
- 1 cup dry instant couscous
- 1 Pinch of cumin ground
- ¼ cup frozen peas
- 2 garlic clove, minced
- 2 green onions chopped
- 1 tablespoon parsley, chopped

Instructions:

1. Sauté garlic with olive oil in a deep pan for 1 minute.
2. Add broth, peas, couscous and rest of the ingredients to the pan.
3. Cook to a boil then reduce its heat then cook for 15 minutes on a simmer.
4. Serve.

CHAPTER 05

HIGH PROTEIN MEALS

Chapter 05: High Protein Meals

Boiled Red Beans

SERVINGS 6   **PREPARATION TIME** 10 minutes   **COOKING TIME** 1 hour 30 minutes

Nutritional Values Per Serving	
Calories	255
Total Fat	0.8g
Saturated Fat	0.1g
Cholesterol	0mg
Sodium	397mg
Total Carbohydrate	46.3g
Dietary Fiber	11.5g
Total Sugars	1.6g
Protein	17g

Meal Prep Suggestion:

Pack these beans with boiled white rice, and sauteed veggies and refrigerate only up to 3 days.

Ingredients:

- 1 pound dried red kidney beans
- 2 bay leaves
- 1 teaspoon salt

Instructions:

1. Soak the beans in a bowl filled with water for 5 hours.
2. Drain and transfer the beans to a saucepan.
3. Add 10 cups water, and salt to the beans.
4. Cook these beans to a boil, then reduce its heat and cook for 90 minutes on a simmer.
5. Garnish with basil and serve.

Chapter 05: High Protein Meals

Stewed White Beans With Pumpkin

SERVINGS 4
PREPARATION TIME 10 minutes
COOKING TIME 2 hours 5 minutes

Nutritional Values Per Serving	
Calories	263
Total Fat	5.4g
Saturated Fat	0.8g
Cholesterol	0mg
Sodium	64mg
Total Carbohydrate	41.9g
Dietary Fiber	10.7g
Total Sugars	4.4g
Protein	14.5g

Meal Prep Suggestion:
This stew goes well with boiled rice and flatbread.

Ingredients:
- 8 ounces dry white beans
- 4 teaspoons olive oil
- 1 large onion, minced
- 1 tablespoon garlic, minced
- 1 serrano chile, sliced
- Kosher salt, to taste
- ¼ teaspoon hot paprika
- 1 tablespoon tomato paste
- 3 cups water
- 15 sprigs cilantro, chopped
- ½ small pumpkin, peeled, diced

Instructions:
1. Add beans to a saucepan and pour in water to cover them.
2. Cook the beans to a boil, reduce its heat and cook for 1 hour then drain.
3. Sauté onion with ¼ teaspoon salt, serrano chili and garlic with oil in a stockpot for 5 minutes.
4. Add tomato paste, and paprika then cook for 1 minute.
5. Stir in beans, water, and cilantro then cook for 35 minutes on a simmer.
6. Add pumpkin and cook for 25 minutes.
7. Serve warm.

Chapter 05: High Protein Meals

Tofu Stuffed Pastry

SERVINGS 4 **PREPARATION TIME** 10 minutes **COOKING TIME** 30 minutes

Nutritional Values Per Serving	
Calories	369
Total Fat	17g
Saturated Fat	5.2g
Cholesterol	17mg
Sodium	586mg
Total Carbohydrate	45g
Dietary Fiber	3.6g
Total Sugars	1.8g
Protein	13.3g

Meal Prep Suggestion:

Pack the unbaked pastries in a sealable container and freeze until ready to bake and serve.

Ingredients:

- 2 pizza dough sheets
- 2 medium potato, peeled and boiled
- 12 vegan mozzarella slices
- 12 tofu slices, crumbled

Instructions:

1. At 400 degrees F, preheat your oven.
2. Layer a cookie sheet with parchment paper.
3. Spread the dough sheets on a working surface into ¼ inch thick sheet.
4. Cut them into 6 rectangles of equal size.
5. Mash potato in a bowl then season with black pepper and salt.
6. Divide this mixture on top of the rectangles and top each with mozzarella and tofu slice.
7. Fold the dough pieces into triangles and place them in a baking sheet lined with parchment paper.
8. Bake the pastries for 30 minutes in the oven and flip them once cooked half way through.
9. Serve warm.

Chapter 05: High Protein Meals

Tofu Falafel Wraps

SERVINGS
4

PREPARATION TIME
10 minutes

COOKING TIME
20 minutes

Nutritional Values Per Serving	
Calories	301
Total Fat	8.7g
Saturated Fat	1.3g
Cholesterol	0mg
Sodium	172mg
Total Carbohydrate	41.5g
Dietary Fiber	12.5g
Total Sugars	8.2g
Protein	17.5g

Meal Prep Suggestion:

Pack the falafels, and other toppings separately in a container with multiple compartments and refrigerate till the serving time.

Ingredients:

Tofu Falafel

- 7 ounces tofu
- 7 ¼ ounces chickpeas, cooked
- 2 garlic cloves
- 1 tablespoon flaxseed
- ½ bunch of parsley
- 2 tablespoons veggie broth
- Black pepper, to taste
- Salt, to taste

Taco

- 4 ounces hummus
- ½ cucumber, julienned
- 1 bunch rocket leaves, chopped
- 1 roma tomato, julienned
- ¼ white onion, sliced
- 2 tablespoon Fresh lemon juice
- 4 tortillas
- Salt and pepper, to taste

Instructions:

1. At 360 degrees F, preheat your oven.
2. Blend tofu with chickpeas, garlic, flaxseed, parsley, broth, black pepper and salt in a blender smooth.
3. Make 1 inch balls out of this mixture and place them in a greased baking sheet.
4. Bake these falafels for 20 minutes in the preheated oven.
5. Spread hummus over the tortillas and add rest of the ingredients along with baked falafels on top.
6. Serve.

Chapter 05: High Protein Meals

Cereal Almond Bars

SERVINGS 8 **PREPARATION TIME** 10 minutes **COOKING TIME** 2 minutes

Nutritional Values Per Serving	
Calories	318
Total Fat	16.4g
Saturated Fat	10.5g
Cholesterol	2mg
Sodium	119mg
Total Carbohydrate	41g
Dietary Fiber	2.3g
Total Sugars	19.1g
Protein	4.5g

Meal Prep Suggestion:

These bars can be stored in a dry and sealable container in the refrigerator.

Ingredients:

- 4 cups crispy rice
- 1 cup old fashioned rolled oats
- ½ cup almonds, sliced
- ½ cup dried cherries
- ½ cup shaved coconut
- ⅓ cup maple syrup
- ⅓ cup coconut oil
- ¼ cup brown sugar
- ⅓ cup almond butter
- 1 teaspoon vanilla extract
- ½ cup dark chocolate chunks

Instructions:

1. Mix coconut oil, maple syrup and sugar to a saucepan and cook to a boil.
2. Toss cereal with coconut, cherries, almond and oats in a 9x13 inches baking pan lined with parchment paper.
3. Pour the coconut oil mixture over the cereal mixture.
4. Allow the mixture to cool and set.
5. Cut into bars and serve.

Chapter 05: High Protein Meals

Muesli Bars

SERVINGS
6

PREPARATION TIME
10 minutes

COOKING TIME
5 minutes

Nutritional Values Per Serving	
Calories	323
Total Fat	14.7g
Saturated Fat	2.3g
Cholesterol	1mg
Sodium	96mg
Total Carbohydrate	46.9g
Dietary Fiber	4.8g
Total Sugars	29.1g
Protein	7.2g

Meal Prep Suggestion:

Wrap these bars in a plastic sheet and refrigerate till serving time.

Ingredients:

- 1 cup brown sugar
- 4 tablespoons almond butter
- ¼ cup cocoa powder
- ¼ cup almond milk
- ½ cup mixed nuts
- 2 cups muesli
- 1 teaspoon vanilla extract

Instructions:

1. Mix milk, butter, cocoa powder, and sugar in a saucepan and cook for 5 minutes.
2. Mix nuts with granola and vanilla in an 8 inch baking pan with parchment paper.
3. Pour the butter mixture over the nuts and refrigerate for 2 hours.
4. Cut the granola into bars and serve.

Chapter 05: High Protein Meals

Saucy Navy Beans

SERVINGS 8   **PREPARATION TIME** 10 minutes   **COOKING TIME** 8 minutes

Nutritional Values Per Serving	
Calories	253
Total Fat	1.6g
Saturated Fat	0.2g
Cholesterol	0mg
Sodium	723mg
Total Carbohydrate	46.8g
Dietary Fiber	13.1g
Total Sugars	8.9g
Protein	16.1g

Meal Prep Suggestion:
Pack these beans with some boiled or fried rice on the side.

Ingredients:
- 2 cups (14 oz) dried navy beans
- 3 x 14oz cans navy beans, drained
- 2 cups vegetable broth
- 1 cup water
- 2 teaspoon vegan worcestershire sauce
- 6 tablespoon ketchup
- 2 tablespoon tomato paste
- 3 tablespoon brown sugar
- 1 tablespoon apple cider vinegar
- ½ teaspoon garlic powder
- ½ teaspoon onion powder
- ½ teaspoon black pepper
- 1 teaspoon salt

Sauce Thickening
- 8 teaspoon cornflour
- ¼ cup water

Instructions:
1. Soak beans in a suitable bowl filled with water for 24 hours then drain.
2. Transfer the beans to a cooking and fill it with water.
3. Cook for 1 ½ hours on a simmer until beans are soft.
4. Drain the beans and keep them aside.
5. Mix the remaining sauce mixture in a saucepan and cook for 5 minutes on a simmer.
6. Stir in cooked beans and mix well then cook for 3 minutes.
7. Serve warm.

Chapter 05: High Protein Meals

Black Chana Fry

SERVINGS 4   **PREPARATION TIME** 10 minutes   **COOKING TIME** 56 minutes

Nutritional Values Per Serving	
Calories	289
Total Fat	12.2g
Saturated Fat	1.5g
Cholesterol	0mg
Sodium	682mg
Total Carbohydrate	33.7g
Dietary Fiber	11.4g
Total Sugars	4.6g
Protein	11.3g

Meal Prep Suggestion:

Store the black chickpea stir fry in the refrigerator and make a spinach bed only before serving.

Ingredients:

- ½ lbs. black chickpeas
- 2 tablespoon olive oil
- 1 teaspoon cumin seeds
- ½ yellow onion, diced
- 1 teaspoon ginger garlic paste
- ¼ teaspoon chili powder
- ½ teaspoon coriander powder
- ¼ teaspoon ground turmeric
- ½ teaspoon garam masala
- Salt, to taste
- 1 pinch of asafoetida
- Water, as required
- 1 tsbp lemon juice
- 1 handful chopped spinach
- Onion rings, to garnish

Instructions:

1. Soak black chickpeas in a bowl filled with water for 6 hours.
2. Drain and rinse the soaked chickpeas.
3. Sauté cumin seeds with oil in a deep pan for 1 minute.
4. Stir in onions then cook for 5 minutes.
5. Add ginger garlic paste, coriander powder, salt, and rest of the ingredients.
6. Sauté for 5 minutes then add 2 cups warm water.
7. Cook on a simmer for 45 minutes until chickpeas turn soft, remove excess liquid if needed.
8. Spread spinach in a bowl and add the black chickpea to the bowl.
9. Garnish with onion rings and serve.

Chapter 05: High Protein Meals

Red Lentil Potato Soup

SERVINGS 6   **PREPARATION TIME** 10 minutes   **COOKING TIME** 69 minutes

Nutritional Values Per Serving	
Calories	260
Total Fat	6.8g
Saturated Fat	1.2g
Cholesterol	0mg
Sodium	1101mg
Total Carbohydrate	35.4g
Dietary Fiber	12.7g
Total Sugars	6.1g
Protein	15.2g

Meal Prep Suggestion:

Enjoy this red lentil potato soup with roasted carrots and broccoli on the side.

Ingredients:

- 2 tablespoon olive oil
- 1 yellow onion, chopped
- 2 garlic cloves, chopped
- 3 ounces tomato paste
- 1 cup dry red lentils
- ½ lb carrots, chopped
- 1 potato, peeled and diced
- 6 cups vegetable broth
- 1 tablespoon cumin
- 1 teaspoon smoked paprika
- ¾ teaspoon salt
- ⅛ teaspoon cayenne pepper

Instructions:

1. Sauté garlic and onion with oil in a large cooking pot for 5 minutes.
2. Stir in tomato paste and cook for 4 minutes.
3. Add carrots, lentils and rest of the ingredients to the pot.
4. Cook the lentils to a boil then cook for 60- minutes on a simmer.
5. Serve warm.

Chapter 05: High Protein Meals

Mixed Lentil Stew

SERVINGS
6

PREPARATION TIME
15 minutes

COOKING TIME
57 minutes

Nutritional Values Per Serving	
Calories	260
Total Fat	6.8g
Saturated Fat	1.2g
Cholesterol	0mg
Sodium	1101mg
Total Carbohydrate	35.4g
Dietary Fiber	12.7g
Total Sugars	6.1g
Protein	15.2g

Meal Prep Suggestion:

This mixed lentils can be best stored in a freezer, and to do so pack it in a small ziplock bag or reaction-free container.

Ingredients:

- 2 tablespoon olive oil
- 1 onion, chopped
- 2 garlic cloves, minced
- 1 large carrot, chopped
- 2 celery ribs, chopped
- 2 cups dried lentils
- 14 ounces crushed tomato
- 6 cups vegetable stock
- ½ teaspoon cumin
- ½ teaspoon coriander powder
- 1½ teaspoon paprika powder
- 2 dried bay leaves
- 1 lemon, zest and juice
- ¼ teaspoon salt
- ¼ teaspoon black pepper

Instructions:

1. Sauté garlic and onion with oil in a large pan for 2 minutes.
2. Stir in carrot and celery then cook for 10 minutes.
3. Add lentils and rest of the ingredients then cook for 40 minutes on a simmer.
4. Puree half of the soup in a blender and return to the pan.
5. Cook for 5 minutes then serve warm.

Chapter 05: High Protein Meals

Korean Eggplant Stew

SERVINGS 4   **PREPARATION TIME** 15 minutes   **COOKING TIME** 15 minutes

Nutritional Values Per Serving	
Calories	216
Total Fat	6.4g
Saturated Fat	0.7g
Cholesterol	0mg
Sodium	464mg
Total Carbohydrate	39.6g
Dietary Fiber	18.1g
Total Sugars	21.9g
Protein	6.6g

Meal Prep Suggestion:

Pack the eggplant meal with some white boiled rice and some extra spices and sauce for garnish.

Ingredients:

- 4 eggplants, quartered and sliced
- 2 tablespoons soy sauce
- 4 teaspoons spring onion, sliced diagonally
- 2 teaspoons sesame oil
- 2 teaspoons Gochugang
- 2 red peppers, sliced
- 2 teaspoons minced garlic
- 2 teaspoons sugar
- 4 pinches black pepper
- 2 teaspoons sesame seeds

Instructions:

1. Sauté eggplant with almond butter in a skillet for 5 minutes per side.
2. Mix garlic, with rest of the ingredients in a bowl and pour over the eggplant.
3. Sautee for 5 minutes and serve warm.

Chapter 05: High Protein Meals

Tuscan White Beans

SERVINGS
4

PREPARATION TIME
15 minutes

COOKING TIME
10 minutes

Nutritional Values Per Serving

Calories	376
Total Fat	7.8g
Saturated Fat	1.1g
Cholesterol	0mg
Sodium	28mg
Total Carbohydrate	57.2g
Dietary Fiber	23.4g
Total Sugars	2.8g
Protein	22.1g

Meal Prep Suggestion:

You can also prepare these beans by using fresh or dried tomatoes.

Ingredients:

- 2 garlic cloves, smashed
- ¼ teaspoon red pepper flakes
- 2 tablespoons olive oil
- ¼ cup tomato paste
- 1 sprig rosemary
- 2 canned cannellini beans
- Parsley, to garnish

Instructions:

1. Sauté garlic and red pepper flakes with oil in a skillet for 1 minute.
2. Stir in rosemary and tomato paste then cook for 2 minutes.
3. Add beans and cook for 5 minutes.
4. Stir in salt, parsley and ½ cup water then cook for 2 minutes.
5. Garnish and serve.

Chapter 05: High Protein Meals

Brussels Sprout Broccoli Stew

SERVINGS 6 **PREPARATION TIME** 10 minutes **COOKING TIME** 40 minutes

Nutritional Values Per Serving

Calories	325
Total Fat	17.5g
Saturated Fat	9.7g
Cholesterol	0mg
Sodium	507mg
Total Carbohydrate	40g
Dietary Fiber	9g
Total Sugars	12.7g
Protein	6.9g

Meal Prep Suggestion:

This stew can be best stored in a freezer, after being packed in a sealable container.

Ingredients:

- 2 medium sweet potatoes, chopped
- 2 carrots, chopped
- 1 cup turnips, chopped
- 1 parsnip, chopped
- 1½ cup broccoli florets
- 1 medium onion, chopped
- 3 tablespoon olive oil
- 1 teaspoon dried thyme
- ½ teaspoon smoked paprika
- ½ teaspoon sea salt
- 1 cup tomato paste
- 1 cup coconut cream
- ¼ teaspoon black pepper
- 2 cups vegetable broth
- 1 cup brussels sprouts
- 1 tablespoon balsamic vinegar
- 1 green pepper, chopped
- Green chilli, to garnish

Instructions:

1. At 425 degrees F, preheat your oven.
2. Toss onion, parsnips, turnips, carrots and sweet potatoes with black pepper, salt, paprika, thyme and oil in a large bowl.
3. Spread the veggie in a baking sheet and roast for 30 minutes.
4. Boil broth in a saucepan and stir in roasted veggies, pepper and broccoli then cook for 5 minutes.
5. Add rest of the ingredients then cook for 5 minutes.
6. Garnish with green chilli.
7. Serve warm.

Chapter 05: High Protein Meals

Tofu Curry

SERVINGS 4   **PREPARATION TIME** 10 minutes   **COOKING TIME** 20 minutes

Nutritional Values Per Serving

Calories	341
Total Fat	23.6g
Saturated Fat	9.1g
Cholesterol	0mg
Sodium	470mg
Total Carbohydrate	23.1g
Dietary Fiber	6.2g
Total Sugars	13.8g
Protein	16.5g

Meal Prep Suggestion:

Enjoy this tofu curry with toasted bread or rice.

Ingredients:

- 1 pound tofu, diced
- 1 onion, chopped
- 1 garlic, chopped
- 3 tablespoons olive oil
- 14 ounces canned tomatoes, chopped
- 1 cup tomato paste
- ½ cup coconut cream
- 2 cups vegetable broth
- 2 bay leaves
- Salt, to taste
- Black peppers, to taste

Instructions:

1. Sauté onion and garlic with olive oil in a large saucepan then cook for 5 minutes.
2. Stir in canned tomatoes and rest of the ingredients then cook for 20 minutes on a simmer.
3. Serve warm.

Chapter 05: High Protein Meals

Crispy Tofu Platter

SERVINGS 4 **PREPARATION TIME** 10 minutes **COOKING TIME** 10 minutes

Nutritional Values Per Serving	
Calories	375
Total Fat	29g
Saturated Fat	3.9g
Cholesterol	0mg
Sodium	882mg
Total Carbohydrate	25.8g
Dietary Fiber	1.9g
Total Sugars	2.7g
Protein	4.1g

Meal Prep Suggestion:

Keep the coated tofu packed and frozen until you are ready to cook and serve instantly.

Ingredients:

- 2 containers firm tofu
- ⅔ cup cornstarch
- 1½ teaspoon salt
- ½ cup oil, for frying
- 2 red onions, chopped
- 1 garlic cloves, minced
- 2 green onions, green part, chopped

Instructions:

1. Mix cornstarch with salt in a bowl.
2. Coat the tofu cubes with the cornstarch mixture.
3. Set a deep fryer with oil over medium heat and heat to 350 degrees F.
4. Deep fry the tofu for 5 minutes until golden brown.
5. Transfer the crispy tofu to a serving plate.
6. Sauté red onion with garlic, green onion and oil in a saucepan for 5 minutes.
7. Spread this mixture over the tofu.
8. Serve warm.

Chapter 05: High Protein Meals

Glazed Tofu

SERVINGS **4**   PREPARATION TIME **15 minutes**   COOKING TIME **10 minutes**

Nutritional Values Per Serving	
Calories	285
Total Fat	22.6g
Saturated Fat	3.8g
Cholesterol	0mg
Sodium	1055mg
Total Carbohydrate	8.1g
Dietary Fiber	2.1g
Total Sugars	3.6g
Protein	17.5g

Meal Prep Suggestion:

This glazed tofu goes well with boiled somen noodles.

Ingredients:

- 2 (14-oz.) packages tofu, drained and diced
- 2 tablespoon hoisin
- 4 tablespoon soy sauce
- 2 tablespoon chili garlic sauce
- 4 teaspoon unseasoned rice vinegar
- 4 tablespoon olive oil

Instructions:

1. Mix the tofu with soy sauce and rest of the ingredients in a bowl.
2. Cover and refrigerate the tofu for 30 minutes.
3. Set a skillet over medium heat.
4. Add tofu along with the marinade and cook for 10 minutes.
5. Serve warm.

Chapter 05: High Protein Meals

Rice with Brown Lentils

SERVINGS | PREPARATION TIME | COOKING TIME
4 | 15 minutes | 45 minutes

Nutritional Values Per Serving	
Calories	384
Total Fat	2.3g
Saturated Fat	0.5g
Cholesterol	0mg
Sodium	786mg
Total Carbohydrate	73.8g
Dietary Fiber	4g
Total Sugars	4.2g
Protein	15.1g

Meal Prep Suggestion:

Pack the cooked rice with some saucy beans and roasted veggies on the side.

Ingredients:

- 1 onion, chopped
- 1 tablespoon garlic powder
- 1½ cups white rice
- ½ cup sweet potato, peeled and diced
- ½ cup brown lentils
- 4 cups vegetable broth
- 1 bunch parsley, chopped
- Salt to taste

Instructions:

1. Sauté onion with oil in a saucepan for 3 minutes.
2. Stir in water, sweet potato, lentils, black pepper, salt and rice then cook for 45 minutes on a simmer.
3. Garnish with parsley and serve warm.

Chapter 05: High Protein Meals

Vegetable Tempeh Stew

SERVINGS 4
PREPARATION TIME 15 minutes
COOKING TIME 15 minutes

Nutritional Values Per Serving	
Calories	299
Total Fat	15.9g
Saturated Fat	3.2g
Cholesterol	0mg
Sodium	85mg
Total Carbohydrate	21.5g
Dietary Fiber	3.2g
Total Sugars	4.1g
Protein	23.2g

Meal Prep Suggestion:

Boiled white or black rice goes well with this soup.

Ingredients:

- 1 tablespoons vegetable oil
- ½ cup onion, diced
- 6 cups water
- 16 ounces tempeh, sliced
- 2 cups carrots, sliced
- 2 cups bok choy, chopped
- ¼ cup cabbage, shredded
- 2 cups enoki mushrooms, sliced
- 3 scallions, diced
- 1 handful of chopped cilantro

Instructions:

1. Sauté onions with oil in a saucepan for 5 minutes.
2. Stir in water, tempeh, veggies and rest of the ingredients.
3. Cover and cook for 10 minutes on a simmer.
4. Serve warm.

Chapter 05: High Protein Meals

Vegetable Gyoza

SERVINGS 8 | **PREPARATION TIME** 15 minutes | **COOKING TIME** 23 minutes

Nutritional Values Per Serving

Calories	242
Total Fat	2.6g
Saturated Fat	0.5g
Cholesterol	2mg
Sodium	782mg
Total Carbohydrate	45.8g
Dietary Fiber	2.8g
Total Sugars	2.6g
Protein	7g

Meal Prep Suggestion:

Pack the uncooked dumplings with chili sauce on the side and cook them right before serving.

Ingredients:

- 12 ounces firm tofu, crumbled
- 5 ounces king oyster mushrooms, chopped
- 2 ounces shiitake mushrooms, chopped
- 3.5 ounces red cabbage, chopped
- 5 ounces cabbage, chopped
- 1 teaspoon salt
- 2 ounces carrot, chopped
- 3 ounces onion, chopped
- 2 green onions, , chopped
- 1 knob ginger, chopped
- 1 clove garlic, chopped
- 2 tablespoon potato starch
- 2 tablespoon soy sauce
- 1 tablespoon miso
- ⅛ teaspoon white pepper powder
- 30 gyoza wrappers

Frying Gyoza

- 1 tablespoon oil
- 1 cup water

Instructions:

1. Chop all the veggies in a food processor and keep them aside.
2. Sauté tofu with mushrooms, oil and rest of the filling ingredients in a deep pan for 7 minutes.
3. Spread a gyoza wrapper on a working surface, and add a tablespoon of the tofu filling at the center.
4. Fold this gyoza wrapper in half and pinch the edges to seal.
5. Make more gyoza dumplings with remaining wrappers and fillings.
6. Set a pan filled with water over medium-high heat and cook to a boil.
7. Drop the dumplings into the water and cook for 5 minutes.
8. Transfer the dumplings to a plate using a slotted spoon.
9. Set a pan with oil over medium heat and sear the dumplings for 2-3 minutes per side.
10. Serve warm.

Chapter 05: High Protein Meals

Tofu Mushroom Dumplings

SERVINGS 4
PREPARATION TIME 15 minutes
COOKING TIME 30 minutes

Nutritional Values Per Serving	
Calories	235
Total Fat	3.8g
Saturated Fat	0.6g
Cholesterol	0mg
Sodium	1749mg
Total Carbohydrate	48.2g
Dietary Fiber	3.1g
Total Sugars	6.4g
Protein	8.5g

Meal Prep Suggestion:

Enjoy the dumplings with spicy chili sauce.

Ingredients:

- 2 cups all-purpose flour
- ½ cup 2 teaspoons water

Filling

- 5 ounces five-spice tofu, chopped
- 1 ⅔ ounces Chinese chives, chopped
- 6 shiitake mushrooms, chopped
- ½ cup carrot, grated
- 1 tablespoon scallions, chopped
- ½ teaspoon ginger, minced
- ¼ teaspoon ground Sichuan pepper
- 1 tablespoon cooking oil
- 2 teaspoon light soy sauce
- ¼ teaspoon sesame oil
- ¼ teaspoon salt, or to taste

Instructions:

1. Mix flour with water in a bowl and knead the dough for 15 minutes.
2. Cover and leave the dough for 60 minutes.
3. Meanwhile, mix tofu with carrot, mushroom, chives, scallions, Sichuan pepper and ginger in a bowl.
4. Sauté this mixture with sesame oil and rest of the ingredients in a skillet for 5 minutes.
5. Divide the prepared dough into three equal parts and roll each into a rope.
6. Cut the ropes into 10 equal sections and spread each into a round circle.
7. Divide the tofu mixture on top of half of the dough circles.
8. Place the remaining circles on top and fold the edges to make a sealed rim.
9. Set a steamer pan with a basket inside over medium heat.
10. Add water to the steamer, and cook it to boil.
11. Place the dumplings in the basket, cover and cook for 10 minutes.
12. Serve.

Chapter 05: High Protein Meals

Water Chestnut Mushroom Fry

SERVINGS
4

PREPARATION TIME
15 minutes

COOKING TIME
8 minutes

Nutritional Values Per Serving	
Calories	152
Total Fat	7.4g
Saturated Fat	0.9g
Cholesterol	0mg
Sodium	289mg
Total Carbohydrate	19.9g
Dietary Fiber	1.5g
Total Sugars	2.1g
Protein	2.8g

Meal Prep Suggestion:

Pack this stir-fry with roasted veggies on the side.

Ingredients:

- 2 cups water chestnuts, quartered
- 2 cups button mushrooms, quartered
- 2 tablespoons oil
- 2 inches ginger chopped
- 2 green chilllies, chopped
- 10 garlic cloves chopped
- 1 medium onion chopped
- Salt to taste
- 2 tablespoons hoisin sauce
- 2 teaspoons soy sauce
- 2 pinches sugar
- 2 teaspoons crushed black peppercorns
- 4 tablespoons corn flour
- 2 small bunches parsley, chopped
- 2 teaspoons vinegar

Instructions:

1. Sauté mushrooms with salt, onion, garlic, green chili and ginger with oil in a non-stick pan for 5 minutes.
2. Add chestnuts and rest of the ingredients then cook for 3 minutes.
3. Mix corn flour with water in a bowl then pour into the stir fry.
4. Garnish with salt, vinegar and chopped parsley.
5. Serve warm.

Chapter 05: High Protein Meals

Rice Bean Platter

SERVINGS
6

PREPARATION TIME
13 minutes

COOKING TIME
25 minutes

Nutritional Values Per Serving	
Calories	371
Total Fat	3.2g
Saturated Fat	0.5g
Cholesterol	0mg
Sodium	28mg
Total Carbohydrate	69.3g
Dietary Fiber	12g
Total Sugars	7.3g
Protein	17.8g

Meal Prep Suggestion:

Pack all the ingredients of the platter separately in the compartments of a container.

Ingredients:

- 1 cup white rice
- 2 cups water
- 1 cup canned red beans
- 1 cup canned chickpeas
- 6 cherry tomatoes
- 1 block tempeh, sliced
- 1 tablespoon vinegar
- Black pepper and salt, to taste
- 1 green onion, chopped
- 1 cucumber, sliced

Instructions:

1. Add water to a suitable saucepan then cook to a boil.
2. Stir in rice and salt to taste then cook until the rice is soft.
3. Meanwhile, mix red beans with black pepper, and salt in a spread in a baking sheet.
4. Place the slices tempeh, chickpeas and cherry tomatoes on the side of the beans.
5. At 350 degrees F, preheat your oven.
6. Bake the beans, tomatoes and tempeh for 10 minutes.
7. Flip the tomatoes, and tempeh slices once cooked halfway through.
8. Divide the rice in the serving plate and add red beans, tomatoes, chickpeas, tempeh and cucumber on the side.
9. Garnish with green onion.
10. Serve.

Chapter 05: High Protein Meals

Chickpea and Carrot Stew

SERVINGS 6   **PREPARATION TIME** 10 minutes   **COOKING TIME** 31 minutes

Nutritional Values Per Serving

Calories	344
Total Fat	12.6g
Saturated Fat	1.6g
Cholesterol	0mg
Sodium	524mg
Total Carbohydrate	47.1g
Dietary Fiber	13.1g
Total Sugars	9.8g
Protein	13.6g

Meal Prep Suggestion:

Serve this chickpea stew with fried rice on the side.

Ingredients:

- 2 (15.5-ounce) cans chickpeas
- ¼ cup olive oil
- 3 medium carrots, chopped
- 1 large yellow onion, chopped
- 1 ¼ teaspoons kosher salt
- 3 garlic cloves, chopped
- 1 ½ teaspoons ground cumin
- ½ teaspoon ground ginger
- ½ teaspoon ground turmeric
- ⅛ teaspoon cayenne pepper
- ½ teaspoon fresh lime juice

Instructions:

1. Sauté carrots with oil in a deep pan for 4 minutes.
2. Stir in onion and salt then cook for 10 minutes.
3. Add cayenne, turmeric, ginger, cumin and garlic then mix well.
4. Cook for 1 minute then add chickpeas and 1 quart of water.
5. Cook for 30 minutes then serve warm.

Chapter 05: High Protein Meals

Spaghetti with Falafel Balls

SERVINGS 4
PREPARATION TIME 15 minutes
COOKING TIME 30 minutes

Nutritional Values Per Serving	
Calories	311
Total Fat	4.5g
Saturated Fat	0.6g
Cholesterol	0mg
Sodium	53mg
Total Carbohydrate	52.7g
Dietary Fiber	9g
Total Sugars	7.2g
Protein	15g

Meal Prep Suggestion:

Pack the cooked pasta and the falafel sauce mixture separately in two container and reheat in the microwave before serving.

Ingredients:

Pasta

- 1 package spaghetti pasta
- 1 jar of crushed tomatoes
- 2 garlic cloves, crushed
- 1 teaspoon chilli flakes
- 1 onion, peeled and chopped
- Cilantro, chopped

Falafels

- 7 ounces Tofu
- 7 ¼ ounces chickpeas, cooked
- 2 garlic cloves
- 1 tablespoon flaxseed
- ½ bunch of parsley
- 2 tablespoons veggie broth
- Pepper, Salt to taste

Instructions:

1. Blend tofu, chickpeas and rest of the ingredients in a blender until smooth.
2. Make 1 inch balls out of this mixture and keep them aside.
3. At 350 degrees F, preheat your oven.
4. Grease a baking sheet and place the balls in the sheet.
5. Bake the falafels for 5 minutes until golden brown.
6. Boil pasta as per the package's instructions then drain.
7. Sauté garlic and onion with oil in a deep pan for 5 minutes.
8. Stir in tomatoes, falafels and chili flakes them cook for 10 minutes with occasional stirring.
9. Add the falafel with sauce on top of the pasta and garnish with cilantro.
10. Serve warm.

Chapter 05: High Protein Meals

Brussel Sprout Tofu Fry

SERVINGS 4   **PREPARATION TIME** 10 minutes   **COOKING TIME** 10 minutes

Nutritional Values Per Serving	
Calories	333
Total Fat	26.5g
Saturated Fat	3.3g
Cholesterol	0mg
Sodium	1325mg
Total Carbohydrate	19.3g
Dietary Fiber	6.1g
Total Sugars	7.3g
Protein	9.7g

Meal Prep Suggestion:

Serve this stir-fry with some roasted tomatoes and mashed potatoes on the side.

Ingredients:

- 6 ounces firm tofu, diced
- 2 tablespoon chilli sauce
- 1½ tablespoon soy sauce
- 3 tablespoon sesame oil
- 1 teaspoon rice vinegar
- 1 tablespoon maple syrup
- 1 pound brussels sprouts
- 4 tablespoons sunflower oil
- Salt, to taste
- 3 ½ ounces spring onion, sliced
- ½ small chilli, deseeded and chopped
- 3 ⅔ ounces cauliflower florets

Instructions:

1. Mix tofu with syrup, vinegar, sesame oil, soy sauce and chili sauce in a bowl.
2. Cover and marinate this tofu for 30 minutes in the refrigerator.
3. Sauté tofu with its marinade in a deep wok for 5 minutes.
4. Stir in Brussel sprout, cauliflower and rest of the ingredients.
5. Sauté for 5 minutes then serve warm.

Chapter 05: High Protein Meals

Pappardelle Pasta

SERVINGS 4
PREPARATION TIME 15 minutes
COOKING TIME 30 minutes

Nutritional Values Per Serving

Calories	389
Total Fat	9g
Saturated Fat	1.1g
Cholesterol	0mg
Sodium	501mg
Total Carbohydrate	68.1g
Dietary Fiber	8g
Total Sugars	2.6g
Protein	12.9g

Meal Prep Suggestion:

Add crumbled vegan parmesan cheese on top before serving.

Ingredients:

- 2 tablespoons olive oil
- ½ medium onion, diced
- ½ teaspoon red chili flakes
- 1 clove garlic, minced
- 14 ounces crushed tomato
- Salt, to taste
- ½ pound, pappardelle pasta

Instructions:

1. Sauté onion with oil in a deep pan for 10 minutes.
2. Stir in garlic and chile flakes then cook for 2 minutes.
3. Add tomatoes then cook for 20 minutes on a simmer.
4. Boil pasta as per the package's instructions then drain.
5. Add half cup pasta liquid to the tomato sauce then cook for 2 minutes.
6. Stir in pasta, mix well and serve warm.

CHAPTER 06

SHEET PAN, INSTANT POT, FREEZER MEALS

Chapter 06: Sheet Pan, Instant Pot, Freezer Meals

Steamed Cabbage Rolls

SERVINGS 4 | **PREPARATION TIME** 10 minutes | **COOKING TIME** 28 minutes

Nutritional Values Per Serving

Calories	293
Total Fat	9.7g
Saturated Fat	2g
Cholesterol	0mg
Sodium	1205mg
Total Carbohydrate	33.5g
Dietary Fiber	4.3g
Total Sugars	3.9g
Protein	21.7g

Meal Prep Suggestion:

Keep the rolls in a sealable container and refrigerate for upto 2-3 days only.

Ingredients:

- 1 ¼ cup water
- ⅔ cup uncooked white rice
- 16 cabbage leaves
- 2 blocks tofu, crumbled
- ½ cup chopped onion
- 2 teaspoons salt
- ½ teaspoon ground black pepper
- Cilantro, to garnish

Instructions:

1. Add water and rice to a cooking pot then cook for 20 minutes on a simmer.
2. Set a large pan with salted water on medium heat and cook to a boil.
3. Place the cabbage leaves in the water and cook for 4 minutes then drain.
4. Mix tofu with black pepper, salt, onion, cooked rice in a bowl.
5. Spread the cabbage leaves on the working surface and divide the mixture on top of the leaves.
6. Roll the cabbage leaves and secure them with a toothpick.
7. Add water to an Instant Pot and set a rack inside.
8. Place steamer basket on top of the rack, and place the rolls in the basket.
9. Secure the Instant Pot's lid and cook for 2 minutes on a Manual mode at 350 degrees F.
10. Release the pressure completely then remove the lid.
11. Transfer the rolls to a plate and garnish with cilantro.
12. Serve.

Chapter 06: Sheet Pan, Instant Pot, Freezer Meals

Eggplant Ratatouille

SERVINGS 6 | **PREPARATION TIME** 15 minutes | **COOKING TIME** 70 minutes

Nutritional Values Per Serving

Calories	235
Total Fat	5.7g
Saturated Fat	0.7g
Cholesterol	0mg
Sodium	368mg
Total Carbohydrate	43.3g
Dietary Fiber	19.7g
Total Sugars	24.1g
Protein	8.7g

Meal Prep Suggestion:

Enjoy this ratatouille with boiled white rice or some flatbread.

Ingredients:

- 4 eggplants, sliced
- 6 roma tomatoes, sliced
- 2 yellow squashes, sliced

Sauce

- 2 tablespoons olive oil
- 1 onion, diced
- 4 garlic cloves, minced
- 1 red bell pepper, diced
- 1 yellow bell pepper, diced
- Salt, to taste
- Black pepper, to taste
- 28 ounces can of crushed tomatoes
- 2 tablespoons fresh basil, chopped

Herb Seasoning

- 2 tablespoons chopped fresh basil
- 1 teaspoon garlic, minced
- 2 tablespoons chopped fresh parsley
- 2 teaspoons fresh thyme
- Salt, to taste
- Black pepper, to taste
- 4 tablespoons olive oil

Instructions:

1. At 375 degrees F, preheat your oven.
2. Sauté bell peppers, garlic and onion with olive oil in an oven-safe pan for 10 minutes.
3. Stir in crushed tomatoes, black pepper, basil and salt then cook until the sauce turns smooth.
4. Arrange the veggies in any suitable sheet pan in concentric circles.
5. Drizzle the tomato sauce on top and add remaining herbs and spices on top.
6. Cover this pan with a foil sheet and bake for 40 minutes.
7. Uncover the pan and bake for 20 minutes.
8. Serve warm.

Chapter 06: Sheet Pan, Instant Pot, Freezer Meals

Eggplant Stir Fry

SERVINGS 4
PREPARATION TIME 15 minutes
COOKING TIME 15 minutes

Nutritional Values Per Serving	
Calories	189
Total Fat	14g
Saturated Fat	2g
Cholesterol	0mg
Sodium	877mg
Total Carbohydrate	16.4g
Dietary Fiber	6.9g
Total Sugars	7.8g
Protein	3.7g

Meal Prep Suggestion:

Serve this eggplant stir-fry with mashed potatoes and tofu skewers on the side.

Ingredients:

- 1 large eggplants, diced
- ¼ cup olive oil
- 1 medium onions, sliced
- 2 garlic cloves, chopped
- 1 zucchini, chopped
- 1 red bell pepper, sliced
- ¼ cup green olives, sliced
- 1 green bell pepper, sliced
- 2 small dried chilies halved
- 2 tablespoons Tamari
- 1 teaspoon black pepper
- ½ teaspoon salt

Instructions:

1. Sauté onion with garlic and oil in a deep pan for 5 minutes.
2. Stir in zucchini, and rest of the ingredients then transfer the veggies to a sheet pan.
3. At 320 degrees F, preheat your oven.
4. Roast the zucchini olive mixture for 10 minutes in the oven.
5. Serve warm.

Chapter 06: Sheet Pan, Instant Pot, Freezer Meals

Eggplant Lasagna

SERVINGS 4 **PREPARATION TIME** 10 minutes **COOKING TIME** 58 minutes

Nutritional Values Per Serving

Calories	229
Total Fat	8.6g
Saturated Fat	5.2g
Cholesterol	39mg
Sodium	1027mg
Total Carbohydrate	17.1g
Dietary Fiber	6g
Total Sugars	10.9g
Protein	20g

Ingredients:

- 2 large eggplants, sliced
- 1 teaspoon sea salt
- Olive oil, to taste
- 5 garlic cloves, minced
- ½ teaspoon red pepper flakes
- 28 ounces crushed san marzano tomato
- 6 leaves fresh basil, sliced
- 15 ounces vegan cashew ricotta cheese
- 2 cups vegan mozzarella cheese, shredded
- 1 cup vegan parmesan cheese, grated
- 2 teaspoons Italian seasoning

Instructions:

1. At 375 degrees F, preheat your oven.
2. Place the eggplant in a colander, drizzle salt on top and leave for 10 minutes.
3. Pat dry the eggplant and keep them aside.
4. Set a griddle pan over medium heat and grease with olive oil.
5. Sear the eggplant slices for 3 minutes per side then transfer to a plate.
6. Sauté red pepper flakes and garlic with olive oil in a pan for 3 minutes.
7. Stir in garlic and sauté for 30 seconds.
8. Add crushed tomatoes and 1 teaspoon salt then cook for 10 minutes.
9. Stir in basil, mix and remove from the heat.
10. Mix Italian seasoning, ¾ cup vegan parmesan, 1½ cups vegan mozzarella and vegan ricotta in a medium bowl.
11. Grease a 9x13 inches sheet pan with cooking spray.
12. Spread 2 dollops of the sauce in the baking dish
13. Top a single layer of eggplant slices on top and add a layer of ricotta mixture on top.
14. Repeat the layers then drizzle parmesan cheese on top.
15. Bake them for 45 minutes then garnish with basil.
16. Serve warm.

Chapter 06: Sheet Pan, Instant Pot, Freezer Meals

Scalloped Potatoes

SERVINGS
6

PREPARATION TIME
10 minutes

COOKING TIME
50 minutes

Nutritional Values Per Serving	
Calories	380
Total Fat	20g
Saturated Fat	17.1g
Cholesterol	0mg
Sodium	348mg
Total Carbohydrate	46.7g
Dietary Fiber	8g
Total Sugars	6.5g
Protein	7.4g

Ingredients:

- ¼ cup almond butter
- 1 large onion diced
- 2 garlic cloves minced
- ¼ cup flour
- 2 cups almond milk
- 1 cup vegetable broth
- ½ teaspoon salt
- ¼ teaspoon pepper
- 3 pounds white potatoes sliced
- Salt and black pepper to taste

Instructions:

1. At 350 degrees F, preheat your oven.
2. Sauté garlic with onion and butter in a skillet for 3 minutes.
3. Stir in flour then mix well for 2 minutes.
4. Reduce its heat then add broth and milk then mix well.
5. Cook for 1 minutes on a boil then add black pepper and salt.
6. Grease a 9x13 inches sheet pan and spread ⅓ of the potatoes at the bottom.
7. Drizzle black pepper, salt and 1/3 cream sauce on top.
8. Repeat the layers, cover with a foil sheet and bake for 45 minutes.
9. Uncover and bake for 45 minutes.
10. Serve warm.

Chapter 06: Sheet Pan, Instant Pot, Freezer Meals

Mushroom Pasta Bake

SERVINGS: 6
PREPARATION TIME: 15 minutes
COOKING TIME: 41 minutes

Nutritional Values Per Serving	
Calories	424
Total Fat	18.9g
Saturated Fat	8.4g
Cholesterol	0mg
Sodium	182mg
Total Carbohydrate	58.9g
Dietary Fiber	5.6g
Total Sugars	31.1g
Protein	8.8g

Meal Prep Suggestion:

Enjoy this pasta bake with crispy tofu potato appetizers on the side.

Ingredients:

- ½ cup dried porcini mushrooms
- 1 pound mixed short pasta
- 6 tablespoons almond butter
- 4 tablespoons all-purpose flour
- 3 cups almond milk
- 2 tablespoons coconut cream
- ½ pound shiitake mushroom, quartered
- ½ pound white button mushrooms, quartered
- Kosher salt and black pepper, to taste
- 4 ½ ounces vegan cheese, grated
- ½ cup vegan parmesan cheese, grated

Instructions:

1. Soak porcini mushrooms in boiling water in a bowl for 20 minutes then drain.
2. Drain, keep the liquid aside and chop the soaked mushrooms.
3. At 375 degrees F, preheat your oven.
4. Boil pasta as per the package's instruction then drain.
5. Sauté flour with butter in a large saucepan for 1 minute.
6. Stir in milk and liquid then cook for 5 minutes on a simmer.
7. Add porcini mushrooms and cream then mix well.
8. Sauté mushrooms with black pepper, salt and 2 tablespoon butter in a saucepan.
9. Stir in pasta, the prepared sauce and rest of the ingredients.
10. Spread this pasta mixture in a greased sheet pan and drizzle cheese on top.
11. Bake for 35 minutes in the preheated oven.
12. Serve warm.

Chapter 06: Sheet Pan, Instant Pot, Freezer Meals

Eggplant Stuffed Bread

SERVINGS 6

PREPARATION TIME 10 minutes

COOKING TIME 50 minutes

Nutritional Values Per Serving

Calories	467
Total Fat	31.4g
Saturated Fat	6.8g
Cholesterol	0mg
Sodium	673mg
Total Carbohydrate	41.1g
Dietary Fiber	6.6g
Total Sugars	4.4g
Protein	6.4g

Meal Prep Suggestion:

Wrap this stuffed bread carefully in a plastic wrap to keep the moisture intact.

Ingredients:

- 1 pound pizza dough
- 1 eggplant, sliced
- 8 ounces marinara sauce
- 1 cup vegan cashew ricotta cheese
- 2 tablespoons olive oil

Instructions:

1. At 425 degrees F, preheat your oven.
2. Spread eggplant in a greased sheet pan and drizzle olive oil on top.
3. Bake the eggplant for 10 minutes until golden brown.
4. Transfer the eggplant to a bowl and keep them aside.
5. Spread the pizza dough in a sheet pan.
6. Add marinara sauce on top, place the eggplant vertically at the center and drizzle cheese on top.
7. Fold the two sides of the pizza dough to cover the filling to make a sealed loaf.
8. Brush the dough with oil and bake for 20 minutes.
9. Serve.

Puff Pastry Pesto Bites

SERVINGS 12   **PREPARATION TIME** 10 minutes   **COOKING TIME** 20 minutes

Nutritional Values Per Serving	
Calories	379
Total Fat	30.6g
Saturated Fat	14.5g
Cholesterol	37mg
Sodium	604mg
Total Carbohydrate	22.4g
Dietary Fiber	1.6g
Total Sugars	1.9g
Protein	5.8g

Ingredients:

- 12 puff pastry square sheets, thawed
- 12 ounces vegan cream cheese
- ½ cup pesto
- 3 tablespoon almond butter, melted

Instructions:

1. At 400 degrees F, preheat your oven.
2. Cut the puff pastry sheets into 6 smaller pieces.
3. Place these squares on two sheet pans.
4. Divide the cream cheese at the center of the squares.
5. Add a dot of the pesto at the center of the squares and fold four corners of the squares towards the center.
6. Brush the butter on top and bake for 20 minutes in the preheated oven.
7. Serve warm.

Chapter 06: Sheet Pan, Instant Pot, Freezer Meals

Pumpkin Chickpea Stew

SERVINGS
4

PREPARATION TIME
10 minutes

COOKING TIME
24 minutes

Nutritional Values Per Serving	
Calories	376
Total Fat	7.1g
Saturated Fat	2.1g
Cholesterol	0mg
Sodium	323mg
Total Carbohydrate	63g
Dietary Fiber	16.4g
Total Sugars	11.2g
Protein	17.8g

Meal Prep Suggestion:
Enjoy this stew with some boiled white rice.

Ingredients:

- 1 tablespoon coconut oil
- 1 yellow onion, diced
- 4 garlic cloves, minced
- 1 inch knob of ginger, grated
- 2 teaspoons cumin
- 2 teaspoons coriander
- 1 teaspoon cinnamon powder
- 1 pinch of red pepper flakes
- 2 carrots, diced
- 2 sweet potatoes, cubed
- 1 small pumpkin, cubed
- 1 can (28 oz) stewed tomatoes
- 3 cups cooked chickpeas
- 3 cups vegetable broth
- ¼ cup raisins
- Salt and black pepper, to taste
- 1 handful baby kale, chopped
- lemon or lime wedges, to serve
- Cilantro, to garnish

Instructions:

1. Sauté onions with oil in an Instant Pot for 5 minutes on Sauté mode.
2. Stir in spices, ginger and garlic then cook for 1 minute.
3. Add tomatoes, broth, chickpeas, raisins, salt, pumpkin, sweet potatoes and carrots.
4. Secure the Instant Pot's lid and cook on High pressure at 350 degrees F for 15 minutes.
5. Once done, release the pressure completely then remove the lid.
6. Stir in rest of the ingredients and cook on Sauté mode for 3 minutes.
7. Serve warm.

Chapter 06: Sheet Pan, Instant Pot, Freezer Meals

Eggplant Pie

SERVINGS 4 | **PREPARATION TIME** 10 minutes | **COOKING TIME** 2 hours 10 minutes

Nutritional Values Per Serving	
Calories	301
Total Fat	13.5g
Saturated Fat	2.4g
Cholesterol	0mg
Sodium	122mg
Total Carbohydrate	43.3g
Dietary Fiber	14.3g
Total Sugars	17.1g
Protein	7.9g

Meal Prep Suggestion:

Serve this pie with sauteed carrots and broccoli.

Ingredients:

- 2 eggplants, sliced
- 2 tablespoon olive oil
- 1 medium red onion, chopped
- 1 yellow bell pepper, chopped
- 1 tablespoon dried mint
- 2 ½ teaspoon anise seeds
- 2 teaspoon ground cumin
- 1 teaspoon smoked paprika
- ½ teaspoon red pepper flakes
- 1 ½ pound Roma tomatoes, chopped
- 2 tablespoon tomato paste
- 3 garlic cloves, minced
- 1 puff pastry sheet
- ⅓ cup whole-wheat breadcrumbs

Instructions:

1. At 375 degrees F, preheat your oven.
2. Grease a sheet pan with cooking spray.
3. Spread the eggplant in this pan and bake for 50 minutes.
4. Meanwhile, sauté onion with oil, pepper flakes, paprika, cumin, anise, mint, and bell pepper for 8 minutes.
5. Stir in tomato paste and tomatoes then cook for 10 minutes.
6. Add garlic and eggplant then cook for 10 minutes.
7. Spread the puff pastry sheet in a greased sheet pan and fill it with the eggplant mixture.
8. Drizzle breadcrumbs on top and bake for 1 hour in the oven.
9. Serve warm.

Chapter 06: Sheet Pan, Instant Pot, Freezer Meals

Shiitake Mushroom Soup

SERVINGS 4 **PREPARATION TIME** 10 minutes **COOKING TIME** 18 minutes

Nutritional Values Per Serving

Calories	170
Total Fat	7.3g
Saturated Fat	1g
Cholesterol	0mg
Sodium	709mg
Total Carbohydrate	24.8g
Dietary Fiber	5.1g
Total Sugars	7.9g
Protein	4.3g

Meal Prep Suggestion:

Enjoy this soup with ramen noodles or boiled rice.

Ingredients:

- 10 ½ ounces shiitake mushrooms
- 5 ounces enoki mushrooms
- 12 butternut squash dumplings
- 1 onion, chopped
- 4 garlic cloves
- 1 cm cube fresh ginger
- 1 tablespoon sesame oil
- 1 litre vegetable stock
- 2 tablespoon soy sauce
- 3 cups water
- 2 carrots, sliced
- 1 green onion, chopped
- Chilli (optional)
- 1 tablespoon olive oil
- Salt and black pepper to taste

Instructions:

1. Sauté onion with oil in an Instant Pot on Sauté mode for 5 minutes.
2. Stir in garlic and ginger then cook for 30 seconds.
3. Add mushrooms and cook for 2 minutes.
4. Stir in rest of the ingredients except dumplings, and secure the lid.
5. Cook on High pressure for 5 minutes at 350 degrees F.
6. Once done, release the pressure completely then remove the lid.
7. Add the prepared dumplings and cook for 5 minutes on Sauté mode.
8. Serve warm.

Chapter 06: Sheet Pan, Instant Pot, Freezer Meals

Potato Tomato Bake

SERVINGS 6 **PREPARATION TIME** 35 minutes **COOKING TIME** 65 minutes

Nutritional Values Per Serving	
Calories	215
Total Fat	5.8g
Saturated Fat	2.8g
Cholesterol	0mg
Sodium	106mg
Total Carbohydrate	36.1g
Dietary Fiber	7.6g
Total Sugars	10.8g
Protein	7.9g

Meal Prep Suggestion:

Enjoy this tomato bake with a refreshing quinoa salad.

Ingredients:

- 2 large potatoes, peeled and chopped
- 10 ½ ounces mixed fresh tomatoes
- 2 garlic cloves, sliced

Cauliflower Sauce

- 1 cauliflower, cut into florets
- 4 tablespoon raw cashew nuts
- 4 tablespoon almond milk
- Juice of 1 lemon
- 1 large garlic clove
- 3 tablespoon olive oil
- Salt, to taste
- ¼ cup vegan parmesan cheese, shredded

Instructions:

1. At 360 degrees F, preheat your oven.
2. Sauté cauliflower with oil and garlic in a skillet for 5 minutes.
3. Puree the cauliflower with cashews and rest of the sauce ingredients.
4. Grease a sheet pan with cooking spray
5. Mix potatoes with the cauliflower sauce, tomato and rest of the ingredients in the prepared pan.
6. Then drizzle parmesan cheese on top.
7. Bake the potatoes for 40-60 minutes until golden brown.
8. Serve warm.

Chapter 06: Sheet Pan, Instant Pot, Freezer Meals

Stir-Fried Eggplant

SERVINGS 4

PREPARATION TIME 10 minutes

COOKING TIME 10 minutes

Nutritional Values Per Serving	
Calories	380
Total Fat	23g
Saturated Fat	3.3g
Cholesterol	0mg
Sodium	1807mg
Total Carbohydrate	21.9g
Dietary Fiber	6.2g
Total Sugars	11g
Protein	8.2g

Meal Prep Suggestion:

Store the eggplants in a meal box with white rice for the serving.

Ingredients:

- 4 tablespoon soy sauce
- 4 teaspoon Shaoxing wine or dry sherry
- 4 teaspoon unseasoned rice vinegar
- 4 teaspoon sugar
- 4 tablespoon sesame oil
- 5 teaspoon minced garlic
- 6 lbs eggplant, sliced
- 2 tablespoon peanut or grapeseed oil
- 8 tablespoon diagonally sliced green onions
- 4 tablespoon sesame seeds, toasted

Instructions:

1. Toss eggplant with garlic and rest of the ingredients in a sheet pan.
2. At 350 degrees F, preheat your oven.
3. Bake the eggplant mixture for 10 minutes.
4. Toss the eggplant once cooked halfway through.
5. Serve.

Chapter 06: Sheet Pan, Instant Pot, Freezer Meals

Green Bean Stir-Fry

SERVINGS 4   **PREPARATION TIME** 20 minutes   **COOKING TIME** 15 minutes

Nutritional Values Per Serving

Calories	277
Total Fat	7.7g
Saturated Fat	0.7g
Cholesterol	0mg
Sodium	338mg
Total Carbohydrate	49.9g
Dietary Fiber	7g
Total Sugars	5.3g
Protein	7.1g

Meal Prep Suggestion:
Serve the stir-fry with grilled tofu skewers.

Ingredients:

- 2 tablespoon refined oil
- 2 cup green french beans
- 5 potatoes peeled and chopped
- ½ cup green peas
- ½ cup green onion
- 8 garlic pods
- 2 carrots peeled and chopped
- 1 teaspoon cumin seeds
- 1 teaspoon cumin powder
- 2 teaspoon coriander powder
- ½ teaspoon turmeric powder
- 1 teaspoon red chilli powder
- ½ teaspoon salt
- ½ teaspoon dry mango powder
- 1 tablespoon coriander leaves chopped

Instructions:

1. Toss carrots with rest of the ingredients in a sheet pan.
2. At 375 degrees F, preheat your oven.
3. Bake the veggies for 15 minutes in the preheated oven.
4. Toss the veggie mixture after 6-7 minutes of cooking.
5. Serve warm.

Chapter 06: Sheet Pan, Instant Pot, Freezer Meals

Sauteed Potatoes And Mushrooms

SERVINGS: 4
PREPARATION TIME: 10 minutes
COOKING TIME: 11 minutes

Nutritional Values Per Serving	
Calories	237
Total Fat	13.8g
Saturated Fat	1.1g
Cholesterol	0mg
Sodium	90mg
Total Carbohydrate	24.2g
Dietary Fiber	5.7g
Total Sugars	3.3g
Protein	8.8g

Meal Prep Suggestion:

Enjoy the potatoes and mushrooms with toasted bread slices.

Ingredients:

- ½ cup water
- 6 tablespoons almond butter
- 16 ounces potatoes, peeled and diced
- 8 ounces white mushroom, sliced
- 2 pinches salt

Instructions:

1. Sauté potatoes with almond butter in an instant Pot on Sauté Mode for 1 minute.
2. Stir in water, salt, and parsley then secure the lid.
3. Cook on manual Mode for 5 minutes then release the pressure completely.
4. Stir in mushrooms and cook for 5 minutes on Sauté mode.
5. Serve warm.

Chapter 06: Sheet Pan, Instant Pot, Freezer Meals

Sandwich with Roasted Vegetables

SERVINGS: 8
PREPARATION TIME: 15 minutes
COOKING TIME: 10 minutes

Nutritional Values Per Serving

Calories	245
Total Fat	10.4g
Saturated Fat	1.8g
Cholesterol	0mg
Sodium	331mg
Total Carbohydrate	35.8g
Dietary Fiber	6.8g
Total Sugars	5.4g
Protein	7.8g

Meal Prep Suggestion:

Add some Dijon mustard and vegan mayo over the rolls for more taste.

Ingredients:

- 8 ounces mushrooms sliced
- 2 green peppers sliced
- 2 jalapeno peppers, diced
- 2 large tomatoes, sliced
- 2 eggplant, sliced
- 1 cup zucchini, sliced
- 1 tablespoon dried oregano
- 1 teaspoon dried thyme
- 1 teaspoon dried rosemary
- 3 garlic cloves minced
- salt and black pepper to taste
- ⅓ cup olive oil
- 4 hoagie rolls, cut in half
- 1 cup vegan mayo
- 1 tablespoon Dijon mustard
- ¼ teaspoon hot sauce

Instructions:

1. At 425 degrees F, preheat your oven.
2. Mix olive oil, black pepper, salt, garlic, rosemary, thyme, and oregano in a bowl.
3. Mix vegan mayo, mustard and hot sauce in a bowl and stir in half of the veggies then mix well.
4. Spread the veggies in a sheet pan then drizzle spice mixture on top.
5. Bake the veggies for 10 minutes.
6. Divide the mayo veggie mixture on top of the hoagie rolls and garnish with remaining half of the roasted veggies.
7. serve.

Chapter 06: Sheet Pan, Instant Pot, Freezer Meals

Sheet Pan Vegetables

SERVINGS: 4
PREPARATION TIME: 10 minutes
COOKING TIME: 10 minutes

Nutritional Values Per Serving	
Calories	104
Total Fat	7.4g
Saturated Fat	1.1g
Cholesterol	0mg
Sodium	769mg
Total Carbohydrate	8.9g
Dietary Fiber	3.2g
Total Sugars	3.3g
Protein	3.7g

Meal Prep Suggestion:

Separately pack the veggies with some quinoa or chickpea salad on the side.

Ingredients:

- 1 broccoli, cut into florets
- 1 tomato, cut in half
- 1 cauliflower, cut into florets
- 1 zucchini, sliced
- 4 mushrooms, sliced
- 2 tablespoons olive oil
- 1 tablespoon salt
- 1 tablespoon black pepper

Instructions:

1. At 350 degrees F, preheat your oven.
2. Set a grill rack in a sheet pan.
3. Mix olive oil, black pepper and salt in a bowl.
4. Brush this mixture over the veggies.
5. Place the veggies on the grill rack and bake for 5 minutes.
6. Flip the veggies and bake for 5 minutes.
7. Serve.

Chapter 06: Sheet Pan, Instant Pot, Freezer Meals

Cauliflower Cakes

SERVINGS 4   **PREPARATION TIME** 10 minutes   **COOKING TIME** 15 minutes

Nutritional Values Per Serving	
Calories	113
Total Fat	3.8g
Saturated Fat	3.2g
Cholesterol	0mg
Sodium	25mg
Total Carbohydrate	17.5g
Dietary Fiber	2.6g
Total Sugars	2.3g
Protein	3.5g

Meal Prep Suggestion:

Enjoy these patties or cakes with tomato sauce.

Ingredients:

- 1 head cauliflower, cut into florets
- ½ cup whole wheat flour
- 4 tablespoons almond milk
- 3 garlic cloves, minced
- 2 tablespoons parsley, chopped
- 3 tablespoons minced scallions
- Olive oil, to cook

Instructions:

1. Add water to an Instant Pot and set a rack inside.
2. Place the cauliflower on the rack, and seal the lid.
3. Cook on Manual mode on high pressure for 5 minutes.
4. Once done, release the pressure completely then remove the lid.
5. Mash the cauliflower in a bowl then stir in rest of the ingredients.
6. Mix well then make 4-6 cakes out of this mixture.
7. Layer a suitable sheet pan with parchment paper and place the cauliflower cakes in it.
8. At 350 degrees F, preheat your oven.
9. Bake the cauliflower cakes for 10 minutes and flip them once cooked halfway through.
10. Serve.

Chapter 06: Sheet Pan, Instant Pot, Freezer Meals

Mushroom Bisque

SERVINGS
4

PREPARATION TIME
10 minutes

COOKING TIME
16 minutes

Nutritional Values Per Serving

Calories	305
Total Fat	20.5g
Saturated Fat	13.4g
Cholesterol	0mg
Sodium	1462mg
Total Carbohydrate	16.6g
Dietary Fiber	3.7g
Total Sugars	4.8g
Protein	9.9g

Meal Prep Suggestion:

Serve this bisque with roasted mushrooms on top.

Ingredients:

- 2 tablespoons almond butter
- 1 small onion, chopped
- 2 garlic cloves, minced
- 1½ pounds fresh mushrooms, sliced
- 4 cups vegetable broth
- ½ cup sherry
- 1½ teaspoons dried thyme
- 1 teaspoon vegan Worcestershire sauce
- 1 teaspoon salt
- ½ teaspoon black pepper
- 4 tablespoons all-purpose flour
- 1 cup coconut cream

Instructions:

1. Sauté onion with almond butter in an Instant Pot for 3 minutes.
2. Stir in garlic then cook for 2 minutes.
3. Add mushrooms and sauté for 3 minutes.
4. Stir in black pepper, salt, Worcestershire sauce, thyme, sherry and broth.
5. Secure the lid and cook on Manual mode for 5 minutes.
6. Once done, release the pressure completely then remove the lid.
7. Switch the Instant Pot to Sauté mode and cook to a simmer.
8. Mix cream with flour in a bowl and add to the soup.
9. Cook this soup on a simmer for 3 minutes while mixing.
10. Puree this soup with an electric mixer until smooth.
11. Serve warm.

Chapter 06: Sheet Pan, Instant Pot, Freezer Meals

Beans Pasta Soup

SERVINGS 4 **PREPARATION TIME** 15 minutes **COOKING TIME** 40 minutes

Nutritional Values Per Serving

Calories	406
Total Fat	17g
Saturated Fat	13.4g
Cholesterol	0mg
Sodium	965mg
Total Carbohydrate	46.7g
Dietary Fiber	9.2g
Total Sugars	3.9g
Protein	19g

Meal Prep Suggestion:

Freeze this pasta soup in a sealable container then thaw and reheat in the microwave for 5 minutes before serving.

Ingredients:

- 2 cans (14 ounces) vegetable broth
- 1 cup almond milk
- 1 cup black beans, rinsed
- 5 ounces fettucini pasta, broken
- 1 tablespoon lime juice
- 1 teaspoon chili powder
- ¼ teaspoon ground cumin
- ¼ teaspoon black pepper

Instructions:

1. Boil broken fettuccini pasta in salted water as per the package's instructions then drain.
2. Add beans and broth to the Instant Pot insert.
3. Put on the lid and seal it by turning its Pressure valve to closed.
4. Select Manual mode, high pressure and cook for 25 minutes.
5. Once done, release the pressure completely then remove the lid.
6. Switch the Instant Pot to Sauté mode.
7. Stir in almond milk, boiled pasta, cumin, lime juice, black pepper and chili powder.
8. Cook this soup for 5 minutes on a simmer.
9. Serve warm.

Chapter 06: Sheet Pan, Instant Pot, Freezer Meals

Garlicky Roasted Potatoes

SERVINGS 6   **PREPARATION TIME** 15 minutes   **COOKING TIME** 55 minutes

Nutritional Values Per Serving	
Calories	231
Total Fat	7.3g
Saturated Fat	1.1g
Cholesterol	0mg
Sodium	404mg
Total Carbohydrate	38.8g
Dietary Fiber	5.7g
Total Sugars	2.7g
Protein	4.4g

Meal Prep Suggestion:

Enjoy the potatoes with a warming bowl of tomato soup on the side.

Ingredients:

- 3 pounds potatoes
- 3 tablespoons olive oil
- 6 garlic, peeled and halved
- 2 tablespoons fresh parsley, chopped
- 1 teaspoon salt
- ½ teaspoon black pepper

Instructions:

1. At 350 degrees F, preheat your oven.
2. Peel and cut the potatoes into quarters.
3. Toss the potatoes with black pepper, salt, and parsley in a sheet pan.
4. Spread the garlic cloves over the potatoes.
5. Roast the potatoes for 55 minutes in the preheated oven.
6. Flip the potatoes once cooked halfway through.
7. Garnish with parsley and serve warm.

Chapter 06: Sheet Pan, Instant Pot, Freezer Meals

Roasted Polenta Pizza

SERVINGS	PREPARATION TIME	COOKING TIME
6	15 minutes	32 minutes

Nutritional Values Per Serving	
Calories	416
Total Fat	12.6g
Saturated Fat	1.7g
Cholesterol	0mg
Sodium	8mg
Total Carbohydrate	69.8g
Dietary Fiber	5.5g
Total Sugars	5.1g
Protein	7.3g

Meal Prep Suggestion:

Pack the polenta in a sealable container and reheat it in the microwave for 5 minutes before serving.

Ingredients:

- 3 cups polenta
- Salt and black pepper, to taste
- Dried oregano, to taste
- 5 tablespoon olive oil
- 5 garlic cloves, chopped
- 1 eggplant, sliced
- 2 large shallots, peeled and sliced
- 1 large red bell pepper, sliced
- 1 (8.5 ounces) can of sun-dried tomatoes

Instructions:

1. At 400 degrees F, preheat your oven.
2. Layer a large sheet pan with baking or parchment paper.
3. Add 9 cups water, 2 tablespoons salt and polenta to a saucepan.
4. Cook to a boil, reduce its heat then cook for 5 minutes with occasional stirring.
5. Add black pepper and 1 tablespoon dried oregano.
6. Remove from the heat, cover and leave for 2 minutes.
7. Spread the polenta in the prepared sheet pan.
8. Sauté garlic, onion, eggplant and bell pepper with oil in a skillet for 5 minutes.
9. Spread the sauteed vegetables, sundried tomatoes over the polenta crust.
10. Bake this pizza for 20 minutes in the preheated oven.
11. Slice and serve.

Chapter 06: Sheet Pan, Instant Pot, Freezer Meals

Sheet Pan Buns

SERVINGS 12
PREPARATION TIME 1 hour 45 minutes
COOKING TIME 25 minutes

Nutritional Values Per Serving	
Calories	420
Total Fat	11.5g
Saturated Fat	8.7g
Cholesterol	0mg
Sodium	401mg
Total Carbohydrate	67.9g
Dietary Fiber	5.5g
Total Sugars	7.2g
Protein	12.8g

Meal Prep Suggestion:

Seal the buns in a ziplock bag then refrigerate until ready to serve. Avoid moisture during their storage.

Ingredients:

- ½ cup almond butter
- 2 cups almond milk
- ½ cup warm water
- 2½ tablespoons active dry yeast
- ⅓ cup sugar
- 2 tablespoons flaxseeds
- 2 tablespoons water
- 2 teaspoons salt
- 7 cups all-purpose flour

To Coat

- 2 tablespoons melted almond butter

Instructions:

1. Soak flaxseed in a bowl with 2 tablespoons water in a bowl for 5 minutes.
2. Mix flour, milk, almond butter, flaxseed mixture and rest of the ingredients in a bowl until smooth.
3. Knead this dough on a working surface.
4. Cover and leave the prepared dough for 1 hour.
5. Punch down the dough then knead the dough again for 1 minute.
6. Divide the kneaded dough into 12 equal sized portions and roll them into balls.
7. Place the buns in a greased baking sheet lined with parchment paper.
8. Brush the buns with butter on top, cover with kitchen towel then leave for 30 minutes.
9. At 375 degrees F, preheat your oven.
10. Bake the buns for almost 25 minutes in the preheated oven.
11. Allow the buns to cool then serve.

Chapter 06: Sheet Pan, Instant Pot, Freezer Meals

Potato Tomato Stew

SERVINGS 8 | **PREPARATION TIME** 10 minutes | **COOKING TIME** 8 minutes

Nutritional Values Per Serving

Calories	150
Total Fat	3.9g
Saturated Fat	0.6g
Cholesterol	0mg
Sodium	659mg
Total Carbohydrate	25.5g
Dietary Fiber	5.9g
Total Sugars	4.3g
Protein	5.3g
Vitamin D	0mcg

Meal Prep Suggestion:

Enjoy these potatoes with fresh salad on the side.

Ingredients:

- 3 large garlic cloves crushed
- 1 red onion diced
- ¼ cup tamari
- 4 carrots chopped
- 2 tablespoons olive oil
- 3 celery stalks chopped
- 1 eggplant, diced
- 1½ lbs. baby potatoes, quartered
- 1 stem of rosemary chopped
- 3 bay leaves
- 2 (14 ounces) can tomatoes
- 1¼ cups vegetable stock
- 2 tablespoons cacao powder

Instructions:

1. Add oil, garlic, onion, tamari and eggplant to the Instant Pot insert.
2. Select the Sauté mode and cook for 5 minutes.
3. Add potatoes, tomatoes, stock and rest of the ingredients.
4. Put on the lid and seal it by turning the pressure valve to closed position.
5. Cook on Manual mode for 8 minutes at High Pressure.
6. Once done, release the pressure completely then remove the lid.
7. Serve warm.

Chapter 06: Sheet Pan, Instant Pot, Freezer Meals

Roasted Veggies with Baby Corn

SERVINGS | PREPARATION TIME | COOKING TIME
4 | 10 minutes | 30 minutes

Nutritional Values Per Serving

Calories	195
Total Fat	8.4g
Saturated Fat	1.2g
Cholesterol	0mg
Sodium	74mg
Total Carbohydrate	30g
Dietary Fiber	6g
Total Sugars	12.5g
Protein	5.6g

Meal Prep Suggestion:

Pack these veggies with boiled white rice in a sealable container and refrigerate.

Ingredients:

- 1 teaspoon dried herbs
- 2 ounces baby corn
- 2 ounces baby carrots, cut in half.
- 2 beets, sliced
- 1 radish, sliced
- 4 cherry tomatoes, cut in half
- Black pepper and salt, to taste
- 2 tablespoons olive oil
- 1 zucchini, sliced
- 1 small cucumber, cut into quarters

Instructions:

1. Toss beets with black pepper, salt and oil in a sheet pan.
2. At 425 degrees F, preheat your oven.
3. Bake the beet slices for 20 minutes then flip once cooked halfway through.
4. Transfer the beets to a plate.
5. Place the carrots, radish, zucchini and corn in the sheet pan, then drizzle black pepper and salt on top.
6. Bake them for 10 minutes and flip once cooked halfway through.
7. Transfer the corn, zucchini and carrots to the beets.
8. Add rest of the ingredients, mix gently then serve.

Mushroom Tomato Risotto

SERVINGS 4 | **PREPARATION TIME** 10 minutes | **COOKING TIME** 11 minutes

Nutritional Values Per Serving	
Calories	341
Total Fat	21.9g
Saturated Fat	2.8g
Cholesterol	0mg
Sodium	1213mg
Total Carbohydrate	19.1g
Dietary Fiber	2.8g
Total Sugars	4g
Protein	15.7g

Meal Prep Suggestion:

Store the risotto in a sealable container with celery sticks in a different compartment and refrigerate until ready to serve. Reheat the risotto for 5 minutes in the microwave for serving.

Ingredients:

- 6 cups vegetable broth
- 3 tablespoons olive oil
- 1 pound portobello mushrooms, sliced
- 1 pound white mushrooms, sliced
- 1 sundried tomato, chopped
- 2 shallots, diced
- 1½ cups Arborio rice
- ½ cup dry white wine
- Salt to taste
- Black pepper to taste
- 3 tablespoons chives, chopped
- 4 tablespoons almond butter

Instructions:

1. Select Sauté mode on the Instant pot.
2. Add olive oil and mushrooms then sauté for 3 minutes.
3. Stir in rice and rest of the ingredients.
4. Put on the lid, and seal it by turning the pressure valve to closed position.
5. Cook on Manual Mode on high pressure for 8 minutes.
6. Once done, release the pressure completely then remove the lid.
7. Serve warm.

Chapter 06: Sheet Pan, Instant Pot, Freezer Meals

Saffron Risotto

SERVINGS 4 **PREPARATION TIME** 10 minutes **COOKING TIME** 13 minutes

Nutritional Values Per Serving	
Calories	347
Total Fat	5g
Saturated Fat	0.9g
Cholesterol	0mg
Sodium	627mg
Total Carbohydrate	59.2g
Dietary Fiber	2g
Total Sugars	0.8g
Protein	8.8g

Meal Prep Suggestion:

Pack the risotto in a sealable container with roasted carrot in a different compartment and refrigerate until ready to serve. Reheat for 5 minutes in the microwave.

Ingredients:

- 1 ½ cups Arborio rice
- 2 shallots, chopped
- 1 teaspoon saffron
- ½ cup white wine
- 3 ¼ cups vegetable broth
- 1 tablespoon olive oil
- Salt and black pepper, to taste

Instructions:

1. Select Sauté mode on the Instant Pot.
2. Add shallots with oil to the instant pot then sauté for 5 minutes.
3. Stir in rice, stock and rest of the ingredients.
4. Cover its lid, and seal it by turning the pressure valve to close position.
5. Select the Manual mode and cook at High pressure for 8 minutes.
6. Once done, release the pressure completely then remove the lid.
7. Mix well, garnish with herbs and serve warm.

Chapter 06: Sheet Pan, Instant Pot, Freezer Meals

Instant Pot Chickpea Stew

SERVINGS 6   **PREPARATION TIME** 10 minutes   **COOKING TIME** 20 minutes

Nutritional Values Per Serving

Calories	318
Total Fat	6.8g
Saturated Fat	0.8g
Cholesterol	0mg
Sodium	189mg
Total Carbohydrate	51.7g
Dietary Fiber	13.9g
Total Sugars	10.2g
Protein	15.1g

Meal Prep Suggestion:

Place the stew in a sealable container then freeze until ready to serve. Thaw the stew at room temperature then reheat in the microwave for 5 minutes.

Ingredients:

- 1 tablespoon olive oil
- 2 ounces carrots, diced
- 1½ cups diced onion
- 1 cup vegetable broth
- 8 ounces potatoes, sliced
- 1 cup canned diced tomatoes
- 2 cups chickpeas, soaked overnight then drain
- 4 cups water
- Salt, to taste
- Black pepper, to taste
- ½ cup chopped flat-leaf parsley

Instructions:

1. Add chickpeas and 4 cups water to the Instant Pot.
2. Cover its lid and seal the lid by turning its valve to a close position.
3. Select the Manual mode and cook at high pressure for 10 minutes.
4. Once done, release the pressure naturally then remove the lid.
5. Drain and transfer the chickpeas to a bowl.
6. Switch the Instant pot to Sauté mode.
7. Add olive oil, onion, and carrot then sauté for 5 minutes.
8. Stir in rest of the ingredients then cover the lid.
9. Seal the lid, and cook for 5 minutes on High pressure on manual mode.
10. Once done, release the pressure completely then remove the lid.
11. Serve warm.

White Bean Salad

SERVINGS	PREPARATION TIME	COOKING TIME
4	10 minutes	20 minutes

Nutritional Values Per Serving

Calories	547
Total Fat	1.6g
Saturated Fat	0.4g
Cholesterol	0mg
Sodium	30mg
Total Carbohydrate	101.1g
Dietary Fiber	25.1g
Total Sugars	8.7g
Protein	36.7g
Vitamin D	0mcg

Meal Prep Suggestion:

These bean can be stored in a dry and sealable container in the refrigerator.

Ingredients:

- 3 cups white beans, soaked overnight, drain
- 2 green bell peppers, diced
- 2 red bell peppers, diced
- 2 yellow bell peppers, diced
- 2 small onions, chopped
- Salt and black pepper, to taste
- 1 tablespoon lemon juice

Instructions:

1. Add white beans and 4 cups water to the instant pot's insert.
2. Cover its lid and seal it by turning its pressure valve to closed position.
3. Select the Manual mode and cook on High pressure for 20 minutes.
4. Once done, release the pressure naturally then remove the lid.
5. Drain and transfer the white beans to a salad bowl.
6. Toss in veggies, black pepper, salt and lemon juice.
7. Mix gently then serve.

Chapter 06: Sheet Pan, Instant Pot, Freezer Meals

Green Bean Mushroom Medley

SERVINGS 4   **PREPARATION TIME** 10 minutes   **COOKING TIME** 6 minutes

Nutritional Values Per Serving

Calories	156
Total Fat	11.8g
Saturated Fat	7.3g
Cholesterol	31mg
Sodium	401mg
Total Carbohydrate	11.6g
Dietary Fiber	3.9g
Total Sugars	4.4g
Protein	3.5g

Meal Prep Suggestion:

Place the vegetable medley in a sealable container then refrigerate. Reheat in the microwave for 5 minutes before serving.

Ingredients:

- ½ pound fresh green beans, diced into 1 inch lengths
- 2 carrots, cut into thick strips
- ¼ cup almond butter
- 1 onion, sliced
- ½ cup canned corn kernel, drained
- ½ lb fresh mushrooms, sliced
- ½ teaspoon seasoning salt
- ¼ teaspoon garlic, peeled and minced
- ¼ teaspoon white pepper

Instructions:

1. Fill the Instant Pot's insert with 2 cups water.
2. Place its trivet inside the pot, and set the steamer basket on it.
3. Add green beans, carrot and mushrooms in the basket.
4. Cover and seal its lid by turning its pressure valve to closed position.
5. Select Steam mode and cook for 6 minutes.
6. Once done, release the pressure completely then remove the lid.
7. Transfer the steamed veggies to a mixing bowl.
8. Toss in rest of the ingredients then mix well.
9. Serve.

Chapter 06: Sheet Pan, Instant Pot, Freezer Meals

Potato Pasta Soup

SERVINGS 4 | **PREPARATION TIME** 10 minutes | **COOKING TIME** 28 minutes

Nutritional Values Per Serving	
Calories	209
Total Fat	8.1g
Saturated Fat	1.3g
Cholesterol	1mg
Sodium	953mg
Total Carbohydrate	32.1g
Dietary Fiber	5.8g
Total Sugars	9.2g
Protein	6g

Meal Prep Suggestion:

Place the pasta potato soup in a sealable container then freeze until ready to serve. Thaw the soup at room temperature then reheat in the microwave for 5 minutes.

Ingredients:

- 2 medium onions, chopped
- 2 tablespoons olive oil
- ½ cup peas
- 4 tablespoons tomato paste
- 2 pounds Yukon Gold potatoes, peeled
- 6 vegetable bouillon cubes
- 2 cups of boiling water
- ¼ cup kale, chopped
- ½ teaspoon crushed red pepper
- 2 cups spring pasta
- 2 tomatoes, diced
- 3 tablespoons chopped mixed herbs
- Salt, to taste

Instructions:

1. Cut the potatoes and carrot using a curvy slicer.
2. Select Sauté mode on the Instant Pot.
3. Add chopped onion and oil to the pot and sauté for 5 minutes.
4. Stir in tomato paste then cook for 5 minutes.
5. Add potatoes, water, crushed pepper and bouillon to the pot.
6. Cover and seal the lid by turning its pressure valve to the closed position.
7. Select manual mode and cook for 8 minutes at high pressure.
8. Once done, release the pressure completely then remove the lid.
9. Meanwhile, boil the pasta as per the package's instructions then drain.
10. Add pasta and kale to the soup and serve warm.

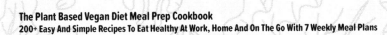

Chapter 06: Sheet Pan, Instant Pot, Freezer Meals

Potato Vermicelli Soup

SERVINGS 4 | **PREPARATION TIME** 10 minutes | **COOKING TIME** 13 minutes

Nutritional Values Per Serving	
Calories	350
Total Fat	7.6g
Saturated Fat	1.1g
Cholesterol	0mg
Sodium	70mg
Total Carbohydrate	64.8g
Dietary Fiber	9.1g
Total Sugars	6.1g
Protein	7.5g

Meal Prep Suggestion:

Store the soup in a sealable container then in the refrigerator and reheat in the microwave before the serving.

Ingredients:

- 6 potatoes, peeled and quarted
- 1 red pepper, chopped
- 1 carrot, chopped
- 1 onion, chopped
- 2 handfuls vermicelli
- Salt, to taste
- Black pepper, to taste
- 1 tablespoon universal vegetable spice
- 1 vegetable bouillon cube
- 2 tablespoons olive oil

Instructions:

1. Select the Sauté mode on the Instant pot.
2. Sauté onion and carrot with oil in the pot for 5 minutes.
3. Stir in potatoes, chopped pepper, water and broth cube.
4. Cover and seal its lid by turning its pressure valve to closed position.
5. Cook on High pressure and manual mode for 8 minutes.
6. Once done, release the pressure completely then remove the lid.
7. Add vermicelli then cook for 10 minutes on Sauté mode.
8. Stir in rest of the ingredients then mix well.
9. Serve warm.

Chapter 06: Sheet Pan, Instant Pot, Freezer Meals

Instant Pot Butternut Soup

SERVINGS 4
PREPARATION TIME 10 minutes
COOKING TIME 30 minutes

Nutritional Values Per Serving

Calories	160
Total Fat	3.3g
Saturated Fat	1.8g
Cholesterol	9mg
Sodium	547mg
Total Carbohydrate	33.7g
Dietary Fiber	6.4g
Total Sugars	10.8g
Protein	3.3g

Meal Prep Suggestion:

Place the soup in a sealable container then freeze until ready to serve. Thaw the soup at room temperature then reheat in the microwave for 5 minutes.

Ingredients:

- ½ medium sweet onion, diced
- 3 cloves garlic, minced
- 4 sage leaves, minced
- 3 sprigs fresh thyme
- 2 ½ pounds butternut squash, peeled, and cubed
- 3 large carrots, chopped
- 1 stalk celery, chopped
- 1 apple, cored and chopped
- 4 cups vegetable stock
- Kosher salt and black pepper, to taste
- ⅓ cup coconut cream, beaten
- 2 tablespoons chopped fresh chives

Instructions:

1. Add onion, garlic, thyme, sage and oil to the Instant pot.
2. Select Sauté mode and cook for 5 minutes.
3. Stir in squash, carrots and rest of the ingredients.
4. Cover the lid, and seal it by turning the pressure valve to closed position.
5. Select Manual mode and cook for 12 minutes on High pressure.
6. Once done, release the pressure completely then remove the lid.
7. Discard the thyme then puree the soup using a hand held blender until smooth.
8. Serve.

Chapter 06: Sheet Pan, Instant Pot, Freezer Meals

Barley Vegetable Stew

SERVINGS	PREPARATION TIME	COOKING TIME
6	15 minutes	20 minutes

Nutritional Values Per Serving

Calories	220
Total Fat	3g
Saturated Fat	0.7g
Cholesterol	0mg
Sodium	1435mg
Total Carbohydrate	37.8g
Dietary Fiber	8.3g
Total Sugars	7g
Protein	12.5g

Meal Prep Suggestion:

Place the barley stew in a sealable container then freeze until ready to serve. Thaw the stew at room temperature then reheat in the microwave for 5 minutes.

Ingredients:

- 2 quarts vegetable broth
- 1 cup uncooked barley
- 1 (14.5 ounce) can diced tomatoes
- 2 carrots, chopped
- 2 stalks celery, chopped
- 1 onion, chopped
- 1 potato, peeled and diced
- 2 bay leaves
- 1 teaspoon salt
- 1 teaspoon white sugar
- ½ teaspoon ground black pepper
- ½ teaspoon garlic powder

Instructions:

1. Add carrots, broth, potato, barley and rest of the ingredients to the Instant Pot.
2. Cover its lid and seal it by turning the pressure valve to closed position.
3. Select manual mode with high pressure and cook for 20 minutes.
4. Once done, release the pressure completely then remove the lid.
5. Serve warm.

CHAPTER 07

KID FRIENDLY RECIPES

Chapter 07: Kid Friendly Recipes

Cauliflower Mash

SERVINGS	PREPARATION TIME	COOKING TIME
4	15 minutes	15 minutes

Nutritional Values Per Serving

Calories	169
Total Fat	11.9g
Saturated Fat	6.6g
Cholesterol	23mg
Sodium	168mg
Total Carbohydrate	13.8g
Dietary Fiber	6.1g
Total Sugars	5.5g
Protein	5.3g

Meal Prep Suggestion:

Pack the cauliflower mash with roasted carrot sticks in a compartmented container then refrigerate until ready to serve.

Ingredients:

- 1 large head cauliflower cut into florets
- 3 tablespoons almond butter
- 3 tablespoons vegan cream
- 6 garlic cloves
- ¼ cup vegan parmesan cheese
- Salt and black pepper to taste

Instructions:

1. Set a steamer with water over medium heat and let it boil.
2. Spread cauliflower florets in the steamer basket and place it in the steamer.
3. Cover and steam the cauliflower for 15 minutes.
4. Drain and transfer the cauliflower to a food processor.
5. Sauté garlic with almond butter in a skillet for 1 minute.
6. Transfer this garlic and almond butter to the cauliflower then blend until smooth.
7. Add black pepper, salt, parmesan cheese and cream then blend again for 1 minute
8. Serve.

Chapter 07: Kid Friendly Recipes

Mash Potatoes

SERVINGS
4

PREPARATION TIME
10 minutes

COOKING TIME
20 minutes

Nutritional Values Per Serving

Calories	293
Total Fat	18.1g
Saturated Fat	6.3g
Cholesterol	0mg
Sodium	305mg
Total Carbohydrate	29.2g
Dietary Fiber	6.3g
Total Sugars	3.5g
Protein	7.7g

Meal Prep Suggestion:

Refrigerate the potato mash with roasted asparagus sticks in a compartmented container.

Ingredients:

- 4 lbs russet potatoes, peeled
- 1 ¼ cups almond milk
- 16 tablespoons almond butter
- 1 ½ teaspoon salt
- 1 tablespoon fresh parsley

Instructions:

1. Peel and cut the russet potatoes into quarters then add to a saucepan.
2. Pour in water to cover the russet potatoes, bring to a boil then cover and cook for 25 minutes until tender.
3. Drain and mash the well cooked potatoes with a fork in a bowl.
4. Stir in rest of the ingredients then mix well.
5. Serve.

Chapter 07: Kid Friendly Recipes

Crispy and Creamy Pasta

SERVINGS
6

PREPARATION TIME
10 minutes

COOKING TIME
25 minutes

Nutritional Values Per Serving	
Calories	450
Total Fat	12.6g
Saturated Fat	4.6g
Cholesterol	21mg
Sodium	523mg
Total Carbohydrate	71.5g
Dietary Fiber	10.1g
Total Sugars	0.8g
Protein	12.5g

Meal Prep Suggestion:
Pack this pasta with roasted bread sticks and carrots.

Ingredients:

- 12 ounces tofu, crumbled
- 1 large garlic clove, minced
- 1 ½ teaspoons kosher salt
- ¾ teaspoon black pepper
- Pinch freshly grated nutmeg
- 2 tablespoons olive oil

Pasta

- 2 tablespoons olive oil
- 1 small yellow onion, chopped
- ½ cup dry white wine
- 1 cup coconut cream
- Salt and black pepper, to taste
- 12 ounces dried tubular pasta
- 1 ½ ounces grated vegan parmesan
- ¼ cup breadcrumbs
- Freshly grated nutmeg, for serving

Instructions:

1. Toast breadcrumbs in a skillet for 3-5 minutes until golden then transfer to a bowl.
2. Boil rigatoni pasta as per the package's instructions then drain.
3. Sauté tofu with salt, nutmeg, black pepper, garlic and oil in a skillet until golden brown.
4. Stir in cream, black pepper, salt, and white wine then cook on a simmer for 5 minutes then mash the mixture well.
5. Fold in boiled pasta and mix well with the creamy tofu sauce.
6. Drizzle vegan parmesan and breadcrumbs on top and serve.

Chapter 07: Kid Friendly Recipes

Creamy Pasta

SERVINGS
4

PREPARATION TIME
10 minutes

COOKING TIME
20 minutes

Nutritional Values Per Serving	
Calories	242
Total Fat	16.4g
Saturated Fat	12g
Cholesterol	23mg
Sodium	263mg
Total Carbohydrate	20.9g
Dietary Fiber	2.1g
Total Sugars	2.2g
Protein	4.1g

Meal Prep Suggestion:

Pack this pasta with roasted carrot sticks.

Ingredients:

- 1 lb fettucini pasta, broken into pieces
- 3 tablespoon almond butter
- 2 teaspoons minced garlic
- 3 tablespoon flour
- 1 cup vegetable broth
- ½ cup pumpkin puree
- ½ cup almond milk
- 2 teaspoons dried parsley
- ¼ teaspoon paprika
- Salt and black pepper to taste

Instructions:

1. Boil pasta as per the package's instructions then drain.
2. Sauté garlic with almond butter in a saucepan for 1 minute.
3. Add flour then mix well for 1 minute.
4. Stir in milk, and broth, mix well then cook until it thickens.
5. Add puree, black pepper, salt, and parsley.
6. Drizzle paprika on top.
7. Serve warm.

Chapter 07: Kid Friendly Recipes

Zucchini Cranberry Muffins

SERVINGS 12 **PREPARATION TIME** 20 minutes **COOKING TIME** 25 minutes

Nutritional Values Per Serving

Calories	111
Total Fat	0.7g
Saturated Fat	0.1g
Cholesterol	0mg
Sodium	153mg
Total Carbohydrate	23.6g
Dietary Fiber	1.7g
Total Sugars	7.2g
Protein	2.5g

Meal Prep Suggestion:

Store the muffins in a sealable jar in the refrigerator while avoiding moisture.

Ingredients:

- 2 cups zucchini, shredded
- 1½ cups whole wheat flour
- ½ cup rolled oats
- 2 teaspoon cinnamon
- 1 tablespoon milled flaxseed
- 1 teaspoon baking powder
- ½ teaspoon baking soda
- ½ teaspoon salt

Wet Ingredients

- ½ cup applesauce
- ¼ cup maple syrup
- 1 tablespoon vanilla extract

Add-Ins

- ¼ cup dried cranberries
- ½ cup fresh cranberries

Instructions:

1. Crush rolled oats in a food processor for 2 minutes then transfer to a mixing bowl.
2. Stir in rest of the dry ingredients then mix well.
3. Add maple syrup, vanilla, and applesauce then stir until smooth.
4. Fold in zucchini shreds and cranberries then mix well.
5. Line two mini muffin trays with paper cups and divide the muffin batter into them.
6. At 350 degrees F, preheat your oven.
7. Bake the zucchini cranberry muffins for 25 minutes until golden brown.
8. Allow the baked muffins to cool.
9. Serve.

Chapter 07: Kid Friendly Recipes

Tofu Patties

SERVINGS 6
PREPARATION TIME 15 minutes
COOKING TIME 14 minutes

Nutritional Values Per Serving	
Calories	115
Total Fat	7.7g
Saturated Fat	1.4g
Cholesterol	0mg
Sodium	50mg
Total Carbohydrate	4.9g
Dietary Fiber	2.3g
Total Sugars	1.4g
Protein	8.1g

Meal Prep Suggestion:

Place the patties on a baking sheet, cover with a plastic sheet and freeze. Cook only right before the serving.

Ingredients:

- 1 (12 ounce) package firm tofu
- 2 teaspoons vegetable oil
- 1 small onion, chopped
- 1 celery, chopped
- 1 tablespoon flaxseed
- 1 tablespoon water
- ¼ cup shredded vegan cheese
- Salt and black pepper to taste
- ½ cup vegetable oil for frying

Instructions:

1. Soak flaxseeds in 1 tablespoon water in a bowl for 5 minutes.
2. Squeeze the excess water out of the tofu then dice it.
3. Sauté onion and celery with oil in a skillet until golden brown then transfer to a bowl.
4. Mash this mixture together then make 6 patties of equal size.
5. Stir in tofu cubes, black pepper, salt, cheese and flaxseed mixture then mix well.
6. Set a skillet over medium heat with oil and sear for 7 minutes per side.
7. Serve.

Chapter 07: Kid Friendly Recipes

Strawberry Pops

SERVINGS: 4
PREPARATION TIME: 4 hours 15 minutes
COOKING TIME: 0 minutes

Nutritional Values Per Serving	
Calories	214
Total Fat	1.3g
Saturated Fat	0g
Cholesterol	0mg
Sodium	4mg
Total Carbohydrate	53.6g
Dietary Fiber	8.4g
Total Sugars	41.9g
Protein	2.8g

Meal Prep Suggestion:

Wrap the pops in plastic sheet then freeze until ready to serve.

Ingredients:

- 15 ounces hulled strawberries, halved
- 3 ounces granulated sugar
- ¼ ounce freeze-dried strawberry powder
- ¾ teaspoon fresh lemon juice
- 3 ounces ice crushed

Instructions:

1. Blend strawberries in a blender until smooth.
2. Add sugar, strawberry powder, lemon juice and ice then puree the mixture.
3. Divide the strawberry into popsicles molds.
4. Insert the popsicle sticks into the popsicles, cover and freezer for 4 hours.
5. Remove from the popsicle molds and serve.

Chapter 07: Kid Friendly Recipes

Mashed Carrots

SERVINGS 6   **PREPARATION TIME** 15 minutes   **COOKING TIME** 20 minutes

Nutritional Values Per Serving

Calories	191
Total Fat	9g
Saturated Fat	0.7g
Cholesterol	0mg
Sodium	157mg
Total Carbohydrate	25.3g
Dietary Fiber	7.2g
Total Sugars	11.9g
Protein	5.3g

Meal Prep Suggestion:

Store the puree with celery sticks to eat with.

Ingredients:

- 2 lbs. carrots, peeled
- 4 tablespoon almond butter
- 2 teaspoons garlic powder
- Salt and black pepper, to taste

Instructions:

1. Boil carrots in a pot filled with water for 20 minutes until soft.
2. Drain and transfer the carrots to a bowl.
3. Mash these cooked carrots with a fork until smooth and lump-free.
4. Add black pepper, salt, garlic powder and butter then mix well.
5. Serve.

Mango Cream Bowl

SERVINGS 4 **PREPARATION TIME** 15 minutes **COOKING TIME** 0 minutes

Nutritional Values Per Serving	
Calories	193
Total Fat	8g
Saturated Fat	6.5g
Cholesterol	0mg
Sodium	7mg
Total Carbohydrate	32.7g
Dietary Fiber	5.2g
Total Sugars	27.7g
Protein	2.4g

Meal Prep Suggestion:

Pack the mango cream with graham crackers or star cookies.

Ingredients:

- 4 medium frozen mangos, peeled and diced
- 6 raspberries, to garnish
- 2 teaspoons maple syrup
- ¼ cup almond milk

Instructions:

1. Add frozen mangos , almond milk and maple syrup in a blender and puree the mixture until smooth.
2. Serve.

Chapter 07: Kid Friendly Recipes

Strawberry Popsicles

SERVINGS 6   **PREPARATION TIME** 15 minutes   **COOKING TIME** 20 minutes

Nutritional Values Per Serving	
Calories	136
Total Fat	6.6g
Saturated Fat	1.5g
Cholesterol	0mg
Sodium	42mg
Total Carbohydrate	17.8g
Dietary Fiber	0.6g
Total Sugars	13.4g
Protein	2.3g

Meal Prep Suggestion:

Store these popsicles in the freezer.

Ingredients:

Cashew Layer

- ½ cup raw cashews, soaked
- 1 ¼ cups coconut milk
- 3 tablespoons maple syrup
- 2 teaspoons vanilla bean paste
- Pinch of salt

Strawberry Layer

- 12 ounces strawberries, washed and hulled
- ½ of a lemon juiced
- 2 tablespoons maple syrup
- ½ teaspoon vanilla bean paste

Instructions:

1. Add strawberries, lemon juice, maple syrup, and vanilla to a blender.
2. Pulse until the mixture pureed and smooth.
3. Divide this mixture into popsicle molds and insert the popsicle in them.
4. Freeze the popsicles for 1 hour.
5. Blend cashews with rest of the cashew layer ingredients in a blender until smooth.
6. Divide this cashew mixture into the popsicle molds.
7. Freeze again for 4 hours then serve.

Chapter 07: Kid Friendly Recipes

Kid's Carrot Rice Soup

SERVINGS 4 **PREPARATION TIME** 15 minutes **COOKING TIME** 35 minutes

Nutritional Values Per Serving	
Calories	214
Total Fat	6.8g
Saturated Fat	2.4g
Cholesterol	8mg
Sodium	253mg
Total Carbohydrate	36.3g
Dietary Fiber	7.6g
Total Sugars	12.7g
Protein	3.1g

Meal Prep Suggestion:

Pack this soup with roasted bread sticks on the side.

Ingredients:

- 1 tablespoon almond butter
- 1 tablespoon olive oil
- 1 large onion, chopped
- 2 pounds sweet carrots, peeled and sliced
- Salt to taste
- ¼ teaspoon sugar
- 2 quarts water
- 6 tablespoons rice
- Black pepper to taste
- 2 tablespoons chopped fresh herbs, to garnish

Instructions:

1. Sauté onion with oil and butter in a soup pot for 5 minutes.
2. Stir in ½ teaspoon salt and carrot then cook for 10 minutes.
3. Add water, and rice and cook for 30 minutes on a simmer.
4. Puree the cooked soup with an immersion blender until smooth.
5. Serve.

Chapter 07: Kid Friendly Recipes

Potato Croquettes

SERVINGS 8   **PREPARATION TIME** 13 minutes   **COOKING TIME** 10 minutes

Nutritional Values Per Serving

Calories	269
Total Fat	2.5g
Saturated Fat	0.2g
Cholesterol	0mg
Sodium	414mg
Total Carbohydrate	55.2g
Dietary Fiber	6.7g
Total Sugars	9g
Protein	6.9g

Meal Prep Suggestion:

Store the uncooked croquettes in a sealable container then freeze. Cook them right before the serving.

Ingredients:

Potato Dough

- 9 potatoes, cooked and mashed
- 1 tablespoon parsley, chopped
- 1 tablespoon all-purpose flour
- 4 tablespoons unsweetened oat milk
- ⅛ teaspoon ground nutmeg
- ¾ teaspoon salt

Breading

- 1 cup all-purpose flour
- 1 cup unsweetened oat milk
- 1 cup breadcrumbs
- ½ teaspoon salt
- Frying oil, to cook

Instructions:

1. Mix mashed potatoes with, parsley, flour, milk, nutmeg and salt in a bowl.
2. Make 2 inches croquettes out of this mixture.
3. Mix breadcrumbs with salt for the coating in a plate.
4. Coat the croquettes with the flour, then dip in the oat milk and coat again with breadcrumbs.
5. Set a deep frying pan with oil over medium high heat.
6. Deep fry the coated croquettes until golden brown then transfer to a plate using a slotted spoon.
7. Serve.

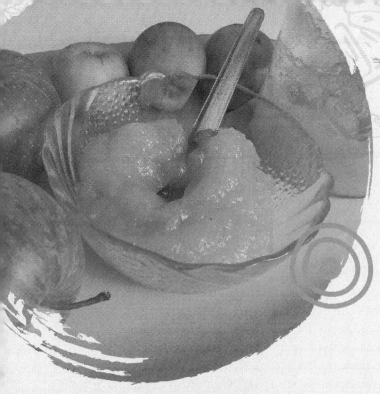

Chapter 07: Kid Friendly Recipes

Cinnamon Apple Meal

SERVINGS 6   **PREPARATION TIME** 10 minutes   **COOKING TIME** 20 minutes

Nutritional Values Per Serving	
Calories	116
Total Fat	0.4g
Saturated Fat	0g
Cholesterol	0mg
Sodium	2mg
Total Carbohydrate	31g
Dietary Fiber	5.5g
Total Sugars	23.2g
Protein	0.6g

Meal Prep Suggestion:

Store this puree with some crackers to eat with.

Ingredients:

- 6 medium apples, peeled, diced
- ¼ cup water
- ½ teaspoon ground cinnamon

Instructions:

1. Add apples, water and cinnamon to a saucepan.
2. Cover and cook the apples for 20 minutes low heat.
3. Puree the cooked apples using an immersion blender.
4. Serve.

Chapter 07: Kid Friendly Recipes

Baby Oatmeal

SERVINGS **4** PREPARATION TIME **15 minutes** COOKING TIME **2 minutes**

Nutritional Values Per Serving	
Calories	176
Total Fat	15g
Saturated Fat	12.8g
Cholesterol	0mg
Sodium	89mg
Total Carbohydrate	10.1g
Dietary Fiber	2.3g
Total Sugars	2.1g
Protein	2.7g

Meal Prep Suggestion:

Pack the oatmeal with pureed avocado, apple, or carrots then add the puree on top before serving.

Ingredients:

- 1 cup rolled old fashioned oats
- 1 cup almond milk
- 1 cup water
- 2 pinches of salt

Instructions:

1. Mix oats , water, salt and milk in a bowl then heat in the microwave for 2 minutes at high heat.
2. Serve.

Chapter 07: Kid Friendly Recipes

Orange Mini Cookies

SERVINGS 12   **PREPARATION TIME** 15 minutes   **COOKING TIME** 10 minutes

Nutritional Values Per Serving

Calories	171
Total Fat	1.2g
Saturated Fat	0.1g
Cholesterol	0mg
Sodium	52mg
Total Carbohydrate	37.7g
Dietary Fiber	1.1g
Total Sugars	17g
Protein	3.1g

Meal Prep Suggestion:

Keep these orange cookies stored in a dry mason jar and keep them in a cool place in the kitchen.

Ingredients:

- 2½ cups all-purpose flour
- 1 teaspoon baking powder
- ¼ teaspoon salt
- 1 cup granulated sugar
- 2 tablespoons orange zest
- 1 cup almond butter
- 2 tablespoons fresh orange juice
- 1 tablespoon flaxseed
- 1 tablespoon water

Instructions:

1. Soak flaxseed in 1 tablespoon water in a bowl for 5 minutes.
2. At 350 degrees F, preheat your oven.
3. Layer two baking sheets with parchment paper.
4. Mix 2 ½ cups flour, ¼ tsp salt and 1 tsp baking powder in a bowl.
5. Beat sugar, zest, butter, flaxseed mixture and orange in a blender then add to the dry mixture.
6. Mix well until smooth then make 2 inches balls out of this mixture.
7. Place the balls in the baking sheet and press each into a cookie.
8. Bake the cookies for 12 minutes and serve.

Chapter 07: Kid Friendly Recipes

Star Cookies

SERVINGS PREPARATION TIME COOKING TIME
24   35 minutes   8 minutes

Nutritional Values Per Serving

Calories	259
Total Fat	12.4g
Saturated Fat	6.2g
Cholesterol	20mg
Sodium	206mg
Total Carbohydrate	34.6g
Dietary Fiber	0.9g
Total Sugars	14.5g
Protein	2.9g

Meal Prep Suggestion:

Keep these star cookies stored in a dry mason jar and keep them in a cool place in the kitchen.

Ingredients:

- 1½ cups almond butter, softened
- ½ cup vegetable shortening
- 2 tablespoons flaxseed meal
- 2 tablespoons water
- 1 cup cane sugar
- 1 cup packed brown sugar
- ¼ cup thawed orange juice concentrate
- 1 teaspoon vanilla extract
- 5 cups all-purpose flour
- 1 teaspoon baking soda
- 1 teaspoon salt

Instructions:

1. Soak flaxseed meal in 2 tablespoons water in a bowl for 5 minutes.
2. Beat butter with sugars and shortening in a mixing bowl for 7 minutes.
3. Add flaxseed mixture, orange juice and vanilla then mix well.
4. Stir in salt, baking soda and flour then mix until smooth.
5. Cover and refrigerate the prepared dough for 20 minutes.
6. Roll out the dough into a ¼ inch thick sheet and use a star shaped cookie cutter to cut cookies out of it.
7. Place the prepared cookies in a baking sheet lined with parchment paper.
8. Bake the star cookies for 8 minutes at 350 degrees F in the oven.
9. Allow the cookies to cool then serve.

Chapter 07: Kid Friendly Recipes

Butternut Squash Puree

SERVINGS   **PREPARATION TIME**   **COOKING TIME**
6   10 minutes   40 minutes

Nutritional Values Per Serving	
Calories	260
Total Fat	17.5g
Saturated Fat	11g
Cholesterol	46mg
Sodium	168mg
Total Carbohydrate	27.9g
Dietary Fiber	2.5g
Total Sugars	14.5g
Protein	1.4g

Meal Prep Suggestion:

Store this pureed squash with carrot sticks to serve.

Ingredients:

- 2 whole butternut squash, halved and seeded
- 6 tablespoons almond butter, melted
- ¼ cup pure maple syrup
- Dash of salt
- Ground cinnamon, for sprinkling

Instructions:

1. At 375 degrees F, preheat your oven.
2. Spread butternut squash in a baking sheet then drizzle butter and salt on top.
3. Bake the squash for 40 minutes in the preheated oven.
4. Transfer the squash to a bowl then mash with a fork.
5. Stir in cinnamon, and maple syrup then mix well.
6. Serve.

Chapter 07: Kid Friendly Recipes

Pink-and-Yellow Cookies

SERVINGS 12
PREPARATION TIME 25 minutes
COOKING TIME 10 minutes

Nutritional Values Per Serving

Calories	321
Total Fat	15.7g
Saturated Fat	9.8g
Cholesterol	41mg
Sodium	223mg
Total Carbohydrate	46.1g
Dietary Fiber	0.3g
Total Sugars	42g
Protein	0.9g

Meal Prep Suggestion:

Keep these cookies stored in a dry mason jar and keep them in a cool place in the kitchen.

Ingredients:

Cookies

- 1½ cups all-purpose flour
- ½ teaspoon baking soda
- ¼ teaspoon salt
- 1 cup almond butter, softened
- ⅔ cup brown sugar
- 1 tablespoon flaxseed meal
- 1 tablespoon water
- 1 teaspoon vanilla extract
- ½ cup almond milk
- ½ teaspoon lemon zest

Glaze

- 3 cups powdered sugar
- 2 tablespoons light corn syrup
- 2 tablespoons lemon juice
- 2 tablespoons water
- Red and yellow food coloring

Instructions:

1. Soak flaxseed meal in 1 tablespoon water in a bowl for 5 minutes.
2. At 350 degrees F, preheat your oven.
3. Layer two baking sheets with parchment paper.
4. Mix flour with salt and baking soda in a bowl.
5. Beat butter with sugar and flaxseed mixture in a mixer for 2 minutes then add dry flour mixture, lemon zest and rest of the ingredients for cookies.
6. Mix well until smooth then drop the cookie dough spoon by spoon on the baking sheets to make several cookies.
7. Bake the cookies for 10 minutes in the oven until golden brown.
8. Meanwhile, mix sugar, water, lemon juice and corn syrup in a bowl. Divide the glaze into two bowls.
9. Add 2 red food color to one bowl and add 3 drops of yellow food color to the other bowl.
10. Dip the cookies in the yellow glaze then place them in the baking sheets and keep them aside for 10 minutes.
11. Coat half of each cookie with the pink glaze and place in the baking sheets then leave for 30 minutes.
12. Serve.

Chapter 07: Kid Friendly Recipes

Animal Pasta Soup

SERVINGS 4 **PREPARATION TIME** 15 minutes **COOKING TIME** 1 hour 23 minutes

Nutritional Values Per Serving	
Calories	281
Total Fat	8.5g
Saturated Fat	1.3g
Cholesterol	0mg
Sodium	761mg
Total Carbohydrate	50.1g
Dietary Fiber	9g
Total Sugars	12g
Protein	5.7g

Meal Prep Suggestion:

Store this soup with roasted asparagus.

Ingredients:

- 1 lb. roma tomatoes
- ½ lb. pumpkin puree
- 14 ½ ounces diced tomatoes canned
- 1 small onion sliced
- 3 stalks celery sliced
- 1 garlic clove, minced
- 1 cup vegetable stock
- 3 sprigs thyme
- ¼ teaspoon oregano dried
- 1-2 teaspoon salt
- ¼ teaspoon black pepper ground
- 2 tablespoons olive oil
- 1 tablespoon maple syrup
- 1 ½ cup dried animal shaped pasta, colorful

Instructions:

1. At 400 degrees F, preheat your oven.
2. Toss halved tomatoes with olive oil, thyme and salt in a baking sheet.
3. Roast the tomatoes for 25 minutes in the oven.
4. Sauté onions with oil in a large pot for 5 minutes.
5. Stir in celery and cook for 2 minutes.
6. Add ¼ tsp dried oregano and garlic then cook for 1 minute.
7. Stir in tomatoes, pumpkin puree, canned tomatoes, black pepper, salt and stock then cook on a simmer for 25 minutes.
8. Stir in maple syrup and cook for 15 minutes then puree the mixture with an immersion blender until smooth.
9. Boil the pasta as per the package's instructions then drain.
10. Add pasta to the soup and serve.

Chapter 07: Kid Friendly Recipes

Bow Tie Pasta Soup

SERVINGS 8
PREPARATION TIME 10 minutes
COOKING TIME 30 minutes

Nutritional Values Per Serving

Calories	467
Total Fat	6.2g
Saturated Fat	0.3g
Cholesterol	0mg
Sodium	156mg
Total Carbohydrate	87.9g
Dietary Fiber	1.7g
Total Sugars	2.8g
Protein	15.2g

Meal Prep Suggestion:

Store this pasta soup along with celery and carrot sticks.

Ingredients:

- 1 tablespoon olive oil
- 1 small onion, diced
- 1 carrot, grated
- 2 ribs celery, diced
- 1 small red bell pepper, diced
- 1 teaspoon dried Italian herb blend
- 4 cups vegetable broth
- 15 ounces tomato paste
- 8 ounces mini bowtie pasta
- Kosher salt
- ¼ cup almond milk

Instructions:

1. Sauté red bell pepper, celery, carrots and onions with oil in a Dutch oven for 8 minutes.
2. Stir in broth, almond milk, tomato paste, and dried herbs then cook to a boil then let it simmer for 10 minutes.
3. Meanwhile, boil the bow tie pasta as per the package's instruction then drain.
4. Puree the cooked soup mixture using an immersion blender.
5. Add the cooked pasta and cook for 2 minutes.
6. Serve warm.

CHAPTER 08
SNACK RECIPES

Chapter 08: Snack Recipes

Zucchini Sticks

SERVINGS
6

PREPARATION TIME
10 minutes

COOKING TIME
30 minutes

Nutritional Values Per Serving	
Calories	144
Total Fat	6g
Saturated Fat	4.9g
Cholesterol	3mg
Sodium	150mg
Total Carbohydrate	20g
Dietary Fiber	3.1g
Total Sugars	2.8g
Protein	4.3g

Meal Prep Suggestion:

Spread the uncooked sticks on a baking sheet then freeze for 2 hours. Once frozen, transfer the zucchini sticks to a ziplock bag as well. Cook the zucchini sticks right before serving to have the best crispiness.

Ingredients:

- 3 medium zucchini
- ⅓ cup flour
- ½ cup almond milk
- 2 garlic cloves, minced
- 1 cup panko breadcrumbs
- ½ cup vegan parmesan cheese, grated
- 2 tablespoons parsley, minced
- 1 teaspoon fresh oregano, minced
- ½ teaspoon paprika
- Salt and black pepper to taste

Instructions:

1. At 425 degrees F, preheat your oven.
2. Layer a baking sheet with parchment paper.
3. Peel the zucchinis and cut them in ½ inch sticks.
4. Spread flour in one plate, and add milk to a bowl and minced garlic in one bowl.
5. Toss breadcrumbs with black pepper, salt, paprika, oregano, parsley, and cheese in a bowl.
6. Coat the zucchini sticks in the flour, dip in the milk and then coat with the breadcrumb mixture.
7. Place the zucchini stick on a baking sheet lined with parchment paper.
8. Bake the zucchini sticks for 30 minutes in the oven.
9. Serve.

Chapter 08: Snack Recipes

Fried Blossoms

SERVINGS 4 **PREPARATION TIME** 15 minutes **COOKING TIME** 6 minutes

Nutritional Values Per Serving	
Calories	181
Total Fat	0.4g
Saturated Fat	0.1g
Cholesterol	0mg
Sodium	587mg
Total Carbohydrate	33.3g
Dietary Fiber	1.1g
Total Sugars	0.1g
Protein	4.4g

Meal Prep Suggestion:

Place the uncooked blossoms in a sealable container then freeze for 2 hours. Once frozen, transfer the blossoms to a ziplock bag as well. Deep fry the blossoms only right before serving to have the best crispiness.

Ingredients:

- 1 ¼ cups all-purpose flour
- 1 teaspoon kosher salt
- 12 ounces beer
- 24 zucchini blossoms
- Salt, to taste
- Vegetable oil, for frying

Instructions:

1. Set a large pot filled with oil up to 2 inches over medium heat.
2. Mix flour with salt in a suitable bowl then stir in beer.
3. Mix well until smooth.
4. Dip the zucchini blossoms in the prepared batter then deep fry them in the hot oil for 3 minutes until golden brown.
5. Transfer to a suitable plate lined with parchment paper.
6. Drizzle salt on top and serve.

Chapter 08: Snack Recipes

Caramel Popcorn

SERVINGS 8
PREPARATION TIME 10 minutes
COOKING TIME 1 hour 5 minutes

Nutritional Values Per Serving	
Calories	123
Total Fat	1.6g
Saturated Fat	0.2g
Cholesterol	0mg
Sodium	376mg
Total Carbohydrate	26.1g
Dietary Fiber	1.7g
Total Sugars	17.9g
Protein	1.7g

Meal Prep Suggestion:

Store the crispy popcorn in a sealable mason jar.

Ingredients:

- 10 cups of popped popcorn
- 1 teaspoon salt
- 1 cup almond butter
- 1 cup light brown sugar
- 2 teaspoons vanilla
- ½ teaspoon baking soda

Instructions:

1. Mix butter, sugar, salt, baking soda and salt in a saucepan then cook for 5 minutes.
2. Spread the popcorn in a baking sheet then pour the butter mixture over the popcorn.
3. Bake the popcorn for 60 minutes at 220 degrees F in the oven.
4. Toss well after every 15 minutes
5. Serve.

Chapter 08: Snack Recipes

Bake Buffalo Cauliflower Wings

SERVINGS
4

PREPARATION TIME
10 minutes

COOKING TIME
30 minutes

Nutritional Values Per Serving

Calories	138
Total Fat	8.6g
Saturated Fat	1g
Cholesterol	0mg
Sodium	966mg
Total Carbohydrate	13.2g
Dietary Fiber	6.2g
Total Sugars	5.6g
Protein	6.1g

Meal Prep Suggestion:

Store the cauliflower florets in a sealable container in the refrigerator and reheat for 1-2 minutes in the microwave before serving.

Ingredients:

- 1 large cauliflower head, cut into small florets
- ½ cup Frank's Red Hot Sauce
- 2 tablespoon almond butter, melted
- 1 tablespoon olive oil
- 1 tablespoon lemon juice
- ½ teaspoon garlic powder
- 1 teaspoon salt
- 1 tablespoons parsley, chopped
- 1 teaspoon sesame seeds

Instructions:

1. At 425 degrees F, preheat your oven.
2. Toss cauliflower florets with almond butter, olive oil, lemon juice, garlic powder, salt, and red hot sauce in a bowl.
3. Spread the cauliflower florets in a baking sheet.
4. Bake the florets for 30 minutes in the preheated oven.
5. Drizzle parsley and sesame seeds on top.
6. Serve.

Chapter 08: Snack Recipes

Tofu Sticks

SERVINGS
4

PREPARATION TIME
10 minutes

COOKING TIME
12 minutes

Nutritional Values Per Serving

Calories	299
Total Fat	14.6g
Saturated Fat	3.2g
Cholesterol	0mg
Sodium	360mg
Total Carbohydrate	36g
Dietary Fiber	2.9g
Total Sugars	3.8g
Protein	8.7g

Meal Prep Suggestion:

Spread the unfried tofu sticks on a baking sheet then freeze for 2 hours. Once frozen, transfer the tofu sticks to a ziplock bag as well. Cook the sticks right before serving to have the best crispiness.

Ingredients:

- 1 tablespoon coconut oil
- 1 (12 to 14 ounce) package tofu
- 3 tablespoons vegetable oil
- ¾ cup almond flour
- ½ teaspoon garlic powder
- Salt and black pepper, to taste
- 1 cup almond milk
- 3 cups Chex Rice Cereal, crushed

Instructions:

1. Cut the tofu in 1x3 inches finger sticks.
2. Pat dry the tofu sticks with paper towel.
3. Mix almond flour with garlic powder, black pepper and salt in a bowl.
4. Coat the tofu sticks with almond flour mixture then dip in the milk and finally with the crushed cereal.
5. Set a pan with oil over medium heat and sear the tofu sticks for 2-3 minutes per side until golden brown.
6. Serve.

Chapter 08: Snack Recipes

Sweet Potato Fries

SERVINGS 4 **PREPARATION TIME** 10 minutes **COOKING TIME** 20 minutes

Nutritional Values Per Serving	
Calories	168
Total Fat	3.7g
Saturated Fat	0.5g
Cholesterol	0mg
Sodium	127mg
Total Carbohydrate	32.5g
Dietary Fiber	4.7g
Total Sugars	0.6g
Protein	1.7g

Meal Prep Suggestion:

Spread the uncooked fries in a baking sheet and freeze for 2 hours. Transfer these fries to a ziplock bag, seal and freeze again until ready to serve. Bake these fries right before serving.

Ingredients:

- 2 pounds sweet potatoes
- 1 tablespoon cornstarch
- ½ teaspoon salt
- 2 tablespoons olive oil
- Black pepper and cayenne pepper, to taste

Instructions:

1. At 425 degrees F, preheat your oven.
2. Layer two baking sheets with parchment paper.
3. Peel and slice the sweet potatoes into ¼ inch thick sticks.
4. Toss the sweet potatoes with cornstarch, salt, olive oil, black pepper, and cayenne pepper in a bowl.
5. Spread the fries in the baking sheets then bake for 20 minutes.
6. Toss the fries and continue baking for 10 minutes.
7. Serve.

Chapter 08: Snack Recipes

Potato Stuffed Rolls

SERVINGS PREPARATION TIME COOKING TIME
12   10 minutes   12 minutes

Nutritional Values Per Serving

Calories	189
Total Fat	4.6g
Saturated Fat	2.4g
Cholesterol	3mg
Sodium	282mg
Total Carbohydrate	31.3g
Dietary Fiber	2.7g
Total Sugars	0.9g
Protein	5.4g

Meal Prep Suggestion:

Place the unfried rolls in a sealable container then freeze for 2 hours. Once frozen, transfer the rolls to a ziplock bag as well. Deep fry the potato rolls right before serving to have the best crispiness.

Ingredients:

- 2 cups russet baked potatoes, cooked
- ½ cup green onion chopped
- 1 cup vegan cheddar cheese shredded
- ½ cup coconut cream
- ¼ teaspoon salt
- ½ teaspoon black pepper
- ¼ teaspoon garlic powder
- ¼ teaspoon onion powder
- 12 spring roll wrappers

To Seal

- 1 tablespoon cornstarch
- ¼ cup water
- Vegetable oil for frying

Instructions:

1. Mash potatoes in a bowl then stir in green onion, cheese, cream, salt, black pepper, garlic powder, and onion powder them mix well.
2. Mix cornstarch with ¼ cup water in a bowl.
3. Spread a roll wrapper on the working surface.
4. Add a tablespoon of the potato mixture at the center of the wrapper.
5. Fold the top and bottom of the wrapper then roll it.
6. Brush the edge of the roll wrapper with the cornstarch mixture then press to seal.
7. Make more rolls in the same way.
8. Place a deep frying pan with oil over medium high heat.
9. Deep fry the rolls for 2-3 minutes per side until golden brown.
10. Transfer the rolls to a plate using a slotted spoon.
11. Serve warm.

Chapter 08: Snack Recipes

Vegetable Spring Rolls

SERVINGS 12 **PREPARATION TIME** 35 minutes **COOKING TIME** 21 minutes

Nutritional Values Per Serving

Calories	247
Total Fat	3.6g
Saturated Fat	0.5g
Cholesterol	10mg
Sodium	449mg
Total Carbohydrate	44.8g
Dietary Fiber	2.8g
Total Sugars	1g
Protein	8.1g

Meal Prep Suggestion:

Place the unfried rolls in a sealable container then freeze for 2 hours. Once frozen, transfer the rolls to a ziplock bag as well. Deep fry the rolls right before serving to have the best crispiness.

Ingredients:

Vegetable Stuffing

- 2 tablespoons oil
- 2 ½ cups cabbage, shredded
- ½ cup carrot, shredded
- ⅓ cup bell pepper, sliced
- ¼ cup french beans, chopped
- ⅓ cup spring onion whites, chopped
- ½ teaspoon crushed black pepper
- 1 tablespoon soy sauce
- 1 teaspoon celery, chopped
- 1 cup cooked noodles
- 3 tablespoon bean sprouts
- 2 to 3 tablespoons spring onion greens, chopped
- Salt to taste
- Oil as required, for deep frying
- 24 spring roll wrappers

Sealing Paste

- 6 tablespoons cornstarch
- 4 tablespoons water

Instructions:

1. Sauté cabbage, carrot and French beans with oil in a skillet for 5 minutes.
2. Stir in rest of the stuffing ingredients then cook for 3 minutes.
3. Mix cornstarch with ¼ cup water in a bowl.
4. Spread a roll wrapper on the working surface.
5. Add a tablespoon of the vegetable mixture at the center of the wrapper.
6. Fold the top and bottom of the wrapper then roll it.
7. Brush the edge of the roll wrapper with the cornstarch mixture then press to seal.
8. Make more rolls in the same way.
9. Place a deep frying pan with oil over medium high heat.
10. Deep fry the rolls for 2-3 minutes per side until golden brown.
11. Transfer the rolls to a plate using a slotted spoon.
12. Serve warm.

Chapter 08: Snack Recipes

Eggplant Fries

SERVINGS 4 **PREPARATION TIME** 10 minutes **COOKING TIME** 15 minutes

Nutritional Values Per Serving

Calories	124
Total Fat	7.5g
Saturated Fat	1g
Cholesterol	0mg
Sodium	5mg
Total Carbohydrate	15g
Dietary Fiber	8.6g
Total Sugars	7.2g
Protein	2.6g

Meal Prep Suggestion:

Store the uncooked eggplant fries in a dry sealable container then freeze. Once frozen, transfer the frozen eggplant to a sealable ziplock bag as well. Bake the fries right before serving.

Ingredients:

- 2 medium eggplants, peeled
- 2 teaspoons garlic powder
- 2 teaspoons dried oregano
- 2 pinches salt and black pepper
- 2 tablespoons olive oil

Instructions:

1. At 425 degrees F, preheat your oven.
2. Cut the eggplant into French fries sticks.
3. Toss the eggplant with black pepper, salt, oregano and garlic powder.
4. Spread the eggplant fries in a baking sheet then bake for 15 minutes in the oven.
5. Flip the fries once cooked halfway through.
6. Serve.

Chapter 08: Snack Recipes

Apple Chips

SERVINGS: 4
PREPARATION TIME: 20 minutes
COOKING TIME: 60 minutes

Nutritional Values Per Serving	
Calories	125
Total Fat	0.4g
Saturated Fat	0g
Cholesterol	0mg
Sodium	2mg
Total Carbohydrate	33.4g
Dietary Fiber	5.7g
Total Sugars	25.3g
Protein	0.6g

Meal Prep Suggestion:

Store the crispy apple chips in a dry sealable mason jar.

Ingredients:

- 4 golden apples, cored and thinly sliced
- 3 teaspoons white sugar
- 1 teaspoon ground cinnamon

Instructions:

1. At 225 degrees F, preheat your oven.
2. Spread the thin apple slices on a baking sheet.
3. Mix cinnamon and sugar in a bowl and drizzle over the apple slices.
4. Bake the apple slices for 1 hour in the preheated oven.
5. Flip the apple slices once cooked halfway through.
6. Allow the apple slices to cool then serve.

Chapter 08: Snack Recipes

Cassava Croquettes

SERVINGS 8 **PREPARATION TIME** 20 minutes **COOKING TIME** 35 minutes

Nutritional Values Per Serving

Calories	230
Total Fat	4.3g
Saturated Fat	3.4g
Cholesterol	0mg
Sodium	67mg
Total Carbohydrate	45.6g
Dietary Fiber	2.5g
Total Sugars	2.7g
Protein	2.7g

Meal Prep Suggestion:

Store the uncooked coated cassava croquettes in a sealable container then freeze. Once frozen, transfer the croquettes to a sealable ziplock bag as well. Deep fry the frozen croquettes right before serving.

Ingredients:

- 2 medium cassavas, peeled
- 1 tablespoon cornstarch
- 2 tablespoons lemon juice
- ½ cup of breadcrumbs
- 1 garlic clove, minced
- ½ cup almond milk
- Cumin, black pepper, and salt to taste
- Frying oil

Instructions:

1. Fill half of a large sized saucepan with water.
2. Add cassava, garlic and lemon juice then cook for 25 minutes.
3. Drain and transfer the cassava to a bowl.
4. Mash the cassava with a fork then add cornstarch and mix well.
5. Take 3 tablespoons of the cassava mixture at a time then shape it into a stick.
6. Make more sticks in the same way.
7. Dip the cassava sticks in the milk then coat with the breadcrumbs.
8. Set a deep frying pan with oil over medium high heat
9. Deep fry the cassava croquettes in the hot oil for 5 minutes until golden brown.
10. Transfer the croquettes to a plate using a slotted spoon.
11. Drizzle salt, black pepper and cumin on top.
12. Serve.

Chapter 08: Snack Recipes

Chocolate Bombs

SERVINGS 8 | **PREPARATION TIME** 1 hour 15 minutes | **COOKING TIME** 0 minutes

Nutritional Values Per Serving	
Calories	182
Total Fat	16.8g
Saturated Fat	8.8g
Cholesterol	0mg
Sodium	76mg
Total Carbohydrate	7.8g
Dietary Fiber	2.1g
Total Sugars	4.2g
Protein	4.8g

Meal Prep Suggestion:

Place these chocolate bombs in a dry sealable container, stack on top of one another and refrigerate.

Ingredients:

- ½ cup peanut butter
- ¼ cup cocoa powder
- ¼ cup melted dark chocolate
- ¼ cup melted coconut oil
- Stevia to taste
- Sliced peanuts to garnish

Instructions:

1. Layer the 8 cups of muffin tray with paper cups.
2. Mix melted chocolate with cocoa powder, nut butter, coconut oil and stevia in a bowl.
3. Divide this prepared mixture into the muffin cups and refrigerate for 1 hour.
4. Garnish with peanut slices and serve

Chapter 08: Snack Recipes

Chocolate Peanut Balls

SERVINGS 12
PREPARATION TIME 70 minutes
COOKING TIME 0 minutes

Nutritional Values Per Serving

Calories	155
Total Fat	6.5g
Saturated Fat	2.2g
Cholesterol	2mg
Sodium	57mg
Total Carbohydrate	23g
Dietary Fiber	2.8g
Total Sugars	16.1g
Protein	3.5g

Meal Prep Suggestion:

Place these balls in a sealable container then refrigerate until ready to serve.

Ingredients:

- 1 ¼ cups Medjool dates pitted
- ¼ cup peanut butter
- ⅔ cup rolled oats
- ⅓ cup crushed nuts
- 1 tablespoon chia seeds
- ⅛ teaspoon kosher salt
- 3 tablespoons cocoa powder
- ½ cup melted dark chocolate
- ¼ cup almond milk

Instructions:

1. Grind dates with oats, nuts and seeds in a food processor.
2. Take a small scoop of the nuts mixture then drop on a baking sheet lined with parchment paper.
3. Drop more scoops in the same way then refrigerate for 30 minutes.
4. Mix melted dark chocolate with almond milk in a bowl.
5. Dip the refrigerated balls in the melted chocolate then place in the baking sheets.
6. Refrigerate the balls for 30 minutes then serve.

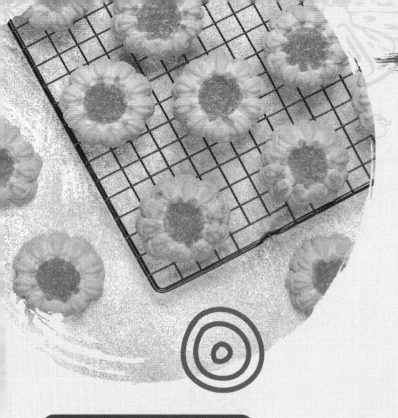

Chapter 08: Snack Recipes

Orange Thumbprint Cookies

SERVINGS 12 | **PREPARATION TIME** 20 minutes | **COOKING TIME** 20 minutes

Nutritional Values Per Serving	
Calories	218
Total Fat	4.8g
Saturated Fat	0.4g
Cholesterol	0mg
Sodium	209mg
Total Carbohydrate	40.4g
Dietary Fiber	1.7g
Total Sugars	21.1g
Protein	4.3g

Meal Prep Suggestion:
Keep these cookies in a cookie jar with sealed lid and avoid moisture and high heat.

Ingredients:
- 2 cups unbleached all-purpose flour
- 1 cup almond flour
- 1 teaspoon salt
- ¼ cup almond butter
- ½ cup brown sugar
- ¼ cup granulated sugar
- ½ teaspoon grated orange zest
- ¾ cup orange marmalade

Instructions:
1. At 325 degrees F, preheat your oven.
2. Mix flours with salt in a suitable mixing bowl.
3. Beat sugars with zest and butter in a mixer for 3 minutes until golden brown.
4. Add dry flour mixture then mix until smooth.
5. Take 1½ teaspoon of the dough at a time and roll it into a ball.
6. Make more balls out of this dough then place in a baking sheet.
7. Place each ball into a flower shape cookie mold, press to get the desired shape then transfer the cookies to a baking sheet.
8. Press the center of each thumbprint cookie to make a dent.
9. Bake the cookies for 10 minutes then add the marmalade at the center of the cookies.
10. Bake again for 10 minutes then allow them to cool.
11. Serve.

Chapter 08: Snack Recipes

Beetroot Chips

SERVINGS 12 | **PREPARATION TIME** 30 minutes | **COOKING TIME** 60 minutes

Nutritional Values Per Serving	
Calories	116
Total Fat	8.6g
Saturated Fat	1.2g
Cholesterol	0mg
Sodium	79mg
Total Carbohydrate	10g
Dietary Fiber	2g
Total Sugars	8g
Protein	1.7g

Meal Prep Suggestion:

Store the crispy beet chips in a sealable dry jar at room temperature.

Ingredients:

- 12 red beets, sliced
- ½ cup olive oil
- 2 teaspoon celery salt

Instructions:

1. At 300 degrees F, preheat your oven.
2. Layer two baking sheets with parchment paper.
3. Mix beets slices with oil and salt in a colander and leave them for 20 minutes.
4. Drain the excess liquid out then spread the beets in the baking sheets.
5. Bake the beets for 45-60 minutes and flip them once cooked halfway through.
6. Serve.

Chapter 08: Snack Recipes

Roasted Chickpeas

SERVINGS 8   **PREPARATION TIME** 15 minutes   **COOKING TIME** 30 minutes

Nutritional Values Per Serving

Calories	185
Total Fat	6.1g
Saturated Fat	0.8g
Cholesterol	0mg
Sodium	30mg
Total Carbohydrate	25.8g
Dietary Fiber	7.4g
Total Sugars	4.6g
Protein	8.2g

Meal Prep Suggestion:

Store the chickpeas in a sealable jar at room temperature.

Ingredients:

- 1 (12 ounces) can chickpeas, drained
- 2 tablespoons olive oil
- 1 pinch salt
- 1 pinch garlic salt
- 1 pinch cayenne pepper

Instructions:

1. Pat dry the chickpeas with a paper towel.
2. Toss the chickpeas with olive oil, garlic salt, salt and cayenne pepper in a bowl.
3. Spread them in a baking sheet lined with parchment paper.
4. At 375 degrees F, preheat your oven.
5. Bake the seasoned chickpeas for 30 minutes until crunchy and golden brown.
6. Serve.

Chapter 08: Snack Recipes

Crusted Kale Chips

SERVINGS 8   **PREPARATION TIME** 15 minutes   **COOKING TIME** 20 minutes

Nutritional Values Per Serving	
Calories	121
Total Fat	1.6g
Saturated Fat	0.2g
Cholesterol	0mg
Sodium	42mg
Total Carbohydrate	21.8g
Dietary Fiber	4.9g
Total Sugars	2.7g
Protein	5.9g

Meal Prep Suggestion:

Add the kale chips to a sealable container and store them at room temperature.

Ingredients:

- 4 cups curly kale leaves
- 1 bunch scallions, chopped
- ½ teaspoon Aleppo pepper, mince
- 1 teaspoon ground cumin
- 1 teaspoon ground coriander seeds
- ½ teaspoon garam masala
- Salt to taste

Batter

- 1 cup chickpea flour
- 3 tablespoons cornstarch
- ½ teaspoon salt
- 1 teaspoon baking powder
- ¾ cup cold sparkling water

Instructions:

1. At 350 degrees F, preheat your oven.
2. Mix garam masala, salt, coriander seeds, cumin, Aleppo pepper and scallion in a bowl.
3. Add kale leaves and gently.
4. Whisk chickpea flour, cornstarch, salt, baking powder and sparkling water.
5. Spread the seasoned kale leaves and coat each with the batter.
6. Place the coated kale leaves in a baking sheet lined with parchment paper.
7. Bake the chips for 15-20 minutes until golden brown.
8. Flip the chips once cooked halfway through.
9. Serve warm.

Chapter 08: Snack Recipes

Air Fried Tofu Nuggets

SERVINGS 8   **PREPARATION TIME** 10 minutes   **COOKING TIME** 15 minutes

Nutritional Values Per Serving	
Calories	121
Total Fat	1.6g
Saturated Fat	0.2g
Cholesterol	0mg
Sodium	42mg
Total Carbohydrate	21.8g
Dietary Fiber	4.9g
Total Sugars	2.7g
Protein	5.9g

Meal Prep Suggestion:

Pack the uncooked crust tofu in a sealable jar, then freeze them to store. Cook just before serving.

Ingredients:

- 1 block high protein tofu, drained
- 2 teaspoons smoked paprika
- ¼ teaspoon black pepper
- ¼ teaspoon salt
- ¼ teaspoon garlic powder

Batter

- 1 cup chickpea flour
- 3 tablespoons cornstarch
- ½ teaspoon salt
- 1 teaspoon baking powder
- ¾ cup cold sparkling water
- 1 cup breadcrumbs

Instructions:

1. Mix the tofu cubes with garlic powder, salt, black pepper and pepper in a bowl.
2. Cover them and refrigerate for 30 minutes.
3. At 350 degrees F, preheat your Air Fryer.
4. Mix the chickpea flour, cornstarch, salt, baking powder, sparkling water in a bowl.
5. Dip the tofu cubes in the batter then coat with the breadcrumbs then shake off the excess.
6. Place the coated tofu cubes in the air fryer basket.
7. Air fry them for 10-15 minutes until golden brown.
8. Serve warm.

Chapter 08: Snack Recipes

White Beans Meatballs

SERVINGS 8   **PREPARATION TIME** 10 minutes   **COOKING TIME** 20 minutes

Nutritional Values Per Serving	
Calories	273
Total Fat	3.3g
Saturated Fat	0.6g
Cholesterol	0mg
Sodium	322mg
Total Carbohydrate	47.6g
Dietary Fiber	11.3g
Total Sugars	4.5g
Protein	15.6g

Meal Prep Suggestion:

Store the unbaked vegan meatballs in a sealable jar in the freezer, then cook before serving.

Ingredients:

- 1 (14 oz) can white beans
- 1 cup frozen spinach
- 3 carrots, chopped
- ½ bell pepper, chopped
- ½ cup sweet corn (canned)
- 1 cup canned green peas
- 1 onion, chopped
- 3 garlic cloves, minced
- 1 cup oat flour
- 1 tablespoon olive oil

Seasoning

- 1 teaspoon cane sugar
- 1 teaspoon salt
- ½ teaspoon turmeric
- ½ teaspoon ground black pepper
- ½ teaspoon dried sage
- ½ teaspoon dried parsley
- 1 tablespoon nutritional yeast

Instructions:

1. At 390 degrees F, preheat your oven.
2. Sauté veggies with oil in a skillet for 10 minutes, then allow them to cool.
3. Add beans and the rest of the ingredients to a food processor.
4. Blend these ingredients for 2 minutes until well-mixed.
5. Place these balls in a baking sheet lined with parchment paper.
6. Bake the bean meatballs for 20 minutes until golden brown.
7. Serve.

Chapter 08: Snack Recipes

Chickpea Stuffed Zucchini Boats

SERVINGS 8   **PREPARATION TIME** 20 minutes   **COOKING TIME** 25 minutes

Nutritional Values Per Serving	
Calories	296
Total Fat	5.2g
Saturated Fat	0.6g
Cholesterol	0mg
Sodium	116mg
Total Carbohydrate	48.8g
Dietary Fiber	14.5g
Total Sugars	10.3g
Protein	16.9g

Meal Prep Suggestion:

Pack the unbaked zucchini boats in a sealable jar in the freezer, then bake before serving.

Ingredients:

- 4 medium zucchini
- ¼ cup (15 g) nutritional yeast
- ½ cup (125 mL) pasta sauce of choice
- 1 (19 ounces) can chickpeas, drained
- 1 pinch of salt and black pepper
- ½ cup vegan parmesan cheese, shredded
- 4 black olives, sliced

Instructions:

1. At 425 degrees, preheat your oven.
2. Cut zucchinis in half lengthwise and remove the seeds from the zucchini.
3. Scoop out some flesh to make space for the filling.
4. Place the zucchini halves in a greased baking sheet.
5. Blend chickpeas with yeast, pasta sauce, black pepper and salt in a food processor.
6. Spoon the chickpea mixture into the zucchini halves.
7. Place the olive slices over the filling and drizzle the vegan cheese on top.
8. Bake the zucchinis for 25 minutes in the preheated oven.
9. Serve warm.

Chapter 08: Snack Recipes

Vegan Buckwheat Muffins

SERVINGS 6   **PREPARATION TIME** 15 minutes   **COOKING TIME** 22 minutes

Nutritional Values Per Serving

Calories	142
Total Fat	8.1g
Saturated Fat	5.9g
Cholesterol	0mg
Sodium	116mg
Total Carbohydrate	17.1g
Dietary Fiber	1.8g
Total Sugars	4.3g
Protein	2.5g

Meal Prep Suggestion:

Store the muffins in a dry and sealable jar in the refrigerator.

Ingredients:

- 1 medium ripe banana, peeled
- ¼ cup almond butter
- ½ cup monk fruit sweetener
- ⅔ cup almond milk
- 1 tablespoon apple cider vinegar
- 2 cups light buckwheat flour
- 2 teaspoons baking powder
- ¼ teaspoon salt
- 1 cup grated carrot
- 2 tablespoons pumpkin seeds to garnish

Instructions:

1. At 350 degrees F, preheat your oven.
2. Mash the peeled banana in a bowl, then stir in almond butter, sweetener, milk, and vinegar.
3. Add buckwheat flour, baking powder, and salt, then mix well until smooth.
4. Fold in carrot, then mix evenly.
5. Line a muffin pan with muffin liners and divide the batter in them.
6. Bake the muffins for 22 minutes in the preheated oven.
7. Allow them to cool, then garnish the muffins with the pumpkin seeds.
8. Serve.

Chapter 08: Snack Recipes

Tahini Date Cookies

SERVINGS	PREPARATION TIME	COOKING TIME
8	15 minutes	10 minutes

Nutritional Values Per Serving

Calories	168
Total Fat	9.1g
Saturated Fat	1.3g
Cholesterol	0mg
Sodium	77mg
Total Carbohydrate	19.2g
Dietary Fiber	3.7g
Total Sugars	4.2g
Protein	4.8g

Meal Prep Suggestion:

Add the cookies to a cookie jar and store them at room temperature.

Ingredients:

- 1 ½ cup oats
- ½ cup tahini
- 1 ½ cup packed soft pitted dates
- ¼ teaspoon sea salt

Instructions:

1. At 350 degrees F, preheat your oven.
2. Blend 1 ½ cups oats in a food processor until finely crushed.
3. Add tahini, dates, and salt, then blend again for 1 minute.
4. Make 12 oat cookies out of this mixture.
5. Place these cookies in a baking sheet lined with parchment paper.
6. Bake the cookies for 10 minutes in the preheated oven.
7. Allow the cookies to cool and serve.

Chapter 08: Snack Recipes

Chocolate Chip Zucchini Muffins

SERVINGS 6 **PREPARATION TIME** 15 minutes **COOKING TIME** 25 minutes

Nutritional Values Per Serving	
Calories	190
Total Fat	8.4g
Saturated Fat	2.4g
Cholesterol	0mg
Sodium	320mg
Total Carbohydrate	27.2g
Dietary Fiber	1.3g
Total Sugars	8.7g
Protein	5.8g

Meal Prep Suggestion:

Pack these muffins in a dry container in the refrigerator.

Ingredients:

- 1 cup zucchini, grated
- 1 cup whole wheat flour
- 1 scoop vegan vanilla protein powder
- ½ teaspoon baking soda
- ½ teaspoon salt
- ⅓ cup cane sugar
- ⅔ cup unsweetened applesauce
- 2 tablespoons olive oil
- 1 teaspoon apple cider vinegar
- ½ cup dark chocolate chips

Instructions:

1. At 350 degrees F, preheat your oven.
2. Place the grated zucchini in a colander and let them strain.
3. Mix flour with sugar, salt, protein and baking soda in a mixing bowl.
4. Stir in vinegar, applesauce, and oil, then mix well until smooth.
5. Fold in zucchini and chocolate chips, then mix evenly.
6. Line the muffin tray with cupcake liners.
7. Divide this batter into the muffin cups.
8. Bake the zucchini muffins for 25 minutes in the preheated oven.
9. Allow the muffins to cool and serve.

Chapter 08: Snack Recipes

Carrot Oat Balls

SERVINGS
6

PREPARATION TIME
15 minutes

COOKING TIME
0 minutes

Nutritional Values Per Serving	
Calories	126
Total Fat	3.9g
Saturated Fat	2.9g
Cholesterol	0mg
Sodium	90mg
Total Carbohydrate	22g
Dietary Fiber	4g
Total Sugars	8.2g
Protein	2.6g

Meal Prep Suggestion:

Store in a sealed container in the fridge for up to 1 week or freezer for up to 3 months.

Ingredients:

- 1 cup rolled oats
- 2 cups packed soft pitted dates
- ¾ cup carrot, grated
- 1 cup unsweetened shredded coconut
- 1 teaspoon cinnamon
- ¼ teaspoon sea salt

To serve

- ½ cup shredded coconut, to coat

Instructions:

1. Blend oats in a food processor for 1 minute.
2. Add dates, carrot, cinnamon and coconut, then blend again for 1 minute.
3. Make 1 inch balls out of this mixture and coat the balls with coconut shreds.
4. Serve.

Chapter 08: Snack Recipes

Chili Garlic Baked Parsnip Fries

SERVINGS 4
PREPARATION TIME 15 minutes
COOKING TIME 37 minutes

Nutritional Values Per Serving

Calories	186
Total Fat	1.6g
Saturated Fat	0.3g
Cholesterol	0mg
Sodium	510mg
Total Carbohydrate	42.9g
Dietary Fiber	11.9g
Total Sugars	11.4g
Protein	3.2g

Meal Prep Suggestion:

Spread the uncooked fries in a sealable container, then freeze them for storage. Cook the fries just before serving.

Ingredients:

- 2 pounds parsnips
- ½ teaspoon olive oil
- 1 tablespoon chilli powder
- 2 teaspoons garlic powder
- 1 teaspoon sea salt

Instructions:

1. At 425 degrees F, preheat your oven.
2. Layer two baking sheets with parchment paper.
3. Peel the parsnips and cut them into French fries sticks.
4. Toss the parsnips with spices and olive oil in a large bowl.
5. Spread the parsnips in the prepared baking sheets.
6. Bake the fries for 25 minutes in the preheated oven.
7. Flip the fries and continue baking for 12 minutes.
8. Serve warm.

Raw Hemp Seed Brownies

Chapter 08: Snack Recipes

SERVINGS 16 | **PREPARATION TIME** 15 minutes | **COOKING TIME** 0 minutes

Nutritional Values Per Serving

Calories	136
Total Fat	6.7g
Saturated Fat	0.5g
Cholesterol	0mg
Sodium	59mg
Total Carbohydrate	18.7g
Dietary Fiber	3g
Total Sugars	14.2g
Protein	4g

Meal Prep Suggestion:

Pack the brownies in a sealable container in the refrigerator.

Ingredients:

- 2 cups packed, soft pitted dates
- 1 cup hemp seeds
- 1 cup raw walnuts
- ⅓ cup cocoa powder
- ½ teaspoon sea salt, optional

Instructions:

1. Blend dates with hemp seeds, walnuts, cocoa powder and salt in a blender for 2 minutes.
2. Spread this dough in an 8 inches baking pan lined with parchment paper.
3. Freeze this dough for 2-3 hours, then cut into 16 squares.
4. Serve.

Chapter 08: Snack Recipes

Carrot Fries

SERVINGS
6

PREPARATION TIME
13 minutes

COOKING TIME
30 minutes

Nutritional Values Per Serving	
Calories	200
Total Fat	4.7g
Saturated Fat	0.7g
Cholesterol	0mg
Sodium	368mg
Total Carbohydrate	38.3g
Dietary Fiber	2.3g
Total Sugars	3.9g
Protein	0.7g

Meal Prep Suggestion:

Spread the uncooked fries in a sealable container, then freeze them for storage. Cook the fries just before serving.

Ingredients:

- 1 pound carrots
- 2 tablespoons tapioca flour
- 2 tablespoons olive oil
- 1 teaspoon sea salt
- ½ teaspoon black pepper
- ½ teaspoon garlic powder
- ½ teaspoon onion powder
- ½ teaspoon thyme
- Parsley, to garnish

Instructions:

1. At 450 degrees F, preheat your oven.
2. Peel and cut the carrots into 4 inches long and ½ inch thick sticks.
3. Toss the carrot sticks with spices and flour in a tray.
4. Add olive oil and mix well.
5. Spread the carrot sticks in a single layer on a baking sheet lined with parchment paper.
6. Bake the carrot fries for 30 minutes in the preheated oven.
7. Flip them once cooked halfway through.
8. Garnish with parsley.
9. Serve warm.

Chapter 08: Snack Recipes

Avocado Fries

SERVINGS	PREPARATION TIME	COOKING TIME
4	10 minutes	15 minutes

Nutritional Values Per Serving	
Calories	208
Total Fat	15.3g
Saturated Fat	2.8g
Cholesterol	0mg
Sodium	318mg
Total Carbohydrate	16.7g
Dietary Fiber	3.6g
Total Sugars	1g
Protein	3g

Meal Prep Suggestion:

Pack the uncooked avocado wedges in a sealable container, then freeze them for storage. Cook the fries just before serving.

Ingredients:

- 2 avocados, ripe
- ½ cup flour
- ½ tablespoon dried oregano
- ½ tablespoon garlic powder
- ½ tablespoon chilli powder
- 1 teaspoon kosher salt
- 2 tablespoons lime juice
- ⅓ cup olive oil
- 1 cup panko

Instructions:

1. Mix flour with salt, chilli powder, garlic powder and oregano in a bowl.
2. Mix olive oil and lime juice in another bowl.
3. Spread the panko on a plate.
4. Peel and cut the avocado flesh into wedges.
5. Dredge the avocado wedges through the flour mixture, dip in the lime mixture then coat with the panko crumbs.
6. Place the coated avocado in a baking sheet lined with parchment paper.
7. Bake the avocado fries for 15 minutes until golden brown.
8. Serve warm.

Chapter 08: Snack Recipes

Onion Rings

SERVINGS
4

PREPARATION TIME
15 minutes

COOKING TIME
10 minutes

Nutritional Values Per Serving

Calories	197
Total Fat	2.1g
Saturated Fat	0.4g
Cholesterol	0mg
Sodium	514mg
Total Carbohydrate	38.1g
Dietary Fiber	3g
Total Sugars	5.1g
Protein	6g

Meal Prep Suggestion:

Pack the uncooked onion rings in a sealable container, then freeze them for storage. Cook the fries just before serving.

Ingredients:

- 2 yellow onions

Dry Mix

- 1 cup panko bread crumbs
- ½ teaspoon paprika
- ¼ teaspoon turmeric
- ¼ teaspoon salt

Wet Mix

- ½ cup flour
- ⅔ cup almond milk
- ½ teaspoon paprika
- ¼ teaspoon turmeric
- ½ teaspoon salt

Instructions:

1. At 450 degrees F, preheat your oven.
2. Mix breadcrumbs with paprika, salt, and turmeric in a bowl.
3. Whisk flour with milk, paprika, turmeric and salt in another bowl until smooth.
4. Peel onions and cut them into ½ inch thick slices cross-sectionally.
5. Separate the onion rings from one another.
6. Dip those rings in the flour batter, then coat with the breadcrumbs.
7. Place these coated onion rings in a baking sheet lined with parchment paper.
8. Bake these rings for 10 minutes in the preheated oven.
9. Serve warm.

Chapter 08: Snack Recipes

Crispy Pepper Poppers

SERVINGS
4

PREPARATION TIME
15 minutes

COOKING TIME
20 minutes

Nutritional Values Per Serving

Calories	217
Total Fat	7.9g
Saturated Fat	1.5g
Cholesterol	0mg
Sodium	1902mg
Total Carbohydrate	28g
Dietary Fiber	5.7g
Total Sugars	6.2g
Protein	8.1g

Meal Prep Suggestion:

Pack the uncooked poppers in a sealable container, then freeze them for storage. Cook the fries just before serving.

Ingredients:

- 16 ounces whole green and red peppers

Cream Cheese Filling
- 6 ounces firm tofu, drained
- ⅓ cup cashews, soaked
- 2 garlic cloves, peeled
- 1 tablespoon lemon juice
- ½ teaspoon salt

Batter
- ½ cup all-purpose flour
- ½ cup soy milk
- 2 teaspoons nutritional yeast
- ½ teaspoon smoked paprika
- ½ teaspoon salt

Breadcrumbs
- ¾ cup medium grind cornmeal
- ¾ cup blanched almond flour
- ¼ teaspoon salt
- Spray oil

Instructions:

1. At 425 degrees F, preheat your oven.
2. Wear the rubber gloves and cut the top of the peppers off.
3. Remove the seeds from inside and make them hollow.
4. Blend all the cream cheese filling ingredients in a blender for 1 minute.
5. Divide this filling in the peppers and stuff them nicely.
6. Mix the cornmeal with the rest of the breadcrumbs ingredients in a bowl.
7. Whisk the soy milk with the rest of the batter ingredients in a bowl until smooth.
8. Dip the whole stuffed peppers in the batter, then coat with breadcrumbs mixture.
9. Place the poppers in a baking sheet lined with parchment paper, then spray them with spray oil.
10. Bake the poppers in the preheated oven for 20 minutes until crispy.
11. Flip the poppers once baked halfway through.
12. Serve warm.

CHAPTER 09

SAUCES, CONDIMENTS AND DRESSING RECIPES

Chapter 09: Sauces, Condiments and Dressing Recipes

Chilli Garlic Sauce

SERVINGS 8 **PREPARATION TIME** 15 minutes **COOKING TIME** 12 minutes

Nutritional Values Per Serving	
Calories	79
Total Fat	0g
Saturated Fat	0g
Cholesterol	0mg
Sodium	141mg
Total Carbohydrate	18.9g
Dietary Fiber	0.1g
Total Sugars	12.5g
Protein	0.1g

Meal Prep Suggestion:

Refrigerate this sauce in a sealable mason jar for long term storage.

Ingredients:

- 1½ tablespoon red chilli flakes
- ½ cup granulated sugar
- ¼ cup rice vinegar
- 3 garlic cloves, minced
- 1 cup water
- 1 pinch sea salt
- ½ tablespoon tapioca flour
- 2 tablespoon water
- 2 teaspoons ginger, grated

Instructions:

1. Add garlic, salt, red pepper flakes, sugar, water and vinegar to a saucepan.
2. Cook on a slow simmer for 10 minutes with occasional stirring.
3. Mix 2 tablespoon water with tapioca flour in a bowl and pour into the pan.
4. Cook for 2 minutes with stirring until the sauce thickens.
5. Pour in a clean mason jar and allow it to cool.
6. Serve.

Chapter 09: Sauces, Condiments and Dressing Recipes

Vegan Buffalo Sauce

SERVINGS 8   **PREPARATION TIME** 10 minutes   **COOKING TIME** 5 minutes

Nutritional Values Per Serving

Calories	100
Total Fat	8.2g
Saturated Fat	1.7g
Cholesterol	0mg
Sodium	79mg
Total Carbohydrate	3.8g
Dietary Fiber	1.3g
Total Sugars	1.7g
Protein	4.2g

Meal Prep Suggestion:

Pack this sauce in a sealable jar in the refrigerator for long term storage.

Ingredients:

- ⅔ cup hot pepper sauce
- ½ cup cold vegan butter
- 1½ tablespoons white vinegar
- 1 tablespoon paprika
- ¼ teaspoon vegan Worcestershire sauce
- ¼ teaspoon cayenne pepper
- ⅛ teaspoon garlic powder
- Salt, to taste

Instructions:

1. Blend garlic powder, salt, cayenne pepper, paprika, Worcestershire sauce, vinegar, butter and hot sauce in a blender for 1 minute.
2. Pour this buffalo sauce into a suitable saucepan.
3. Cook it to a boil, then remove from the heat.
4. Pour in a clean mason jar and allow it to cool.
5. Serve.

Chapter 09: Sauces, Condiments and Dressing Recipes

Gochujang Sauce

SERVINGS	PREPARATION TIME	COOKING TIME
6	15 minutes	5 minutes

Nutritional Values Per Serving

Calories	69
Total Fat	0.1g
Saturated Fat	0g
Cholesterol	0mg
Sodium	44mg
Total Carbohydrate	16.7g
Dietary Fiber	0.1g
Total Sugars	12.9g
Protein	0.8g

Meal Prep Suggestion:

Refrigerate this sauce in a small canning jar for long term storage.

Ingredients:

- 1 cup filtered water
- ¼ cup date syrup
- 2 tablespoon rice wine
- 2 teaspoons garlic powder
- 1 tablespoon rice flour
- ½ cup gochugaru (Korean pepper powder)
- ⅓ cup doenjang paste (fermented Korean soybean paste)

Instructions:

1. Mix water, Korean pepper power, doenjang paste, date syrup, rice wine, garlic powder and rice flour in a saucepan.
2. Cook this sauce until it thickens.
3. Pour this thick pepper sauce into a clean bowl and allow it to cool.
4. Serve.

Chapter 09: Sauces, Condiments and Dressing Recipes

Sweet Chilli Sauce

SERVINGS: 6
PREPARATION TIME: 15 minutes
COOKING TIME: 0 minutes

Nutritional Values Per Serving

Calories	52
Total Fat	1g
Saturated Fat	0.3g
Cholesterol	0mg
Sodium	197mg
Total Carbohydrate	10.2g
Dietary Fiber	0.6g
Total Sugars	2.7g
Protein	0.9g

Meal Prep Suggestion:

Store this sauce in a bottle, then place it in the refrigerator.

Ingredients:

- 2 chargrilled red capsicum (jarred)
- 1 small red chilli, chopped
- 2 large roasted garlic cloves
- 1 teaspoon ginger, grated
- 1 tablespoon of maple syrup
- Juice of ½ a lime
- Salt and black pepper to taste

Instructions:

1. Blend red capsicum with red chilli and the rest of the ingredients in a blender until smooth.
2. Pour in a clean bottle and serve.

Chapter 09: Sauces, Condiments and Dressing Recipes

Avocado Hummus

SERVINGS	PREPARATION TIME	COOKING TIME
8	10 minutes	0 minutes

Nutritional Values Per Serving

Calories	211
Total Fat	18.6g
Saturated Fat	3.1g
Cholesterol	0mg
Sodium	212mg
Total Carbohydrate	9.9g
Dietary Fiber	3.5g
Total Sugars	1.4g
Protein	4g

Meal Prep Suggestion:

Store this hummus with celery and carrot sticks in a container, then refrigerate for storage.

Ingredients:

- 2 tablespoon lemon juice
- 2 garlic cloves, crushed
- 15 ounce can chickpeas drained
- ⅓ cup tahini
- 4 tablespoon cold water
- 1 medium avocado, peeled and sliced
- ½ teaspoon sea salt
- ½ teaspoon cumin
- 2 tablespoon olive oil
- Parsley leaf, to garnish

Instructions:

1. Blend chickpeas with avocado and the rest of the ingredients in a food processor until smooth.
2. Garnish with a parsley leaf.
3. Serve.

Chapter 09: Sauces, Condiments and Dressing Recipes

Pumpkin Hummus

SERVINGS 6
PREPARATION TIME 10 minutes
COOKING TIME 0 minutes

Nutritional Values Per Serving	
Calories	121
Total Fat	3.4g
Saturated Fat	0.5g
Cholesterol	0mg
Sodium	409mg
Total Carbohydrate	19.7g
Dietary Fiber	4.1g
Total Sugars	1.8g
Protein	4g

Meal Prep Suggestion:

Store this hummus with cucumber sticks in a container, then refrigerate for storage.

Ingredients:

- 1 small garlic clove, minced
- 15-ounce can chickpeas
- ¾ cup pumpkin puree
- ½ teaspoon kosher salt
- 1 ¼ teaspoon ground cumin
- 2 tablespoons lemon juice
- 1 teaspoon maple syrup
- 1 tablespoon olive oil
- A splash of soy milk
- Parsley, to garnish

Instructions:

1. Blend chickpeas with pumpkin puree and the rest of the ingredients in a food processor until smooth.
2. Garnish with a splash of soy milk and parsley.
3. Serve.

Chapter 09: Sauces, Condiments and Dressing Recipes

Beet Root Hummus

SERVINGS 12 | **PREPARATION TIME** 15 minutes | **COOKING TIME** 60 minutes

Nutritional Values Per Serving

Calories	183
Total Fat	4g
Saturated Fat	0.5g
Cholesterol	0mg
Sodium	514mg
Total Carbohydrate	29.1g
Dietary Fiber	8.1g
Total Sugars	6.3g
Protein	9.2g

Meal Prep Suggestion:

Store this hummus in a container, then refrigerate it for storage.

Ingredients:

- 3 cups canned chickpeas, drained
- ½ pound beetroot
- 2 garlic cloves, minced
- ¼ cup 2 tablespoon tahini
- 1¼ teaspoon salt
- 1 teaspoon cumin
- ¾ cup cold aquafaba (chickpea liquid)
- 5 tablespoon lemon juice

To Garnish
- 1 tablespoon fresh parsley to garnish
- 2 teaspoons white sesame seeds to garnish
- 2 tablespoon olive oil to garnish

Instructions:

1. At 390 degrees F, preheat your oven.
2. Place the beetroots on foil sheet squares and place them in a roasting pan.
3. Fold the edges of the foil sheet up and slightly scrunchy the edges to make a parcel.
4. Add some water to cover the bottom of the pan.
5. Bake the beetroots for 60 minutes in the preheated oven.
6. When done, allow the beetroots to cool down, then cut into slices.
7. Blend the beetroot slices with aquafaba, lemon juice and tahini in a blender for 30 seconds.
8. Add chickpeas and the rest of the ingredients, then blend again for 1 minute.
9. Spread the hummus in a serving bowl and garnish with sesame seeds, olive oil and parsley.
10. Serve.

Chapter 09: Sauces, Condiments and Dressing Recipes

Chickpea Hummus

SERVINGS 12 **PREPARATION TIME** 10 minutes **COOKING TIME** 0 minutes

Nutritional Values Per Serving

Calories	180
Total Fat	7.2g
Saturated Fat	1g
Cholesterol	0mg
Sodium	27mg
Total Carbohydrate	22.7g
Dietary Fiber	6.7g
Total Sugars	3.9g
Protein	7.8g

Meal Prep Suggestion:

Store this hummus with celery and carrot sticks in a container, then refrigerate for storage.

Ingredients:

- 1 (15-ounce) can chickpeas
- ¼ cup lemon juice
- ¼ cup tahini
- 1 small garlic clove, minced
- 2 tablespoons olive oil
- ½ teaspoon ground cumin
- Salt to taste
- 3 tablespoons water

To Garnish
- Dash ground paprika or sumac for serving
- 2 fresh basil leaves to garnish
- 2 teaspoon toasted white sesame seeds to garnish
- 2 tablespoon olive oil to garnish

Instructions:

1. Blend chickpeas with tahini and the rest of the ingredients in a food processor until smooth.
2. Garnish with oil, sesame seeds, paprika and basil leaves.
3. Serve.

Chapter 09: Sauces, Condiments and Dressing Recipes

Mango Chutney

SERVINGS
4

PREPARATION TIME
10 minutes

COOKING TIME
25 minutes

Nutritional Values Per Serving

Calories	65
Total Fat	1.2g
Saturated Fat	0.2g
Cholesterol	0mg
Sodium	150mg
Total Carbohydrate	13.7g
Dietary Fiber	0g
Total Sugars	11.2g
Protein	0.1g

Meal Prep Suggestion:

Store this hummus in a container, then refrigerate it for storage.

Ingredients:

- 1 teaspoon olive oil
- 1 champagne mango, peeled and diced
- ½ inch ginger grated
- ½ teaspoon red chilli flakes
- 1 garlic clove, chopped
- ¼ teaspoon salt
- ¼ teaspoon Asafoetida
- 2 tablespoons cider vinegar
- 2 tablespoons raw sugar
- ⅛ teaspoon cinnamon clove
- ⅛ teaspoon cardamom
- ⅛ teaspoon nutmeg powder

Instructions:

1. Add mango cubes, oil, ginger and the rest of the ingredients to a saucepan.
2. Cook this mango mixture for 25 minutes on low heat with frequent stirring.
3. Remove this sauce from the heat and allow it to cool.
4. Transfer to a clean jar or can then seal.
5. Serve.

Chapter 09: Sauces, Condiments and Dressing Recipes

Cashew Sauce

SERVINGS
8

PREPARATION TIME
10 minutes

COOKING TIME
0 minutes

Nutritional Values Per Serving

Calories	198
Total Fat	15.9g
Saturated Fat	3.1g
Cholesterol	0mg
Sodium	297mg
Total Carbohydrate	11.5g
Dietary Fiber	1.1g
Total Sugars	1.7g
Protein	5.3g

Meal Prep Suggestion:

Store this sauce in a sealable container, then refrigerate for storage.

Ingredients:

- 2 cups cashews
- 1 ¼ cup water
- 2 garlic cloves, peeled
- 1 teaspoon salt

Instructions:

1. Soak cashews in a suitable bowl filled with water for 2 hours.
2. Drain and transfer the soaked cashews to a blender.
3. Add water, salt and garlic, then puree the mixture.
4. Garnish with herbs.
5. Serve.

Chapter 09: Sauces, Condiments and Dressing Recipes

Peri Peri Sauce

SERVINGS: 8 | PREPARATION TIME: 10 minutes | COOKING TIME: 0 minutes

Nutritional Values Per Serving

Calories	128
Total Fat	12.7g
Saturated Fat	7.2g
Cholesterol	0mg
Sodium	154mg
Total Carbohydrate	4.6g
Dietary Fiber	1.7g
Total Sugars	2g
Protein	1.2g

Meal Prep Suggestion:

Store this sauce with celery and carrot sticks in a container, then refrigerate for storage.

Ingredients:

- 1 long red cayenne chilli pepper
- 1 large red bell pepper, chopped
- 2 tablespoon lemon juice
- 1½ tablespoon smoked paprika
- ½ teaspoon salt
- 1 tablespoon dried oregano
- 4 garlic cloves, crushed
- 1½ tablespoon balsamic vinegar
- 1½ tablespoon white wine vinegar
- ½ teaspoon ground black pepper
- 3 tablespoon olive oil
- 1 cup coconut milk

Instructions:

1. Blend chilli pepper with red bell pepper and the rest of the ingredients except the coconut milk in a food processor for 1 minute.
2. Stir in coconut milk and mix well.
3. Serve.

Chapter 09: Sauces, Condiments and Dressing Recipes

Green Sauce

SERVINGS: 12
PREPARATION TIME: 10 minutes
COOKING TIME: 0 minutes

Nutritional Values Per Serving

Calories	82
Total Fat	5.6g
Saturated Fat	1g
Cholesterol	0mg
Sodium	399mg
Total Carbohydrate	6.9g
Dietary Fiber	1.5g
Total Sugars	2g
Protein	2.4g

Meal Prep Suggestion:

Store this green sauce in a sealable mason jar, then refrigerate for storage.

Ingredients:

- 1½ cups fresh parsley
- 1 cup mint
- 2 tablespoons lemon juice
- 1 tablespoon lime juice
- 2 garlic cloves, chopped
- ½ cup cashew nuts, soaked
- 1 small serrano chilli pepper
- 1½ tablespoons white miso
- 2 tablespoons olive oil
- 6 tablespoons water
- ¼ cup capers
- Salt, to taste
- Black pepper, to taste
- 1 tablespoon maple syrup

Instructions:

1. Add cashews, herbs and the rest of the ingredients to a food processor.
2. Blend this herb mixture until smooth.
3. Serve.

Chapter 09: Sauces, Condiments and Dressing Recipes

Chimichurri Sauce

SERVINGS 12   **PREPARATION TIME** 15 minutes   **COOKING TIME** 0 minutes

Nutritional Values Per Serving

Calories	75
Total Fat	8.4g
Saturated Fat	1.2g
Cholesterol	0mg
Sodium	80mg
Total Carbohydrate	0.5g
Dietary Fiber	0.2g
Total Sugars	0.1g
Protein	0.1g

Meal Prep Suggestion:

Pack this chimichurri sauce in a sealable canning jar, then refrigerate it for storage.

Ingredients:

- ½ cup parsley, packed
- ¼ cup cilantro
- 3 tablespoon red wine vinegar
- 2 garlic cloves, minced
- 1 teaspoon oregano
- ¼ teaspoon ground cumin
- ½ teaspoon chilli flakes
- ½ cup olive oil
- ½ teaspoon sea salt
- Pine nuts to garnish

Instructions:

1. Add parsley, oregano and the rest of the ingredients to a food processor.
2. Puree this mixture until smooth.
3. Garnish with pine nuts.
4. Serve.

Chapter 09: Sauces, Condiments and Dressing Recipes

Walnut Spinach Pesto

SERVINGS
12

PREPARATION TIME
15 minutes

COOKING TIME
0 minutes

Nutritional Values Per Serving

Calories	105
Total Fat	10.4g
Saturated Fat	1g
Cholesterol	0mg
Sodium	198mg
Total Carbohydrate	2g
Dietary Fiber	0.8g
Total Sugars	0.2g
Protein	2.7g

Meal Prep Suggestion:

Store this walnut spinach pesto in a sealable canning jar, then refrigerate for storage.

Ingredients:

- 1 ½ cup tightly packed spinach
- 1 teaspoon salt
- 4 garlic cloves
- ¼ cup olive oil
- 1 cup dry roasted walnut
- 1 ½ tablespoon lemon juice
- 1 teaspoon agave syrup

Instructions:

1. Blend spinach, basil and the rest of the ingredients in a blender until smooth.
2. Serve.

Chapter 09: Sauces, Condiments and Dressing Recipes

Basil Pesto

SERVINGS	PREPARATION TIME	COOKING TIME
12	10 minutes	0 minutes

Nutritional Values Per Serving	
Calories	119
Total Fat	12.4g
Saturated Fat	1.5g
Cholesterol	0mg
Sodium	166mg
Total Carbohydrate	2g
Dietary Fiber	0.9g
Total Sugars	0.3g
Protein	1.8g

Meal Prep Suggestion:

Store this pesto in a sealable mason jar, then refrigerate it for storage.

Ingredients:

- 1 packed cup basil leaves
- 2 packed cup spinach leaves
- 1 teaspoon garlic cloves, minced
- 2 tablespoons lemon juice
- 2 tablespoons nutritional yeast
- ½ cup pine nuts
- ½ cup olive oil
- 1 teaspoon coarse salt
- ½ teaspoon black pepper

Instructions:

1. Blend spinach, basil and the rest of the ingredients in a blender until smooth.
2. Serve.

Chapter 09: Sauces, Condiments and Dressing Recipes

Thousand Island Sauce

SERVINGS: 12
PREPARATION TIME: 10 minutes
COOKING TIME: 0 minutes

Nutritional Values Per Serving

Calories	106
Total Fat	7.8g
Saturated Fat	3.2g
Cholesterol	0mg
Sodium	188mg
Total Carbohydrate	7.8g
Dietary Fiber	1.1g
Total Sugars	3.2g
Protein	2.9g

Meal Prep Suggestion:

Store in a sterilized jar, then refrigerate.

Ingredients:

Vegan Mayo
- 1 cup raw cashew nuts, soaked
- 2 tablespoon nutritional yeast
- ⅛ teaspoon mustard powder
- 1 teaspoon dried garlic
- ½ cup coconut milk
- 2 tablespoon lemon juice
- ½ teaspoon salt

Sauce
- ½ teaspoon paprika
- ¼ cup 2 tablespoon ketchup
- 3 tablespoon sweet pickle relish
- 3 tablespoon 1 teaspoon lemon juice
- ¼ teaspoon salt

Instructions:

1. Drain and blend the cashews with the rest of the mayo ingredients in a blender until smooth.
2. Add paprika, ketchup, relish, lemon juice and salt.
3. Mix well and serve.

Chapter 09: Sauces, Condiments and Dressing Recipes

Vegan Tzatziki Sauce

SERVINGS 8   **PREPARATION TIME** 15 minutes   **COOKING TIME** 0 minutes

Nutritional Values Per Serving

Calories	104
Total Fat	8g
Saturated Fat	1.6g
Cholesterol	0mg
Sodium	123mg
Total Carbohydrate	6.8g
Dietary Fiber	0.7g
Total Sugars	1.2g
Protein	2.9g

Meal Prep Suggestion:

Keep the tzatziki sauce in a sealable container, then refrigerate.

Ingredients:

- 1 cup cucumber, peeled and grated
- 1 cup raw cashews, soaked
- ¾ cup water
- 1 ½ tablespoons lemon juice
- 2 ½ teaspoons distilled white vinegar
- 3 garlic cloves, minced
- ½ teaspoon sea salt
- 1 pinch ground black pepper
- 1 ½ tablespoons fresh dill

Instructions:

1. Pat dry the grated cucumber and keep it aside in a bowl.
2. Blend cashews with water, lemon juice, vinegar, garlic, salt, black pepper and dill.
3. Pour this mixture over the cucumber and stir well.
4. Serve and garnish with dill.

Chapter 09: Sauces, Condiments and Dressing Recipes

Cranberry Sauce

SERVINGS
8

PREPARATION TIME
10 minutes

COOKING TIME
20 minutes

Nutritional Values Per Serving

Calories	75
Total Fat	0.1g
Saturated Fat	0g
Cholesterol	0mg
Sodium	75mg
Total Carbohydrate	17.9g
Dietary Fiber	2.5g
Total Sugars	14.2g
Protein	0.1g

Meal Prep Suggestion:

Pack the cranberry sauce in a suitable canning jar, then refrigerate it for storage.

Ingredients:

- 3 cup cranberries, pitted
- 1 ½ cup apple, peeled and diced
- ⅓ cup granulated sugar
- ¾ cup water
- ¼ teaspoon salt

Instructions:

1. Add apple, cranberries, sugar, water and salt to a saucepan.
2. Add cook this cranberry mixture for 20 minutes until soft with occasional stirring.
3. Allow the sauce to cool, then serve.

Chapter 09: Sauces, Condiments and Dressing Recipes

Satay Peanut Sauce

SERVINGS 12   **PREPARATION TIME** 10 minutes   **COOKING TIME** 0 minutes

Nutritional Values Per Serving	
Calories	98
Total Fat	8.4g
Saturated Fat	2.4g
Cholesterol	0mg
Sodium	120mg
Total Carbohydrate	4.1g
Dietary Fiber	1.2g
Total Sugars	2.3g
Protein	3.4g

Meal Prep Suggestion:

Pack this satay peanut sauce in a sealable canning jar, then refrigerate it for storage.

Ingredients:

- 1 cup dry roasted peanuts
- ⅓ cup water
- 2 garlic cloves, minced
- ½ teaspoon dark soy sauce
- 2 teaspoons sesame oil
- 2 tablespoons brown sugar
- ½ tablespoon coconut aminos
- ½ teaspoon tamarind paste
- ½ teaspoon cayenne pepper
- ⅓ cup coconut milk

Instructions:

1. Blend peanuts with garlic and the rest of the ingredients in a food processor until smooth.
2. Serve.

Chapter 09: Sauces, Condiments and Dressing Recipes

Dairy-Free Béchamel Sauce

SERVINGS 8 **PREPARATION TIME** 10 minutes **COOKING TIME** 10 minutes

Nutritional Values Per Serving	
Calories	72
Total Fat	4.4g
Saturated Fat	0.8g
Cholesterol	0mg
Sodium	45mg
Total Carbohydrate	6.4g
Dietary Fiber	0.8g
Total Sugars	2.5g
Protein	1.9g

Meal Prep Suggestion:

Store this bechamel sauce in a sealable dry jar in the refrigerator.

Ingredients:

- 1 onion, peeled and sliced
- 13 ½ ounces soy milk
- 3 ½ ounces water
- 1 ½ teaspoon vegetable stock powder
- 2 cloves
- 2 bay leaves
- ¼ teaspoon grated nutmeg
- 3 tablespoon cornflour
- 2 tablespoon vegetable oil
- Pinch of salt
- Pinch of pepper

Instructions:

1. Cook onion slices, nutmeg, stock powder, cloves, bay leaves, milk and water in a saucepan, then cook for 20 minutes.
2. Use a slotted spoon to discard the bay leaves, cloves and onion.
3. Mix corn flour with oil in a bowl and pour into the saucepan.
4. Stir well and cook the sauce until it thickens.
5. Garnish with black pepper.
6. Serve.

Conclusion

I hope you enjoyed this cookbook and the plant-based meal prep recipes contained within it. Are you going to give these simple and practical recipes a try? If you are, then remember the tips and tricks shared in this book.

Hopefully all your false preconceived notions you had about being too busy to cook have been dispelled. This book provided all the tools you need to eat better and prepare healthy meals for yourself. It started with outlining the benefits of a plant-based diet and the many upsides of meal prepping. Within these pages is advice on what to do and not do when it comes to preparing meals ahead of time.

Included in this cookbook are seven different types of weekly meal plans. It covers breakfast dishes, lunch, dinner, high-protein plant-based meals, insta-pot, freezer, and sheet pan meals. There's kid friendly recipes, snacks, sauces, and condiments. Overall, there's 200 plus meals for you to try.

Most plant-based dieters find it difficult to switch to a plant-based diet as they barely get enough time to cook at home. Every busy foodie requires delectable yet simple and quick recipes in order to incorporate all plant-based products into his diet without feeling compelled to give up too soon. The recipes shared in this cookbook can make the entire process of following the plant-based diet easy.

There is a plethora of plant-based cookbooks available today. What separates this collection from the others is that it contains well-written meal plans and meal prepping guides. Because without these vital planning tools, all you have is healthy recipes with no way to properly utilize them. The recipes in this book also have detailed nutritional profiles making it simple to keep track of your daily caloric consumption.

This book is the result of my own struggles with living a healthier plant-based lifestyle. I was fortunate enough to have the financial means to make the mistakes needed to learn what works and what doesn't. Through a lot of trial and error, I cracked the code! And it's my intense desire to share this with you, the reader and hopefully the world. Do give this cookbook a read, choose your favorite plant-based meals, follow the meal plans as per your needs, and see how quickly your health improves! Once you are done with this experience, share it with your friends and relatives as well to spread healthy ideas around. Best of luck on your journey towards a better healthier diet!

References

7 Benefits of Meal Prepping - Selecthealth.org. selecthealth.org/blog/2019/08/7-benefits-of-meal-prepping.

Bustard, By: Denise, and Denise Bustard. "How to Meal Prep- A Beginner's Guide." *Sweet Peas and Saffron,* 19 Mar. 2021, sweetpeasandsaffron.com/how-to-meal-prep/.

Fit-Fresh, and Fit-Fresh. "Benefits of Meal Prep: Top 10 Reasons Why You Should Meal Prep." *Fit Fresh Blog,* 26 May 2017, blog.fit-fresh.com/benefits-meal-prep-top-10-reasons-meal-prep.

"How to Meal Prep: A Beginner's Guide for Perfect Make-Ahead Meals." *Bulletproof,* 3 Sept. 2021, www.bulletproof.com/diet/healthy-eating/how-to-meal-prep-beginners-guide/.

Joseph, Luis B., et al. "Best Kitchen Tools for Healthy Meal Prep." *Eating Bird Food,* 29 Sept. 2021, www.eatingbirdfood.com/meal-prep-kitchen-tools/.

Masur, Lauren. "The Ultimate Grocery List, According to Meal Prep Experts." *Kitchn,* Apartment Therapy, LLC., 1 Apr. 2021, www.thekitchn.com/meal-prep-grocery-list-23139177.

"Meal Prep Grocery List: Easy and Healthy Shopping!" *The Fit Father Project,* 11 Nov. 2020, www.fitfatherproject.com/meal-prep-grocery-list/.

Petre, Alina. "How to Meal Prep - A Beginner's Guide." *Healthline,* Healthline Media, 14 Dec. 2020, www.healthline.com/nutrition/how-to-meal-prep#methods.

Petre, Alina. "How to Meal Prep - A Beginner's Guide." *Healthline,* Healthline Media, 14 Dec. 2020, www.healthline.com/nutrition/how-to-meal-prep#methods.

Petre, Alina. "How to Meal Prep - A Beginner's Guide." *Healthline,* Healthline Media, 14 Dec. 2020, www.healthline.com/nutrition/how-to-meal-prep#time-management.

Alphabetical List of Recipes

A

Air Fried Tofu Nuggets 274
Animal Pasta Soup 254
Apple Chips 266
Apple Cinnamon Waffles 100
Avocado Fries 284
Avocado Hummus 292
Avocado Toast 93

B

Baby Oatmeal 249
Bake Buffalo Cauliflower Wings 260
Barley Vegetable Stew 234
Basil Pesto 302
Bbq Tofu Wraps 109
Beans Pasta Soup 220
Beet Root Hummus 294
Beetroot Chips 271
Berry Smoothie Bowls 82
Bircher Muesli 88
Black Chana Fry 181
Black Rice Meal 136
Blueberry Almond Oatmeal (Vegan, High-Protein) 75
Blueberry Muffins 96
Boiled Red Beans 174
Bow Tie Pasta Soup 255
Breakfast Burrito 94
Breakfast Cookie Bites 89
Breakfast Cookies 90
Breakfast Enchiladas 80
Broccoli, Carrot And Potato Soup 118
Broccoli, Mushrooms Quinoa Bowl 164
Brussel Sprout Tofu Fry 198
Brussels Sprout Broccoli Stew 186
Butternut Squash Puree 252

C

Caramel Popcorn 259
Carrot Fries 283
Carrot Oat Balls 280
Carrot Quinoa Bars 85
Cashew Sauce 297
Cassava Croquettes 267
Cauliflower Cakes 218
Cauliflower Mash 236
Cereal Almonds Bars 178
Chickpea & Sweet Potato Breakfast Hash 77
Chickpea and Carrot Stew 196
Chickpea Hummus 295
Chickpea Omelets 68
Chickpea Rice 155
Chickpea Stuffed Zucchini Boats 276
Chickpeas Creme Soup 123
Chili Garlic Baked Parsnip Fries 281
Chilli Garlic Sauce 288
Chimichurri Sauce 300
Chocolate Baked Oatmeal 98
Chocolate Bombs 268
Chocolate Chip Zucchini Muffins 279
Chocolate Peanut Balls 269
Cinnamon Apple Meal 248
Coconut Chia Oats 81
Cranberry Orange Muffins 70
Cranberry Sauce 305
Cream Of Broccoli Soup 120
Creamy Pasta 239
Crispy and Creamy Pasta 238
Crispy Pepper Poppers 286
Crispy Tofu Platter 188
Crusted Kale Chips 273
Curried Chickpea Bowls 113
Cutlets Cauliflower 153

D

Dairy-Free Béchamel Sauce 307

E

Edamame Quinoa Salad 166
Eggplant Casserole 142
Eggplant Fries 265
Eggplant Lasagna 204
Eggplant Pie 210

Eggplant Ratatouille	202
Eggplant Stir Fry	203
Eggplant Stuffed Bread	207

F

Farfalle Pasta With Chickpea	146
Fried Blossoms	258
Fruity Flapjacks	97

G

Garlicky Roasted Potatoes	221
Glazed Tofu	189
Gochujang Sauce	290
Grain Free Granola	91
Greek Couscous Salad	114
Green Bean Curry	03
Green Bean Mushroom Medley	230
Green Bean Stir-Fry	214
Green Sauce	299
Green Smoothie Bowl	92
Greens Soup	121
Grilled Eggplant Rolls	158

H

Herbed Couscous	172

I

Instant Pot Butternut Soup	233
Instant Pot Chickpea Stew	228
Italian Chickpea Soup	124

J

Jerk Spiced Tofu	112

K

Kid's Carrot Rice Soup	246
Kimchi	171
Korean Barbeque Tofu	111
Korean Eggplant Stew	184

L

Lemon Sauteed Cabbage	169
Lentil Soup With Mixed Veggies	126
Lentil Soup With Mushrooms	150
Lentil Soup	125
Lunch Wrap	106

M

Mash Potatoes	237
Mashed Carrot	243
Mediterranean Vegan Bowls	104
Miso Soup With Mushrooms	152
Mixed Lentil Stew	183
Muesli Bars	179
Mushroom Bisque	219
Mushroom Broccoli Stir Fry	102
Mushroom Cauliflower Rice	107
Mushroom Pasta Bake	206
Mushroom Soup	149
Mushroom Soup With Green Vegetables	151
Mushroom Tofu Soup	154
Mushroom Tomato Risotto	226
Mushrooms Broccoli Stir Fry	159

N

Noodles With Tofu	141

O

Onion Rings	285
Orange Mini Cookies	250
Orange Thumbprint Cookies	270
Overnight Zoats	95

P

Pappardelle Pasta	199
Pasta Salad With Tomato And Broccoli	128
Pasta With Lentil Sauce	129
Pasta With Vegetables And Chickpeas	144
Peanut Butter And Banana Mini Muffins	79
Penne Pasta With Pesto Sauce	127
Penne Pasta With Tomato Sauce	131
Peri Peri Sauce	298
Pink-and-Yellow Cookies	253
Potato Croquettes	247

Potato Kale Burger 163
Potato Pasta Soup 231
Potato Stuffed Rolls 263
Potato Tomato Bake 212
Potato Tomato Stew 224
Potato Vermicelli Soup 232
Puff Pastry Pesto Bites 208
Pumpkin Chickpea Stew 209
Pumpkin Hummus 293
Pumpkin Pie Quinoa 84

Q

Quiche Muffins With Sun-Dried Tomatoes And Spinach 78

R

Raw Hemp Seed Brownies 282
Red Lentil Potato Soup 182
Rice Bean Platter 195
Rice Stuffed Butternut Squash 162
Rice with Brown Lentils 190
Rice With Chopped Carrots 135
Rice With Vegetables 134
Rigatoni with Tomatoes, and Zucchini 168
Roasted Chickpeas 272
Roasted Polenta Pizza 222
Roasted Veggies with Baby Corn 225
Rotini Pasta Salad With Arugula 167
Rustic Gnocchi Pasta 148

S

Saffron Risotto 227
Salad With Roasted Eggplant And Kale 145
Sandwich with Roasted Vegetables 216
Satay Peanut Sauce 306
Saucy Navy Beans 180
Sauteed Potatoes And Mushrooms 215
Sauteed Zoodles 130
Savoury Vegan Muffins 76
Scalloped Potatoes 205
Sheet Pan Buns 223
Sheet Pan Vegetables 217
Shiitake Mushroom Soup 211
Soup Of Broccoli And Spinach 122
Spaghetti with Falafel Balls 197
Spicy Tomato Soup 147
Star Cookies 251

Steamed Cabbage Rolls 201
Steamed White Beans In Tomato Sauce 157
Stewed White Beans With Pumpkin 175
Stinky Tofu 156
Stir-Fried Eggplant 213
Strawberry Almond Baked Oatmeal 73
Strawberry Pops 242
Strawberry Popsicles 245
Stuffed Aubergine Rolls 138
Stuffed Cabbage Rolls 161
Sweet Chilli Sauce 291
Sweet Potato Fries 262

T

Tahini Date Cookies 278
Tempeh Stir Fry 116
Tempeh Vegetable Quinoa Bowls 105
Thai Quinoa Salad 115
The Best Vegan Banana Bread 71
Thousand Island Sauce 303
Three Colors Pasta 132
Thumbprint Cookies 86
Tofu And Rice Platter 139
Tofu Curry 187
Tofu Falafel Wraps 177
Tofu Mushroom Dumplings 193
Tofu Patties 241
Tofu Sticks 261
Tofu Stuffed Pastry 176
Tofu With Zucchini Noodles 110
Traditional Pizza 160
Tropical Smoothie Bowls 83
Tuscan White Beans 185

V

Vegan Borsch Soup 119
Vegan Bowl With Cashew Pesto 108
Vegan Breakfast Burrito 67
Vegan Buckwheat Muffins 277
Vegan Buffalo Sauce Recipe 289
Vegan Poke Bowl 133
Vegan Pumpkin Muffins 69
Vegan Quiche 66
Vegan Tater Tot Breakfast Casserole 74
Vegan Tzatziki Sauce 304
Vegan Waffles 87
Vegetable Gyoza 192

Vegetable Meatballs With Zucchini Noodles 140
Vegetable Spring Roll's 264
Vegetable Tempeh Stew 191
Vegetarian Eggplants Stew 143
Vegetarian Meal Salad 165
Veggie Tofu Scramble 72
Vermicelli Soup 117

W

Walnut Spinach Pesto 301
Water Chestnut Mushroom Fry 194
White Bean Salad 229
White Beans Meatballs 275
White Rice Cakes 170

Z

Zucchini Bread 99
Zucchini Cranberry Muffins 240
Zucchini Sticks 257

Index of Ingredients

A

Active dry yeast 160, 223
Agave 73, 301
Aleppo pepper 273
All-purpose flour 66, 79, 99, 120, 147, 149, 193, 206, 219, 223, 247, 250, 215, 253, 258, 286
Allspice 119
Almond butter 82, 83, 120, 147, 162, 170, 178, 179, 184, 205, 206, 208, 215, 223, 226, 230, 237, 243, 250, 251, 252, 253, 259, 260, 270, 277
Almond flour 86, 89, 90, 261, 270, 286
Almond milk 73, 76, 78, 79, 82, 83, 87, 90, 95, 96, 99, 100, 151, 179, 205, 206, 212, 220, 223, 237, 239, 244, 249, 253, 255, 257, 261, 267, 269, 277, 285
Almonds 73, 75, 88, 136, 140, 178
Aniseed 153
Apple 88, 92, 100, 233, 248, 266
Apple cider vinegar 180, 277, 279, 305
Apple sauce 70, 71, 85, 86 96, 240, 279
Arborio rice 226, 227
Arugula 158, 167
Asafoetida 260, 475
Asparagus 133, 139
Avocado 67, 93, 94, 109, 113, 133, 284, 292
Avocado oil 111, 119

B

Baby carrots 133, 136, 139, 225
Baby corn cobs 136
Baby hearty greens 121
Baby spinach 66, 67, 72, 106, 113
Baking powder 69, 70, 71, 73, 76, 78, 87, 97, 100, 240, 250, 273, 274, 277
Baking soda 69, 70, 71, 79, 85, 86, 99, 157, 240, 251, 253, 259, 279
Balsamic vinegar 140, 158, 167, 186
Bananas 71, 79, 82, 83, 85, 90, 92, 95, 277
Basmati rice 135, 155
Bbq sauce 109, 111
Bean sprouts 133, 264
Beer 258
Beets 119, 225, 271, 294
Berry chia jam 97
Black beans 80, 220

Black chickpeas 181
Black rice 136
Black salt 78
Breadcrumbs 185, 316, 370, 386, 402, 421, 434, 455
Broccoli 49, 107, 117, 127, 139, 141, 143, 145, 147, 149, 157, 159, 183, 218, 228, 270, 330
Brown lentils 201, 278
Brown rice 80, 130
Brown sugar 88, 99, 178, 179, 180, 253, 259, 270
Butler soy curls 67
Button mushrooms 105, 194, 206

C

Cabbage 111, 115, 119, 121, 130, 133, 161, 165, 169, 171, 191, 192, 201, 264
Cane sugar 99, 251, 275, 279
Canned chickpeas 104, 113, 114, 123, 124, 144, 146, 155, 195, 196, 272, 276, 292, 293, 294, 295
Cannellini beans 157, 185
Capers 299
Cardamom 296
Carrots 68, 85, 105, 115, 116, 118, 119, 121, 123, 124, 125, 126, 129, 133, 134, 135, 136, 139, 141, 155, 157, 158, 159, 165, 171, 182, 183, 186, 191, 192, 193, 196, 209, 210, 211, 214, 224, 225, 226, 228, 230, 231, 232, 233, 236, 243, 246, 255, 264, 275, 277, 280, 283, 292
Cashew nuts 108, 212, 245, 286, 297, 299, 303, 304
Cassava 267
Cauliflower 107, 112, 146, 153, 198, 212, 217, 218, 236, 260
Cauliflower rice 107
Cayenne powder 67, 125, 182, 196, 262, 272, 289, 298, 306
Celery 118, 119, 121, 124, 132, 149, 150, 183, 224, 226, 233, 234, 241, 254, 255, 264
Celery salt 271
Chargrilled red capsicum 291
Cherry tomatoes 94, 114, 132, 139, 160, 167, 195, 225
Chex rice cereal 163, 261
Chia seeds 72, 81, 82, 83, 89, 90, 91, 92, 97, 98, 269
Chickpea flour 68, 273, 274
Chickpeas 177, 197, 209, 228
Chilli flakes 110, 123, 197, 300
Chives 76, 78, 193, 226, 233
Chocolate chips 71, 79, 98, 279
Cider vinegar 296
Cilantro 113, 117, 175

Cinnamon powder 69, 73, 79, 84, 85, 89, 91, 95, 96, 98, 99, 100, 113, 209, 240, 248, 252, 266, 280
Cinnamon clove 296
Cloves 307
Cocoa powder 85, 86, 95, 98, 179, 268, 282
Coconut cream 120, 146, 147, 149, 170, 186, 187, 206, 219, 233, 238, 263
Coconut milk 81, 97, 98, 103, 245, 298, 303, 306
Coconut oil 69, 73, 78, 86, 90, 91, 100, 178, 209, 261, 268
Coconut shreds 280
Coconut sugar 70, 85, 87, 159
Collard greens 126
Condensed tomato soup 161
Cooked rice 139
Coriander leaves 109, 131, 161, 162
Coriander ground 140, 181, 183, 209, 214, 273
Corn flour/cornstarch 180, 307
Cornmeal 286
Cranberries 70, 91, 240, 305
Cremini mushrooms 108
Crushed nuts 89 269
Cucumber 104, 114, 138, 177, 195, 225, 293, 304
Curry powder 103, 125, 126, 162

D

Dark chocolate 71, 90, 178 268, 269, 279
Date syrup 209
Dill 119, 138, 304
Doenjang paste 290
Dried basil 132
Dried cherries 178
Dried chives 76, 78
Dried cranberries 70, 91 240
Dried Italian herbs 145, 255
Dried oregano 114, 118, 128, 132, 216, 222, 254, 265
Dried porcini mushrooms 206
Dried rosemary leaves 216
Dried sage leaves 275
Dried shiitake mushrooms 154, 192, 193, 206, 211
Dried thyme leaves 76, 121, 123, 126, 150, 186, 216, 219
Dried tomatoes 78, 127, 168, 222
Dry white wine 148, 149, 226, 238

E

Edamame 115, 133, 166
Eggplant 135, 138, 142, 143, 145, 158, 162, 184, 202, 203, 204, 207, 210, 213, 216, 222, 224, 265
Enchilada sauce 80

F

Fennel powder 156
Flaxseeds 74, 76, 85, 95, 96, 140, 161 177, 197, 223, 240, 241, 250, 251, 253
Flour 205, 218, 239, 257, 275, 277, 279, 283, 284, 285, 290
Frozen bananas 82, 83
Frozen blueberries 75
Frozen mango 244
Frozen peas 127, 140, 172
Frozen spinach 275
Frozen tater tots 74
Frozen veggies 166

G

Garam masala 181, 273
Garlic cloves 119, 122, 123, 124, 125, 126, 129, 130, 131, 133, 139, 140, 141, 143, 144, 145, 148, 149, 150, 152, 156, 157, 159, 164, 165, 166, 167, 168, 177, 182, 183, 185, 188, 194, 196, 197, 202, 203, 204, 205, 209, 210, 211, 212, 216, 218, 219, 221, 222, 224, 236, 257, 275, 286, 288, 291, 292, 294, 297, 298, 299, 300, 301, 302, 304, 306
Garlic paste 116, 181
Garlic powder 67, 76, 77, 94, 180, 234, 243, 260, 261, 263, 265, 274, 289, 290
Garlic salt 134
Ginger 84, 102, 110, 111, 115, 116, 133, 139, 141, 152, 159, 165, 166, 171, 181, 192, 193, 194, 196, 209, 211, 288, 291, 296
Ginger paste 116
Gochujang 111
Gram flour 153
Grape tomatoes 168
Grapeseed oil 213
Green apple 92
Green bell peppers 74, 94, 111, 129, 203, 229
Green chiles 67
Green beans 103, 116, 136, 230
Green olives 106, 203
Green onions 107, 111, 113, 115, 152, 156, 162, 171, 172, 188, 192, 195, 211, 213, 214, 263
Green peas 136, 214, 275
Green peppers 129, 186, 216
Ground almonds 140
Ground cinnamon 85, 248, 252, 266
Ground coriander 140
Ground cumin 94, 126, 210, 273, 295
Ground flax 79, 90
Ground ginger 166, 196
Ground nutmeg 85, 247
Ground oats 89
Ground turmeric 94, 134
Ground vanilla bean 84, 245

H

Hemp hearts 85
Hemp seeds 282
Hot sauce 289
Hummus 104, 106, 177

I

Israeli couscous 108, 172
Italian salad dressing 132
Italian seasoning 124, 129, 204

J

Jerk seasoning 112

K

Kalamata olives 128
Kale 78, 108, 145, 148, 152, 163, 209, 231, 273
Ketchup 111, 180, 303
Kiwi 95
Korean radish 171

L

Leek 171
Lemon juice 75, 77, 96, 99, 104, 108, 113, 114, 125, 126, 138, 169, 181, 229, 242, 245, 253, 260, 267, 286, 292, 294, 295, 298, 301, 303, 304
Lemon zest 253
Light buckwheat flour 277
Lime juice 93, 220, 284, 299

M

Mango 83, 162, 214, 244, 296
Maple syrup 67, 75, 79, 81, 86, 88, 89, 91, 102, 110, 115, 116, 17, 198, 240, 244, 245, 252, 254, 291, 293, 299
Matcha tea powder 81
Medjool dates 269
Mini bowtie pasta 255
Mint 138, 210, 299
Mirin 102
Molasses 89
Monk fruit sweetener 277
Mustard powder 114, 153, 216, 303

N

Noodles 130, 140, 141, 152, 171, 189, 211, 264
Nut butter 89, 116
Nutmeg powder 69, 70, 84, 85, 238, 247, 296, 307
Nutritional yeast 67, 68, 286

O

Oat flour 86, 89, 97, 100, 275
Oat milk 88, 92
Oats 88, 89, 90, 95, 96, 97, 98, 178, 240, 249, 269, 278, 280
Olives 106, 132, 276
Onion 75, 104, 114, 115, 117, 120, 126, 128, 159, 163, 168, 181, 182, 188, 196, 209, 210, 224, 238, 285
Onion powder 67, 74, 180, 263
Orange extract 70
Orange marmalade 270
Orange zest 270

P

Panko breadcrumbs 257, 284, 285
Papaya 83
Paprika 74, 76, 93, 94, 123, 175, 182, 183, 186, 210, 239, 257, 274, 285, 286, 289, 295, 298, 303
Parsley 108, 114, 129, 143, 145, 149, 150, 151, 156, 172, 177, 185, 190, 194, 197, 202, 215, 218, 221, 228, 237, 239, 247, 257, 260, 275, 283, 292, 293, 294, 299, 300
Parsnips 186, 281
Pasta 117, 127, 128, 129, 131, 132, 144, 146, 148, 167, 168, 197, 199, 206, 230, 231, 238, 239, 254, 255, 276
Pasta sauce 276
Peanut butter 79, 86, 110, 115, 186, 269
Peanut flour 89
Peanuts 77, 115, 268, 306
Pearled couscous mix 114
Pecans 84
Pesto 72, 208
Pine nuts 72, 158, 300, 302
Pineapple 112, 133
Pitted dates 278, 280, 282
Plain flour 76
Plant-based milk 70, 71, 84
Popped popcorn 259
Potatoes 262, 263, 103, 118, 119, 123, 148, 151, 153, 156, 163, 168, 176, 182, 186, 190, 192, 198, 203, 205, 212, 214, 215, 221, 224, 228, 231, 232, 234, 237, 247, 262, 263
Powdered sugar 70, 253
Pumpkin 175, 209
Pumpkin puree 69, 84, 239, 254, 293
Pumpkin seeds 91
Purple cabbage 121, 130, 133, 115

Q

Quinoa 104, 105, 115, 133, 160, 164, 166
Quinoa flakes 84
Quinoa flour 85

R

Raisins 88, 144, 209
Rapeseed oil 140
Raspberries 82, 244
Raw sugar 296
Red bell pepper 74, 77, 105, 111, 115, 143, 159, 202, 203, 222, 229, 255, 298
Red cabbage 115, 192
Red hot sauce 260
Rice vinegar 107, 110, 111, 115, 116, 133, 139, 154, 189, 198, 213, 288
Roasted peanuts 77
Roll wrappers 263, 264
Rolled oats 81, 86, 88, 89, 90, 95, 96, 97, 98, 240, 269, 280
Rosemary 121, 123, 143, 185, 216, 224
Rotini pasta 128, 132, 167
Russet potatoes 237

S

Salsa 67, 80, 94, 112, 138
Sambal oelek 133, 139
Sesame oil 102, 107, 110, 111, 116, 133, 139, 165, 166, 184, 193, 198, 211, 213, 306
Scallions 163, 191, 193, 218, 273
Seitan 94
Serrano chilli pepper 175, 299
Sesame seeds 111, 116, 133, 139, 152, 159, 260, 294, 295
Shiitake mushroom 192, 193, 206, 211
Smoked paprika 74, 94, 186, 210, 286
Snap peas 102
Soy milk 66, 69, 96, 286, 293, 307
Soy sauce 67, 102, 103, 107, 110, 111, 115, 116, 130, 141, 154, 159, 165, 166, 184, 189, 192, 193, 194, 198, 211, 213, 264
Soy yogurt 88
Spaghetti pasta 197
Spinach 66, 67, 72, 78, 92, 94, 106, 113, 122, 146, 181, 275, 301, 302
Sriracha 77, 107
Strawberries 73, 242, 245
Sun-dried tomatoes 168
Sunflower oil 103, 198
Sunflower seeds 91
Sweet corn 275
Sweet onion 133, 139, 233
Sweet pickle relish 303
Sweet potatoes 77, 186, 190, 209, 262

T

Tahini 77, 145, 278, 292, 294, 295
Tamari 111, 133, 139, 203, 224
Tamarind paste 306
Tapioca flour 283, 288
Tempeh 74, 105, 116, 191
Thyme 76, 121, 123, 126, 140, 142, 147, 149, 150, 186, 202, 216, 219, 233, 254, 283
Tofu 66, 67, 72, 78, 80, 82, 103, 108, 109, 110, 111, 112, 114, 127, 130, 133, 139, 141, 145, 154, 156, 161, 165, 166, 167, 176, 177, 187, 188, 189, 192, 193, 197, 198, 201, 203, 206, 214, 238, 241, 261, 274, 286
Tomato paste 103, 113, 124, 129, 168, 175, 180, 182, 185, 186, 187, 210, 231, 255
Tomato puree 140
Tomatoes 72, 78, 94, 103, 104, 106, 108, 109, 117, 126, 131, 138, 138, 140, 142, 143, 144, 155, 177, 183, 187, 197, 199, 202, 204, 209, 210, 212, 216, 217, 224, 228, 231, 234, 254
Tortillas 67, 80, 94, 106, 109, 177
Turmeric 67, 78, 94, 120, 134, 181, 196, 214, 275, 285

V

Vanilla extract 71, 73, 86, 96, 100, 178, 179, 240, 251, 253
Vegan butter 289
Vegan cashew ricotta cheese 207
Vegan cheddar cheese 170, 263
Vegan cheese 66, 72, 76, 158, 206, 276
Vegan cream 74, 236
Vegan cream cheese 74, 208
Vegan fish sauce 171
Vegan margarine 66
Vegan mayo 163, 216
Vegan mozzarella 142, 160, 176, 204
Vegan parmesan cheese 127, 142, 199, 204, 206, 212, 236, 238, 257, 276
Vegan tempeh sausage patties 74
Vegan Worcestershire sauce 180, 219
Vegetable broth 118, 119, 120, 121, 123, 124, 126, 134, 136, 147, 151, 159, 172, 180, 182, 186, 187, 190, 205, 209, 219, 220, 226, 227, 228, 234, 239, 255
Vegetable stock 122, 125, 149, 183, 211, 224, 233, 254
Vegetable stock powder 307
Vermicelli pasta 117, 232

W

Walnuts 85, 88, 282
White beans 175, 229, 275
White button mushrooms 206
White long-grain rice 134
White mushroom 215, 226

White pepper 230
White potatoes 205
White sesame seeds 295
White sugar 234, 266
White vinegar 304
White wine 148, 149, 168, 226, 227, 238
Whole meal flour 76
Whole wheat wraps 94
Whole-wheat flour 210

Y

Yellow food coloring 253
Yellow onion 74, 117, 120, 126, 168, 181, 182, 196, 209, 238, 285
Yellow pepper 163
Yellow squash 168, 202

Z

Zucchini 72, 76, 95, 99, 105, 110, 111, 127, 140, 143, 168, 203, 216, 217, 225, 240, 257, 258, 276, 279

Manufactured by Amazon.ca
Bolton, ON